SCRE PUBLICATION 73

ISBN 0 340 25745 8 (boards)
      0 340 25746 6 (limp)

Printed and bound in Great Britain for Hodder and Stoughton Educational, a division of Hodder and Stoughton Ltd, Mill Road, Dunton Green, Sevenoaks, Kent, by Macdonald Printers (Edinburgh) Limited, Edgefield Road, Loanhead, Midlothian.

CONTENTS

PART IIIC

SUMMARY, GENERAL DISCUSSION, AND
POSSIBLE IMPLICATIONS OF THE STATISTICAL
STUDY OF THE IMPACT OF THE LREHV SCHEME

PART IV

POSSIBLE IMPLICATIONS OF THE BACKGROUND
DATA FOR HOME VISITING AND THE DESIGN
OF HOME VISITING PROGRAMMES

PART V

RECOMMENDATIONS FOR ACTION AND
FURTHER RESEARCH

ACKNOWLEDGMENTS

This report owes its existence to the concern, energy, and enthusiasm of Ian MacFadyen, who was, at that time, the administrator responsible for the Lothian Home Visiting scheme. Not only did he play a key role in the organising and directing of the scheme itself, but he encouraged and facilitated an evaluation exercise which he knew must be, if it were to be useful, critical as well as possibly laudatory. His confidence in inviting constructive criticism has, in the event, been fully vindicated.

No less important has been the support given to the project by the Scottish Education Department, which both financed the SCRE evaluation and contributed to the membership of the committee that guided the work of the project.

Beyond that, the Home Visitors' "facilitator", Dorothy Bremner, and the Home Visitors themselves—Catherine Frame, Margaret McKay, Hazel Stuart, Vera Harrison, Irene Brydon, Jennifer Alderson-Shaw, and Aileen Burshall—have all contributed in invaluable ways to the production of the report, quite apart from their contribution to the Home Visiting itself. My colleague, Gail McCail, who has prepared two complementary reports on the study, contributed in many ways to clarifying the ideas set down in Part I of this report.

The members of the Advisory Committee on the project, under the Chairmanship of Arnold Morrison, raised many questions which were later pursued. They also contributed in crucial ways to obtaining the Manpower Services Commission grant which provided the funds which were used to carry out the statistical study on which so much of this report is based. Bryan Dockrell gave encouragement and inspiration in his own inimitable manner, and Gerald Osborne, Brenda Stoneham and John Powell, as professional and technical editors, instilled clarity into the report where none existed previously.

Many colleagues in this country and in the United States have also contributed in various ways to the report. Particular mention should be made of Willem Van der Eyken, Margaret Harrison, Candy Sullivan, Phyllis Levenstein, Jane Stallings, and John Love.

Despite the thanks that must go to all these people, the lion's share of the credit for this particular report must go to Margaret Berrill and Evelyn Ward, who interviewed approximately 500 families as part of the statistical study. Not only did they interview them, they worked on the development of the questionnaires, the tabulation of the responses, and the preparation of the report itself. To them, and to the parents who were interviewed, we owe an immense debt of gratitude. Sally Lawrie and Barbara Hallyburton typed and retyped the various drafts of the questionnaires and the emerging report with endless patience.

Finally, I owe my wife thanks, not only for putting up with the fact that I have not been available for many "spare-time" activities since I came to Edinburgh, but also for duplicating large sections of the various drafts of the report and keeping track of the references. Without her help and support this report would have taken still longer to produce, and been still less informative than it is.

JOHN RAVEN

Scottish Council for Research in Education

November 1979

DOCUMENTS AVAILABLE ON REQUEST

FROM THE SCOTTISH COUNCIL FOR RESEARCH IN EDUCATION*

APPENDICES

    A   Main Tables to this Report.

    B   Non Contact, Refusal Rates, and Demographic Data on the Samples involved in the Statistical Study.

    C   The Interview Schedules used in the Statistical Study.

    D   Development of the Interview Schedules used in the Statistical Study.

OTHER PAPERS

Ian MacFadyen: The Lothian Region Educational Home Visiting Scheme—a paper prepared for a Lothian - Strathclyde meeting.

The EHVs: Teacher in the Year 2,000?—a paper prepared for Lothian-Strathclyde Meeting.

The Evolution of the Evaluation.

What's in a Name? Is the project best thought of as an Evaluated Innovation, a Service or Action Research?

*Prices on Request

NATURE AND PURPOSE OF THE REPORT

The purpose of this report is to present the results of an Evaluation of the Lothian Region Educational Home Visiting Scheme.

The purpose of an evaluation is to assess the effects of a programme of activity with a view to doing two things: firstly, finding out whether it represents a justifiable expenditure and, secondly, finding ways in which it might be improved.

To assess its impact, two styles of research have been utilised. One strategy made use of an "illuminative" approach. This meant developing a better understanding of the practical operation of the scheme with a view to discerning what its effects were likely to be. The other strategy was more traditional, and involved comparing the answers Home Visited mothers gave to a series of interview questions with answers obtained from other mothers drawn from the same areas of the city as the mothers who had had Home Visits and a contrasting sample of High Status mothers. Since it cannot be claimed that these two groups represent control groups in the strict sense of the word, they are referred to in this report as "bench-mark" groups.

Three strategies have been adopted in our quest for ways in which the scheme might be improved. First, we have attempted to clarify the possible theoretical bases of some of the processes of development and social functioning with which the Educational Home Visitors have been trying to grapple. Secondly, we have examined our data on the effects which the scheme appears to have had, and not had, with a view to obtaining clues as to ways in which it might be improved. Thirdly, we have examined the data obtained from the two bench-mark samples with a view to abstracting what it has to tell us about parents' priorities in child-rearing, the causes and implications of variance between parents' priorities, and the types of intervention which might be appropriate to different sorts of family in different circumstances.

In the chapters which follow, the illuminative material will be reviewed first. After reviewing its possible implications for the long term development of the children, communities, and society concerned, we turn to the statistical data on the impact of the programme on the mothers directly involved. Finally, we review the material obtained from the two bench-mark samples with a view to discerning what, if anything, it may have to tell us about the design of Home Visiting Programmes.

PART I

THE LOTHIAN REGION EDUCATIONAL HOME VISITING SCHEME

A BRIEF OVERVIEW OF THE LOTHIAN REGION EDUCATIONAL HOME VISITING SCHEME AND THE EVALUATION

This chapter will provide the reader with a brief—if somewhat over-simplified—picture of both the Lothian Region Educational Home Visiting Scheme, which was established by Ian MacFadyen, Lothian Region Divisional Educational Officer, and the Evaluation, which was undertaken by the Scottish Council for Research in Education.

The Context of the Lothian Region Educational Home Visiting Scheme

The Lothian Region Educational Home Visiting Scheme had its roots in a number of research traditions. The first of these was that associated with the Plowden Report (1966), the work of J.W.B. Douglas (1968), Elizabeth Fraser (1959), and the National Children's Bureau (Wedge *et al* (1973)) in the U.K. and the Coleman Report (1966) in the United States. These studies showed that many children seemed to do less well at school than even their measured intelligence would predict. The second was the widely held view, promulgated by Peaker (1971), Coleman (1966), and Davé (1963), that some two-thirds of the variance in school performance among pupils of the same age could be attributed to home background. The third was the equally widely held view (largely attributable to Bloom (1964)) that the variance in cognitive/academic ability was well established by the time children were five years of age. Taken together with the conclusions of the two previously mentioned sets of research, this suggested that variance in educational performance had something to do with early experience in the home. The work of Bernstein (1971) and Tough (1973) suggested that the relevant early experiences had something to do with the use of language. Fifthly, and finally, Bronfenbrenner's (1974) review of the research literature on the effectiveness of intervention programmes designed to boost cognitive development and educational performance had suggested that their effects were less likely to "wash out" if the mother were involved directly as an agent of intervention. Levenstein's (1970, 1972, 1975, 1976, 1978) and Kellaghan's (1977) programmes of intervention, in particular, seemed to hold out great promise.

The Lothian Region Educational Home Visiting Scheme

The scheme began with a single Educational Home Visitor who was attached to a nursery school which made a particular effort to promote parental involvement. At the end of the first year of Visiting, Ian MacFadyen interviewed many of the parents who had been visited and was so impressed by what they said that he recommended that the number of Home Visitors be increased to six on an experimental basis. In order to assess the value of the experiment he also arranged for an independent evaluation to be undertaken by the Scottish Council for Research in Education with funds from the Scottish Education Department. At this point the original Home Visitor ceased Home Visiting as such for personal reasons, but continued to provide support for some mothers' activities, and was later appointed as "facilitator" for weekly Educational Home Visitors' Meetings. Five of the six new Educational Home Visitors, who were all trained teachers, were appointed to the staffs of five schools in areas of the Region which were judged to be socially disadvantaged. The sixth worked with families who had handicapped children. Their brief was, in the context of the research literature alluded to above, to work with two- to three-year-old children in their homes and in their parents' presence for about one hour a week. The length of time the visiting would be kept up was left open, but has turned out to be about nine months on average. The objective of the weekly visits was to encourage the mother to play a more active role in promoting the educational development of her children. It was suggested that the Educational Home Visitors should begin by involving the child in activities in which language was used to extend his imagination, and then seek to involve the mother in such activities. However, it was envisaged from the start that, as the Home Visitors became more comfortable in their new role, these activities would be extended to include encouraging the mother to take a more active role in relation to the formal educational system and to participate in activities which would lead her to become more confident and outgoing. It was envisaged that this would in turn influence the development of her children.

The Home Visitors each visited about ten families per week. Thus, about 180 families were visited in the first two years of operation. This made the Project one of the largest of its kind in the world.

The Educational Home Visitors (EHVs) were encouraged to exercise their professional judgment as to how best to interpret the brief they were given and the research materials they read. They were also encouraged to decide how best to relate their activities to the needs of individual families, schools, and communities. It is recognised that this would lead to considerable variation between the Home Visitors, and an effort was made to select Visitors who, while open to feedback, would have sufficient confidence in their own judgment not to require continual reassurance or direction.

The extent of the variance which did occur is documented in other reports on the evaluation (McCail, 1980a, 1980b) but a hint of it may be given by saying that the first Visitor "agonised" over the Kellaghan and Levenstein approaches but found that they "left her cold". She discussed with her Head Teacher whether she should tell Ian MacFadyen this, and they decided not to do so.

The formal criterion for selecting families for visiting was that they should be likely to benefit in some way from the visiting. It was made clear that this benefit might be social—such as the mother becoming more outgoing—as well as educational in the narrower sense of the word. In practice, many, but by no means all, of the families recommended for visiting by the schools, social workers, or health visitors were "deprived" or "problem" families. Nevertheless it was emphasised that it was important for all the EHVs to visit a cross-section of families. Indeed, despite its location in socially disadvantaged areas and its focus on "families who might benefit", the EHVs were given explicit instructions to avoid families in which the social problems might prevent them focussing on the educational activities which lay at the heart of the Project. Thus the families who were judged to be the "most likely to benefit" were not necessarily the most "needy".

As the study progressed, these social problems, the mother's inability to lead her life satisfactorily, her isolation, and her inability to get satisfactory treatment from the social services, have come to be seen as more and more central to the achievement of the Project's goals. Although one of the Home Visitors did manage to stand out against this broader viewpoint for about two years, she became the most anxious of all the EHVs about her apparent inability to influence the children's cognitive development, and has now come to believe that isolation and depression are central to the mother's unwillingness to become involved in the activities she is trying to encourage.

The Evaluation

The evaluation was set up as a one-man, two-year Project, without other research back-up. It was set up as a "descriptive" and "illuminative", rather than a statistical, study although it was intended that some questionnaire and test data should be collected. Not only was it intended to monitor the development in the EHVs understanding of their task, it was also intended to assess the impact of the Project on the schools concerned, the subsequent development of the children, and on the wider communities in which the Home Visiting took place. It was intended that this should be done by studying the operation of the Project and setting it in the context of other Home Visiting Projects in Britain and the United States.

Despite the general agreement that the Project should be "illuminative" and "descriptive", rather than statistical, the ambiguity of these terms, the desired breadth of the evaluation, and a level of funding which made it impossible to tackle more than a fraction of the issues, made for continuous unease about the evaluation. This was exacerbated by the fact that the researcher who had prepared the original, agreed, research proposal for the SED left after working on the Project for three months and was replaced by the author, and his colleague, Gail McCail (who has prepared a companion publication* describing the activities of the Educational Home Visitors in some detail) who each worked on a half-time basis. We both had rather different backgrounds, orientations, and research styles from the researcher initially appointed to the Project.

The unease about the evaluation was further exacerbated by Ian MacFadyen's desire for "hard" data on the effectiveness of the programme. He had a number of precise questions to which he wanted answers † although he acknowledged that the questions were difficult and recognised that answers could not be obtained within the two years allocated to the Project. Initially, he had seen the administration of IQ tests to the children as a major part of the evaluation. Having

---

* McCail (1980)

† Ian MacFadyen makes his reasons for seeking to have the project evaluated clear in the following quotation:

"A number of precise questions however remain unanswered. For example:

  (a) To what extent, if any, will the programme enable the children to take greater advantage of the later educational opportunities available to them?

  (b) To what extent will the programme improve and extend the support of the mother for the child throughout his educational career?

  (c) To what extent, if any, will the programme encourage in the mother a more

been convinced that the prior task was to examine the impact of the programme on the parents, he repeatedly asked what methods were to be used to assess that impact, and the context in which he raised this question implied that he had not fully accepted the "illuminative" evaluation model.

The author joined the Project because he saw it as an opportunity to develop the methodology which was required to provide accountability in relation to social and educational policy. At the time of joining the Project there seemed to him to be no way in which an evaluation which would provide answers to the sort of question being asked by Ian MacFadyen (eg about the long-term effects of the programme on the children's cognitive development and school careers) could be carried out with the resources currently allocated to it. However, both the Home Visiting Scheme and the evaluation were set up in such a way as to imply continuity of funding and he therefore expected that, in the longer term, it *would* be possible to answer a number of such questions.

The Statistical Study

In point of fact it rapidly became clear that there were many questions which could be tackled through a formal evaluation exercise if funds could be obtained.

It also became clear that the funds to develop relevant question-naires and collect *background* data from the areas in which the Home Visiting was taking place might be obtained under the Job Creation Programme. Although these funds would cover only inexperienced—and changing—personnel, they were the only funds available and, with the agreement and assistance of the SCRE Advisory Committee on the Evaluation, they were sought and obtained.

> out-going attitude to her own life? What effect will that have on the children, and on the family?
>
> (d) What effect will the programme have on the cognitive activity, the intellectual development, and the use of language on the part of the child?
>
> (e) What will be the effect of the programme on the mother/child relationship and what effect will that have on the mother and the child separately?
>
> In an attempt to answer some of these difficult questions, the Education Committee has asked the Scottish Education Department to set up a research project to observe, monitor, and evaluate the home visitor programme, a research project which will take some two/three years to conduct but the results of which may well be of major significance in the educational world."

It may be commented that there is no way in which "hard" answers to some of these questions could possibly be obtained without a longitudinal study lasting more than two to three years!

Under the circumstances, it was decided at the outset that the personnel appointed to the Job Creation Project should be kept well away from the Home Visited mothers. However, having seen the interview schedules which were evolved, and having read the interim report on the Job Creation Project, Ian MacFadyen became convinced that parallel data should be collected from a sample of Home Visited mothers as soon as possible. He urged that this data should be collected immediately despite the author's feeling that the interview schedules should first be modified to collect data on the parents' perceptions of the Home Visiting itself. When it became apparent that additional funding would not be obtained, the author reluctantly concurred and collected the data despite its known inadequacies.

CHAPTER 2

THE BACKGROUND TO, AND OPERATION OF, THE LOTHIAN REGION EDUCATIONAL HOME VISITING SCHEME

IAN MACFADYEN

In Chapter 1 reference was briefly made to the main research traditions which provided a context for the Lothian Region Educational Home Visiting Scheme. In this chapter the Divisional Educational Officer responsible for initiating and running the Project gives his own retrospective account of the background to the scheme. The chapter is an edited version of a Paper prepared for the Education Section Conference of the British Psychological Society, in the autumn of 1978.

The Background to the Scheme

Towards the end of the '60s and during the early '70s a number of generalised movements were beginning to present as more clearly delineated expressions of concern. The cognitivists, now firmly established as a group—in the USA at least—were claiming that the traditional provision for early childhood education, with its emphasis on affective aspects of growth, ignored the cognitive development of children and thus was "selling the children short". The more extreme disciples of the movement, like Bereiter and Engelmann (1966), and Omar Kayham Moore*, were demonstrating what could be achieved by intensive, highly structured and totally dehumanised programmes of intervention. Of more interest to me in this movement was the work of Levenstein (1970, 1972), who conducted what she described as "a Verbal Interaction Programme". She hypothesised that, in the crucially important phase of educational development before the child began formal schooling, the most influential factor was the "caretaker", usually the mother. Thus it would be appropriate to improve the capacity of the mother as the agent of educational development. Levenstein therefore employed what she called Toy

---

* See Pines (1969), pp 68-86

Demonstrators, who were initially trained social workers, to visit the mother in the home. The basic intentions behind the visits were

1. to demonstrate how one might obtain the maximum educational, perceptual, conceptual and motor stimulation from commercially available toys and books;
2. to demonstrate how one might exploit such materials for verbal interaction with the child;
3. to reinforce feelings of competence in mother and child;
4. to encourage the educational relationship between mother and child.

The experiment was of particular interest in that, not only did it demonstrate that the gains in IQ scores were longer lasting than those in other experiments, but much more importantly, it did so within a setting which was comprehensible and natural, ie within the family setting. The project accepted that the major factor influencing the child's educational development was the mother and set out to enhance her relationship with her child.

Another major influence leading to the establishment of the project was the results of the studies of the 1957 cohort by the National Children's Bureau. These were to have a profound effect upon the society in general and educational thinking in particular. One piece of evidence which was of particular significance was that which appeared as the report *From Birth to Seven* (1972). The evidence indicated that certain socially disadvantaged children—even below the age of seven years—had parents who were less likely to consult the teacher, were themselves more destructive and aggressive, were more prone to maladjustment, were more likely to speak unintelligibly and have poor oral ability, were more likely to have poor general knowledge, were poor readers, were poorer at arithmetic and were less creative.

Not only that, but these socially disadvantaged children demonstrated these disadvantages very shortly after beginning formal schooling. This suggested that, for whatever reason, children were arriving at school apparently improperly equipped to cope with school activities. The National Children's Bureau suggested that while, demonstrably, the children were not equipped to cope with the school it was possible that the school, with its middle class characteristics, was designed for one set of children rather than the other. But, whatever its cause, the Bureau highlighted an apparent mis-match between the efforts of the school on the one hand and the attitudes of the parents on the other.

At about the same time Joan Tough (1973) was conducting extended observations of young children's language. Eventually she concluded that whereas all children use language to protect their rights, demonstrate interests, indicate pleasure, needs, and frustrations and direct their own and others actions, the educationally advantaged children were able to demonstrate a more extensive use of language to:

—report on past experience
—collaborate towards an agreed aim
—predict and anticipate events
—see casual relationships
—problemise imaginatively
—create symbolic representations
—justify their behaviour
—reflect on their own and other people's feelings

We recognise those as the very linguistic skills which are demanded by the learning experiences created by the teacher—and not only in the Primary School. The Nursery School appears to make similar demands without fully comprehending the difficulties faced by the children who have not mastered such complex skills.

Joan Tough also remarked on differences in the verbal interaction of the mother-child dyad. In the case of the educationally advantaged child the mother shares meaning with the child. Her comments are designed to lead the child to further thought. She makes comparisons, encourages recall, encourages concentration and attempts to explain situations. In the case of the educationally disadvantaged child the mother engages in this activity to a much more limited extent.

Joan Tough's early work has been the subject of much criticism. However, it can be said to have made a highly significant contribution to an understanding of educational development in children and to the nature of the educational experience provided in schools.

Mention may be of one other influential, local, factor. On the one hand there appeared to be a new groundswell of interest in education. Parents were no longer content to be informed by schools of their children's "progress". Parent-teacher associations were beginning to spring up in various places; community groups began to demand a voice in educational affairs. Education Committees found themselves the somewhat unwilling bridegrooms at the altar of consultation. Schools began to talk of parent involvement. The Playgroup movement, which had struggled to achieve recognition on the educational stage, suddenly found itself at the centre of a political storm.

More disturbingly, there appeared to be an alarming situation in relation to young married couples, particularly young wives living in high flats. It wasn't simply that they appeared to be isolated and very lonely, it seemed as if they did not have the will to overcome their most acute problems. The conventional and well tried methods had proved fruitless; they avoided any kind of social activity, including contact with neighbours. The traditional "evening class" was an anathema to them, even when designed specifically as a result of their suggestions. They avoided contact with schools, nursery, primary and secondary. It was as if, having been married, had children, been housed in local authority developments, they had literally accepted their fate.

But the problem went deeper. There appeared to be indications that a number of young mothers saw themselves as having failed with regard to their children. The reasons for this were imprecisely stated but were variously expressed as, for example,

—an inability to cope with childish activities
—disappointment that children were not as the advertising media displayed them
—lack of assistance from grandparents, neighbours, older siblings, schools, doctors and other professionals
—inability to live up to the expectations of others including their own children
—disappointment at not being able to provide the best for their children (whatever that might be)
—a feeling of guilt at having negative sentiments in relation to their children.

And yet they were not without personal ambition for their children. A small survey conducted in 1974 in the Lothian Region indicated that, contrary to popular belief, 99% of parents described themselves as "interested in the education of their children".

This led to two thoughts:

1. It was difficult to imagine that those parents accepted such a situation willingly. Education might not be able to provide a ready solution, but it could be argued that it had no small part to play in assisting young parents to overcome their difficulty.

2. It was difficult to imagine that such a situation would provide fertile soil for the intellectual growth of the youngsters involved. The degree of commitment and the effort available to promote the educational development of their children would in all probability be in direct ratio to the enthusiasm or otherwise with which they viewed their own situation.

These then were the major factors which led to the establishment of the Educational Home Visiting Project. That these factors could be challenged on a number of grounds did not seem to be a great obstacle; one might wait for years before hypotheses were finally turned into generalised truths. It seemed that the subject matter which these factors covered was pressing enough to warrant some action. The question was: What kind of action?

The developments which have been summarised seemed to point separately and collectively to some initiative which would bring together the educational world and the parents in the parents' home in such a way as to encourage and enhance the educational development of the child: hence the institution of the Lothian Home Visiting Scheme.

The Operation of the Lothian Region Home Visiting Scheme

The Visitors are attached one each to a nursery school or to a primary school with a nursery class.

The reasons for adopting this pattern were three-fold.

1. Similar experiments elsewhere in Britain at that time were marked by the temporary quality of their existence or by the indeterminate place in space of the Visitor. Such "insecurity" of tenure did not seem to be in the best interests of staff and hence of the project itself.

2. The nursery school or class provided the nearest educational equivalent to serve as a home base for the Visitor with all that that entails—services, colleagues, professional communication and refreshment.

3. In the Head teacher the Visitor could find a helpmate, a guide, someone to discuss problems with.

Each Visitor has approximately 10-12 homes which she visits weekly, spending about an hour per week in each home. The remainder of the time is spent recording results, discussing findings with the evaluators, working in the nursery school or class, or in organising parents' meetings and other activities designed to promote the growth of the mothers' feelings of motivation, confidence or competence and involvement in the formal school system.

The Visitor visits homes of children at the pre-school stage, i e between two and three years old. We felt this to be the optimum point of contact in that the educational relationship between the child and the mother would be unlikely to have crystallised. The child is young enough to adapt to a changed pattern of activity on the part of the mother, the mother not yet far enough into motherhood to be unable to reflect upon the quality of the interaction with her child.

The express purpose of visiting the home is to encourage and enhance the mother's unique and irreplaceable role in the educational development of her children. The Visitors begin by working with the child but move as quickly as possible to an involvement of the mother in the activity. Quite often the mother expects the Visitor to "teach" her child and does not expect to be involved other than as an interested bystander. The Visitors get over this problem in a number of ways.

—By structuring the activity to include the mother
—By encouraging the child to involve his mother
—By talking to the mother about her child, her home, and the activities of the visit
—By leaving books and other materials behind
—By discussing activities undertaken by the mother with the child between visits

The Visitor normally takes with her some concrete object in order to give focus to the visit. Sand, water, coloured paper, building bricks, toys, playdough—anything in fact which will draw the attention of the child and mother. At the same time, however, the Visitors are themselves encouraged to persuade the mother that any object, and any household activities—such as making beds, washing, hoovering, and ironing—can be used to focus the attention of her and her child.

The use of language plays a very important part. The mothers are encouraged to use language in such a way as to share meaning with their children, to collaborate in activity, to predict, to explain, to hypothesise and to test that hypothesis, to demonstrate casual relationships, and to stretch the imagination of the child. At the same time, however, mothers are encouraged to avoid too great concentration on such activity because it is taxing for both child and mother.

It was the intention that the Home Visiting aspect of the project would be supported by the school in a variety of ways. This has happened to a greater extent in some areas than others. In the most active schools, the mothers are invited to visit the school, to use the mothers' room, to join in work with the children in the school, to devise and take part in a variety of what might be called informal further education activities, ie classes in hostess catering, flower arranging, family swimming, keep-fit, and child development. In addition they are encouraged to take part in social activities organised by the school, coffee mornings, fund-raising activities, parents' outings, children's outings. The purpose of such activity is on the one hand to close the gap between home and school and on the other to provide some opportunity, however small, for the mother to participate in activities outwith her own home. In other words what begins as an interest in her child may well continue as a determination to promote her own opportunities for self-fulfilment, which, it is hoped, will have a profound rejuvenating effect upon her life and in turn on the educational development of her child.

No Home Visitor is expected to work in homes where there are special problems of relationships. Occasionally one comes across homes in which the marital relationships are very unsound and even some cases where the mother-child relationship is distinctly odd. The Visitors, being on the pioneering periphery of educational development, have quite enough to cope with without entering into some of the most difficult areas of human activity.

The Visitors build up their lists of children to be visited from a number of sources. The intention is that lists should be varied and not filled with what might be termed problem children or families. In fact it is positively beneficial to the group as a whole, and to the Visitor, to have within the group at least one mother who is relatively outgoing in her personality. Quite often the local social worker or health visitor will suggest that a mother and her child be added to the list to be visited.

A place is available at the nursery school or class when the child reaches the age of 3-3½ years if the mother requires it. This is as much a precaution as anything else. A series of Home Visits having been begun, it would make little sense if the parent found that there was no opportunity for communication with the educational world between the age of three and five. It is still a matter of choice of course whether the child attends part-day or full-day.

The precise point at which the Visiting should cease is a matter of debate. The original thought was that it should cease when and if it became clear that the mothers had understood what the Visitor's message had been. This has proved impracticable for two fundamental reasons:

1. In many instances the mother and the child have come to regard the Visitor as a friend and as an indispensable part of their lives. The announcement by the Visitor that she would have to stop visiting has led on numerous occasions to tears, particularly on the part of the mother. This seems to suggest that one of the major

objectives of the scheme, to increase the sense of self-sufficiency in the mother, may not have been entirely successful.

2. The Visitors seem now to be convinced that the intense contact cannot be replaced simply by some kind of loose communication between the mother and the school. It will need to be replaced by a much more carefully structured system of communication between home and school not only at nursery level but at primary school also. What form that should take, it is, as yet, difficult to foresee although a number of ideas are now beginning to emerge.

The Visitors are all qualified teachers. The reason for adopting this policy was that teachers, by and large, would be able to think through the theoretical basis of the project and in its practical application more quickly than other people by virtue of their knowledge and experience. This is not to say that other workers could not be equally effective. We have, like Levenstein, begun to use non-professional volunteers— mothers who have themselves been through the programmes. Whether they will be effective remains to be seen.

More important than the qualifications of the Visitors was their degree of sensitivity. Each Visitor was selected above all else for her capacity to work with adults in their homes without displaying an intolerant or patronising air, for her capacity to offer her professional skills without giving offence or undermining the confidence of the mother, for her capacity to be critical of her own efforts, and for her capacity to engender confidence, trust and a positive response from the mothers.

PART IIA

THE ILLUMINATIVE STUDY:
INTRODUCTION

CHAPTER 3

THE DESIGN OF THE ILLUMINATIVE STUDY AND THE AUTHOR'S ORIENTATION

As we have seen, the evaluation of the Scheme fell into two rather separate parts. The first was an illuminative study designed to examine the operation of the project with a view to discerning what its effects were likely to be. The second was a statistical study in which the attitudes and behaviour of mothers who had had Home Visits were compared with the attitudes of two bench-mark samples. In this chapter the objectives and methodology of the "illuminative" study will be reviewed and followed by some information about the background and interests of the author. It is hoped that this information will enable the reader to set the author's views in an appropriate context. The design of the statistical study will be discussed in Chapter 14.

The objective of the "illuminative" or "descriptive" study was to develop a better theoretical understanding of the processes which were involved in one way or another in the scheme. Set in the context of existing psychological and sociological research and theory, this understanding was expected to enable us to discern what the effects of the scheme would be likely to be. Such an approach has a large number of merits. One is not confined to talking about effects which can be measured with the resources and methodology currently available. Thus, we would be able to provide some information on the probable effects of the scheme on outcomes which we would be unable to assess, statistically, with the resources available to us. For example, we would be able to estimate its effects on schools, community members, and administrators not directly involved in the Project. We would also be able to provide information on its probable *long-term* effects on the families, children, schools and communities concerned. If we had mounted a conventional longitudinal study it would have been necessary to have waited years before we could provide such information. We would also be able to talk about the probable effects of the programme on outcomes for which reliable and valid measures do not exist at the present time. Such outcomes might include the probable effects of the programme on the development of initiative, self-confidence, and inter-personal sensitivity on the part of both mother and child. In this way we would be able to avoid the lop-sided nature of many evaluations which fail to discuss what are often the most important outcomes of the educational processes which are being evaluated because those outcomes cannot be "measured" with the techniques and resources to hand. We would be able to discuss the probable effects of particular "styles" of visiting although these effects would get buried in a mass of "non-effects" in any statistical study which it would be possible to carry out in a Project of this size. To partial out such effects and extricate them from possible contaminating variables would require not only an extremely large research design but also extremely sophisticated analytic procedures. Last, but not least, it would be possible to provide feed-back to help the Educational Home Visitors (EHVs) in their work, long before it would be possible to provide them with the results of any statistical study which "showed" what was working and what was not working. By making theoretically important processes explicit, the long-term objective of any evaluation—improving the services which were being offered—would be achieved more quickly.

None of the above should be taken to mean that we are unaware of the need to check inferences from theory and personal observation against fact and systematic observation by more people. It is simply to state the case for supplementing traditional research styles with "illuminative" research.

For this part of the study, data were collected in a number of ways. Open-ended interviews were carried out with the administrators responsible for the intervention and the evaluation, the EHVs, other members of the staffs of the schools to which they were attached, and some of the parents who were visited. The parents were sometimes interviewed in groups, sometimes in the presence of the EHV concerned, and sometimes alone. The evaluators attended several of the mothers' group meetings and virtually all the weekly meetings of the EHVs. At these meetings they contributed to on-going discussion, sometimes in provocative ways, and also raised specific questions for discussion. The Educational Home Visitors kept notes on their visits, diaries of their activities, and prepared reports on their progress with all the families they visited. They tape-recorded some of their visits and the evaluators accompanied them on others.

None of these methods of collecting data was expected on its own to give an objective account of the operation and impact of the Project, and all methods of collecting data were expected to "contaminate" the operation of the project in some way: the EHVs could not be expected to give a complete and accurate account of their objectives, activities, and difficulties in a single interview. The presence of notebook and pencil, tape-recorder, or an observer could always be expected to influence what was said and done in interviews, in group meetings, or on Home Visits. The mere asking of questions of administrators, head teachers, mothers, or Home Visitors was likely to make certain issues more salient and influence the direction of the project.

Nor was the objective of providing a complete and accurate account of everything that happened necessarily thought to be desirable. What one observes, records and describes is inevitably influenced by one's implicit or explicit theoretical framework and one's assumptions and by what one expects will have a significant effect. The effects which one can label and think about are themselves a product of the current state of development of one's science. If, in a project of this sort, we could give an impression of the general flavour of what seems to most of those involved to be significant aspects of its operation and impact—and draw attention to a few variables, processes, issues and impacts which have been overlooked in previous studies, our work would, we thought, be fully justified.

In order to get a better grasp of the aspects of operation of the project which should be considered significant and the effects that the project was likely to have, an attempt was made to come to terms with the vast early-childhood-intervention literature. Visits were paid to many other projects in this area in the United Kingdom and in the United States of America. It was also hoped that these visits would enable us to discover formal evaluation instruments which could be incorporated into later stages of this project. Unfortunately this hope was not fulfilled. Rather, we gained an impression of a field permeated by studies which had, on the whole, made use of poor conceptual frameworks, research designs, methodologies and instrumentation.

The Assumptions and Theoretical Perspectives of the Author

In order to help the reader to "objectivise" the necessarily selective account of the project which will be presented, and in order to help him to understand why the author has collected and focussed on certain sub-sets of data, an attempt must now be made to share with the reader some of the author's assumptions, his theoretical stance and his reasons for adopting particular viewpoints. The remainder of this chapter therefore tells the reader about the author and not about the project. It is hoped, however, that it will give the reader some insight into why the author is telling him certain things about the Project and omitting others. Those who are interested only in the Project may skip over the remainder of this chapter.

The author joined the Project for two main reasons: Firstly, he was acutely conscious of the need to greatly increase investment in the evaluation of social, and particularly, educational, policy. Secondly, he was particularly interested in trying to find ways of assessing the impact of educational programmes on values, attitudes, perceptions, expectations and behaviour. As he saw it, the project was aimed, in the first instance, at influencing the actions the mothers thought it was important to undertake with their children, the qualities they wanted their children to develop, their expectations of the consequences of undertaking certain activities with their children, and their actual day-to-day behaviour.

The author was anxious to work on the evaluation of social policy for a number of reasons. Firstly, he had realised (Raven, 1975, 1976) that control of the way in which something like 75% of GNP is spent now rests with "The Government" (i e national and local government and their associated bureaucracies). Thus the economic market-place as the means of evaluating the quality of provision, providing and administering variety of provision, and influencing the direction in which development will take place has, for the best of reasons, largely been neutralised. But the political system as the only alternative means of formulating, administering and evaluating policy in such a socialised economy is grossly overloaded. A system to replace the economic market-place and supplement the political must therefore be developed. In such a system, he felt, social scientists had a crucial role to play in helping society to develop the concepts, understandings, structures and tools which are required to formulate, administer and evaluate policy—and, in particular, to administer and evaluate policies which allow people with different priorities to be catered for in different ways.

To come closer to the present project, his research had also suggested that the measures which were needed to assess the adequacy with which the educational system was reaching the goals which the large majority of the pupils, ex-pupils, parents, teachers, employers, and employees set for it were measures of values, motivational dispositions, perceptions, expectations, and feelings of confidence and personal efficacy. The methodology required to assess these qualities was in many ways similar to that needed to assess the impact of the Lothian Region Educational Home Visiting Project on just such qualities. The Lothian Region Project was in effect an adult education project which was intended to influence values, perceptions, expectations, motivation and behaviour.

In addition to these general attitudes toward policy evaluation and education, the author also brought with him some beliefs and expectations (again derived from his previous research) much more closely related to the subject matter of the present project.

In the first place, he was extremely sceptical about the widely held view that home background was responsible for the lion's share of the variance in academic attainments. He had in fact carried out a path analysis of some data in which Davé's questionnaire had been administered to a sample of parents of primary school children and the results correlated with a wide range of measures of the children's school attainment (Raven, 1977). What he found was that some 75% of the variance in school performance could be predicted from what Davé (1963) had labelled "home process" variables. *But* 67% of the variance could be predicted from scores on a verbal intelligence test. When the effect of IQ was partialled out, only 8% of the variance was left to be accounted for by "home process" variables. Given the high level of inter-correlation between the variables, it was not possible to choose between an explanation of the variance in school performance based on variance in parental attitudes and an explanation based on IQ. In terms of its practical implications this is most unfortunate— because it is widely assumed that while parents' attitudes are open to influence, IQ is not. It also emerged that many of the "home process" variables were themselves arguably best thought of as surrogates for the child's ability. Thus, parents' estimates of how long they expected their children to stay at school were bound to be influenced by their estimates of their children's ability.

Having carried out an extensive path analysis on this data—using each of the 19 parental attitude composite variables (some of which would be expected to be more dependent on home process variables than others)—without advancing understanding of the importance of home background one iota, he concluded (*a*) that the case for asserting that home process variables were primarily *responsible* for the variance in educational performance of the children was far from established, and (*b*) that the only way to proceed toward a better understanding was to make use of an experimental design in which an attempt would be made to influence educational outcomes. He therefore saw the Lothian Region Educational Home Visiting Project as an attempt to do just this.

Secondly, other aspects of his previous research had made him extremely sceptical about the assertion that parental attitudes and values were primary determinants of school and life performance. His research had confirmed the widely held, if not well documented, view that the qualities which parents wish their children to develop, and which pupils wish to develop, vary markedly with socio-economic status. However, it also showed something else. When one studied secondary school pupils who expected to be upwardly or downwardly mobile, one found that the qualities which pupils wished to develop were as characteristic of the groups they expected to enter as they were of those they were leaving. Thus, downwardly mobile pupils, who had presumably been brought up in homes which, like other high socio-ecomonic status households, stressed independence, originality, responsibility, and thinking for oneself (see data reported below), were much more likely than others from the same backgrounds to stress the importance of developing obedience and conformity, and having rules to guide their lives laid down for them, which tend to be characteristic of low socio-economic status families. Similarly, pupils who expected to be moderately upwardly mobile were more likely than others)—without advancing understanding of the importance of and responsibility (Raven, 1976, 1977). (It should be stressed that this is not a complete summary of the results—for example, upwardly mobile pupils who were jumping several status categories were less interested than *any* of their peers in the development of such qualities as an interest in the communities in which they were going to live).

Thus, while confirming the relationship between social and educational attitudes and socio-economic status found in the literature, and confirming the ecological relevance of these attitudes and expectations (which had been so much emphasised by Kohn (1969)), his data (like that reported by Havighurst (1962), and the Newsons (1978)), had suggested that, in many cases, children's attitudes did *not* simply reflect their parents' attitudes. Rather the pattern of relationships suggested some anticipatory socialisation effects similar to those noted by Kinsey (1948) in relation to sexual attitudes and behaviour. As in Kinsey's case, it appeared that the attitudes and behaviours involved could have been learned neither from parents nor from members of the status groups which the pupils expected to enter. Something pretty fundamental therefore seemed to be operating, and this challenged both the notion that such attitudes and values are simply transmitted to children (and, as a result, affected their school performance) and the view that it was important to encourage more "working class" children to accept the "middle class" value system so that they could "take advantage of what the school system had to offer". Rather the results suggested that it was important to respect this variance in values and attitudes when making provision for education and that, by so doing, one would *not* run the risk of creating a caste society—provided one created flexible structures in which pupils could move from one value system to another as they developed.

A third set of perspectives which the author brought with him to his task—and which structured the way in which he saw the Project and his interpretation of the data he collected—had to do with his previous work on the value of schooling. Essentially, this research shows that teachers, pupils, ex-pupils, parents and employers are right to believe that the primary objective of education is to foster such qualities as initiative, confidence that one can deal with new situations and new people, and the ability to learn without instruction. And it suggests that their view that the current educational system—for understandable reasons—does very little to foster these qualities is also correct. However, it also shows that schools are right to do what they do do—to focus on getting pupils through examinations. This is because these certificates are important prerequisites to a decent way of life despite the fact that the activities required to obtain them confer few benefits on their pupils. The backwash of this pre-occupation to infant level was noted by several of the Educational Home Visitors.

What these results show is that teachers, parents, pupils and this Project have a serious dilemma. Children must be helped to pass examinations because of the extrinsic benefits conferred on them by these certificates. But the activities which lead to the acquisition of these certificates confer few educational benefits on pupils—and may actually stunt the growth of the children's competence. Thus schooling in one sense (getting examination certificates) is extremely important, whilst, in another sense (promoting growth and development) it is probably unimportant. Thus, the project's goal of leading parents to "value" schooling and to do with their children the things which need to be done in order to help their children to adjust to school and do well there, is, in a sense, extremely questionable. But equally, in another sense, it is extremely important—for, as most parents, pupils and teachers know, school success *is* extremely important as a key to gaining respect and material well-being in our society.

Knowledge of this dilemma naturally led the author to emphasise the importance of collecting particular data on the impact of the Lothian Region Educational Home Visiting Scheme and to interpret that data in particular ways. It also led him to be particularly sensitive to those who argued that one of the most important goals of the project was to lead the parents concerned to a position from which they could argue that schools should change so that they could help pupils to develop the qualities they needed to lead their chosen way of life rather than force them to opt in to a way of life which they did not particularly value in order to gain respect and a minimum standard of living in our society.

A fourth fact about the author which should be recorded is that he has, for many years, been pre-occupied with the conceptualisation, assessment and development of motivational dispositions like adaptability, innovativeness, and creativity. As we have seen, most people believe that these qualities lie at the heart of educational objectives despite the fact that, at least, in Ireland, Belgium, and the United States they are sadly neglected in practice (Raven *et al*, 1959, 1969, 1973, 1975, 1977). The author has been rather more heavily involved in research in this area than in research dealing with the conceptualisation, measurement and development of abilities or attainments like intelligence, reading or science. This long standing interest has naturally led him to be more receptive to remarks which could be construed as relating to these pre-occupations and concerns than other researchers might have been. Since his theoretical formulation of the *nature* of these qualities and their development also asserts that they have centrally to do with values, indeed that the most important problem facing educationalists is to come to terms with values, it is to be expected that he would be more sensitive than other researchers might have been to those aspects of the present project which have been concerned with the growth of general competence rather than focussing only on success in the school system, and that he would be more aware of the value-related issues which permeate the project despite its avowed emphasis on cognitive development— which is often assumed, despite the work of Spearman and Piaget, to be relatively value-free.

A fifth and final perspective which the author brought with him to his task is derived from his work on creativity and innovativeness (Raven and Molloy, 1969; Raven, 1975; Raven and Dolphin, 1978). This suggests that advance in scientific understanding comes about most quickly, not by following the British civil service type tradition which emphasises a cautious quest for certainty before publishing one's tentative conclusions, but by assembling material to argue a position which then leads to public debate. The author's primary concern is, therefore, not to be *right*, but to argue a position which, through public debate, will lead to advance in understanding. He therefore does not feel obliged to consider every possible alternative explanation and interpretation of his observations and results *before* publishing them. This, of course, conflicts with the expectations of those who commissioned this study—for this Report cannot claim to be impersonal, complete, and "objective". And not only because of the puny resources available to the researchers but also because the attempt to be complete and objective is misguided. Such an attempt would mean focussing on data and interpretations which, while highly selected, pretended to be value-free and non-controversial. It would therefore mean neglecting crucial issues for which an adequate theoretical framework, concepts and measures have not been developed. In other words it would mean failing to discuss the most important issues and failing to report on the most important things one has learned (Donnison, 1972). The set of data we have chosen to collect and publish—whether statistical or descriptive—has been selected because we, personally, perhaps for some barely understood reason, *felt* that it was important, and what we saw in it and chose to highlight is also a subjective decision. More than that, we have built the scraps of information we have collected together into a pattern which is at the same time a great deal more than, and a great deal less than, what we observed. The author makes no apology for this. He believes that the notion that a single social scientist, working in a field as important, as open, and under-researched as this one, *could* be objective is totally disfunctional. What we need is more people with different pre-occupations and perspectives researching the area and hotly debating their conclusions, not a more pedantic approach to this particular publication which, after all, represents but a drop in the ocean.

CHAPTER 4

THE INTERNATIONAL CONTEXT OF THE LOTHIAN REGION EDUCATIONAL HOME VISITING SCHEME AS AN EVALUATED EXPERIMENTAL PROGRAMME

The purpose of this chapter is to provide a brief review of evaluations of intervention programmes which have at least something in common with the Lothian Region Educational Home Visiting Scheme. It was originally intended to provide both a map of related programmes—whether evaluated or not—and a fairly thorough review of relevant evaluation studies, so that the probable effects of the Lothian Scheme could be more readily assessed and compared with alternatives. To this end the author visited a large number of relevant programmes in the United Kingdom and the United States and read through a mountain of evaluation studies. For a variety of reasons—including constraints of time and space, as well as the quality of much of the material—it is not possible to include a thorough review of this material here. A review of the United States material collected together by the author is, however, being published in Van der Eyken (1980), where a review and evaluation of several British Studies will also be found. A summary of the range of programmes available also appears in McCail (1980). Here brief reference will be made to a number of the most relevant programmes.

The United States Programme

The US intervention programme has three main components: Headstart, Follow-through and Homestart.

The scale of the operation may be indicated by the fact that, since 1965, between ten and two hundred billion dollars has been invested each year in such programmes. Over six million children have been involved at a cost, at current prices, of something of the order of three thousand dollars each. Some two hundred million dollars have been invested in the evaluation of these programmes.

The particular variant of the scheme which is initiated at any site is chosen, administered and evaluated on a local basis. What typically happens is that several groups of academics and practitioners proffer a number of alternative programmes from which one or two are chosen by local groups for implementation.

Headstart was initiated, not by the Office of Child Development, but by the Office of Economic Opportunity. In those early days community development objectives loomed large—and remarkably successful the programmes were in achieving them (Marris and Rein, 1972). However, in the wake of the movement, best signalled by the names of Bloom (1964) and Coleman (1966), toward a belief in the central importance of early environment, Headstart was increasingly seen as being primarily concerned with educational activities with a *cognitive* emphasis. The original focus became secondary. A quote from Zigler, the first Director of the Office of Child Development, which states the educational/cognitive point of view particularly clearly, will be found below. Some argue that the change of emphasis from controversial but attainable goals to non-controversial but hard-to-attain goals was deliberate: the Community Development programmes were *too* successful in enabling people to bring effective pressure to bear on authorities, and this threatened vested interests. (The same point has been made in relation to the British Community Development programmes).

Zigler's Headstart was based on the belief that what happened to children before they started school was of critical importance to their subsequent educational development. A variety of centre-(institution-) based and home-based programmes were therefore initiated to demonstrate what could be done to boost children's development in the early years. Later, the Federal government initiated Headstart Planned Variation to place more emphasis on assessing the relative merits of alternative programmes rather than "showing what could be done".

It was recognised from the beginning that Headstart alone would be unlikely to have a permanent effect on children's educational development. Provision was therefore made, in *Follow-through*, for a variety of further activities to strengthen and build on the gains the children were expected to make.

The term "Homestart" referred to a specific type of Headstart programme. This involved home-based intervention designed to encourage the mothers to play a more active role in promoting the educational development of their children.

Reflecting their origins in the Office of Economic Opportunity, and despite Zigler's somewhat narrower orientation, all Headstart programmes were multi-pronged, involving educational activities for parent and child, health care, and improvement of the economic, social and physical environment. Despite the variety of models, *all* Headstart programmes were supposed to follow guidelines laid down by the Office of Child Development, which included the following *educational* objectives:

Provide children with a learning environment and living environment which will help them to develop socially, intellectually, physically and emotionally . . .

Involve parents in educational activities to enhance their role as principal influence on the children's education and development . . .

Assist parents to increase their knowledge, understanding, skills, in child growth and development . . .

Build ethnic pride, develop a positive self concept, enhance individual strengths . . .

Encourage children to solve problems, initiate action, explore, experiment, question . . .

Provide adequate indoor and outdoor space, materials, equipment and time for children to use large and small muscles . . .

Provide for on-going observation, recording and evaluation of each child's growth and development for the purpose of planning action suited to individual needs . . .

Provide for parent participation in planning the educational programme . . . and classroom . . . and home activities . . .

Provide parent training in the observation of growth and development.

The *health* component includes:

Provide a comprehensive health scheme . . . medical, dental, mental health, and nutrition . . .

Provide the child's family with the necessary skills and understandings . . .

Provide for a thorough health screening . . . vision testing . . . hearing . . . immunisation . . .

Provide extensive community mental health care.

The *nutrition* component includes:

Provide food to meet nutritional needs . . .

Educate parents in the selection and preparation of food, money management, consumer education.

The *social service* component includes:

Furnishing information about available community schemes and how to use them . . .

Follow up to assure delivery of needed assistance . . .

Establishing a role of advocacy and spokesman of Headstart families . . .

Helping . . . parent groups work with other neighbourhood and community groups with similar concerns . . .

Help to ensure better co-ordination between community agencies.

The *parent involvement* component includes:

Direct involvement in decision making . . .

Participation in classroom activities . . .

Providing methods and approaches for involving parents in experiences which will lead to enhancing the development of their skills, self-confidence, and sense of independence.

This comprehensive approach was retained in Follow-through. And yet the Stanford Research Institute were able to identify over eighty different models of intervention—each replicated at sites all over the country.

The *range* of models is breathtaking, ranging from primary emphasis on encouraging the adult members of the communities concerned to develop the civic perceptions, expectations, and abilities required to gain control over the wider political and administrative process, through giving parents the right to hire and fire teachers, assess pupils' progress in school and determine school curriculum (in order to ensure their relevance to the needs of their own culture), having parents come into classrooms to model effective human behaviour for the pupils, project-based education designed to enhance motivation, and conventional but individualised programmes based on one-to-one instruction, to highly structured programmes designed to teach children particular words and phrases.

Altogether, well over ten thousand programmes have been run and evaluated, and the very variety of the programmes and evaluations has helped to ensure that it would be difficult to systematise, analyse and assess them.

Given the variety of the goals pursued by project sponsors, attempts at national evaluations have, not surprisingly, proved difficult. At one point the Stanford Research Institute, which had been awarded the contract for the national evaluation of Follow-through, started trying to develop evaluation instruments geared to the goals of the sponsors (to, it must be admitted, an impossible time scale) only to find itself confronted, first, by an edict from the Office of Child Development to concentrate on assessing the programme's effects on IQ and academic performance, and, subsequently, with the loss of their contract.

Despite the activities of his colleagues, quoted above, Zigler, the Director of the Office of Child Development defined the goals of the programmes as being to enhance "the ability to master formal concepts, to perform well at school, to stay out of trouble with the law, and to relate well to adults and other children" (1973).

Several thousand evaluation studies have been carried out. It is clearly impossible for any single researcher, particularly one engaged in substantive research of his own, to get hold of, let alone evaluate these reports. To facilitate the process of evaluation the US Department of Health Education and Welfare has commissioned a number of reviews of the literature emerging from this vast enterprise. These reviews are, unfortunately, flatly contradictory. Thus, whereas Mann *et al* (1977) concludes that, of 62 schemes selected for their quality, 49 showed a beneficial effect and only 13 did not, and Brown (1977) came to the conclusion that the 13 studies which did not appear to show a beneficial effect were unsatisfactory for one reason or another (thereby concluding that there were *no* studies which did *not* show a benefit). Hawkridge *et al* (1968) and McLaughlin (1977) came to exactly the opposite conclusion. Hawkridge *et al* concluded that, out of over one thousand studies, only twenty-one met a criterion of improved academic or intellectual function, while McLaughlin *et al*, after reviewing forty "exemplary" studies which had at one time or another reported benefits (including the studies referred to in more detail below) concluded that:

"At the outset (of this exercise) it was expected that a major proportion of the effort would involve reconciliation of different, but apparently valid, studies: however, this turned out not to be a substantial problem. . . . The major problem was to draw *any* valid substantive conclusions from *any* of the studies".

Nevertheless, notwithstanding all the arguments, a number of conclusions do emerge from this literature:

1. Despite the breathtaking range of programmes, involving manipulation of every conceivable set of variables known to the author, no *dramatic* effects of any of the programmes have been demonstrated except that perhaps, given a little encouragement,

"deprived" adults are very good at coming together to bring such effective pressure to bear on the bureaucratic and administrative machinery that steps have to be taken to put a stop to such programmes of adult education.

2. *None* of the programmes has been able to have a dramatic and lasting effect on IQ. It is *not* the case that, as *was* widely believed at the start of the programme, simply doing such things as talking to children would dramatically raise their IQs and school performance. Whatever the variance in school perform-ance *is* due to it is *not* principally due to *any* of the obvious variables which were thought to lie behind it when the program-mes were implemented. (We may note in passing that one reason why the designs of the evaluation studies look so poor is that these studies were based on the assumption that the effects of intervention *would* be dramatic, and therefore demonstrable despite minor defects in experimental design and instrumentation).

3. If they are able to opt into the programmes, high socio-economic status children benefit *more* from the programmes than do low socio-economic status children (Palmer (1976), Jensen (1974)).

4. The range of outcomes which has been assessed does not do justice to the range of outcomes which one would expect to follow from such programmes. Thus one finds Love (1976) emphasising that thousands of parents *have* learned important things and come to feel, and to be, more competent and capable of leading their lives in the way they want to lead them than they were before, but that this effect does not show up in the studies which have been made.

4. No one style of intervention has been shown to be superior to others (although Stallings' (1974) evaluation of some of the Follow-through programmes does show that traditional school programmes depress the ability to perceive and think clearly, while "open" education programmes enhance this ability but depress performance in the three Rs).

6. One of the reasons for the messiness of the area is that programmes have not been sufficiently clear about whether they were service-oriented or research-oriented. The result has been a lack of theoretical basis in the interventions, fluidity in the processes the effects of which the researchers were supposed to be studying, and insufficient funds for the development of appropriate instrumentation (Haney, 1976).

7. While the Lothian Project represents but a drop in the ocean in comparison with the vast US involvement in such programmes, in terms of the *evaluation* studies it is one of the largest, most theoretically based, and most systematically evaluated projects in the world.

8. Whereas Headstart began with a community-development orientation, and, as a result of political rows, found itself deflected on to the less threatening goal of promoting cognitive development, the Lothian Project began with a focus on cognitive development, and, as a result of the Home Visitors' experiences, came to see the community-development goal as central to the achievement of its cognitive and educational objectives.

Studies of Particular Relevance

Despite the fact that pressures of space have led us to omit most of the material we have reviewed, it is necessary to summarise a few studies that are of particular importance from the point of view of evaluating the Lothian Scheme.

AMERICAN PROJECTS

Homestart, one of the best evaluated programmes, was aimed at the poor. Through regular weekly visits lasting about an hour and a quarter each, the families in the project were encouraged not only to play with their children, but to improve their health care, nutrition and to make better use of community resources.

Each Home Visitor worked, on average, with about ten or eleven families. The visitors themselves, though they were paid, were given very little (slightly over $5,000 a year) for work that often involved them in 50-60 hours a week. They were called "para-professionals" in that 90% of them had little or no formal training, and did not generally have much experience of working with families or of providing the varied child development, nutrition and health services that the programme called for. "In fact", said the Final Report on the project, "not being 'professional' was viewed by many project staff as an asset, making it easier to establish a close and trusting relationship with parents".

Homestart set out, through its home visiting programme, its group meetings and its back-up service of professional workers, to change the attitudes and child-rearing practices of parents, and at the same time to make families more self-reliant in their use of community facilities. As compared to a control group, Homestart families, after only a year in the programme, certainly showed changes of behaviour. They were more inclined to let their children help around the home, spent time reading to their children and helping them with drawing, provided more books and toys, talked to their children more often, were more involved in the community, and were generally doing those things which the Homestart visitors had encouraged them to do. (Although, notably, when asked whether they used specific community services like housing or job training, Homestart mothers reported a greater uptake than "controls" of only one out of 15 possible agencies).

The children, too, were significantly ahead of "controls" in terms of measurements on a Pre-school Inventory, a language scale and a child talk score. There was a statistically significant relationship between the frequency and length of time of home visiting and both parent and child outcomes. Where Home Visitors had made fewer than three visits a month, or where the visits fell below 1½-2 hours, there the language development of the children grew more slowly (Love, J. *et al*, 1976). However, children visited for two years did not do better than those visited for only one year.

When Homestart families and children were compared with children who had gone through Headstart programmes, only small differences could be detected.

"Although the minor differences that were found suggest that Homestart's advantage is in producing a more positive effect on the mother-child relationship, there were actually very few (such differences) . . . it must be concluded that the two programs had very similar effects on parents."

(Love, 1976)

Bearing in mind that Headstart programmes were largely centre-based "teaching" projects with a minimum of home visiting or often even parental involvement, this is thought-provoking, because it suggests that, while home visiting can of itself result in important changes, these are quantitatively (and perhaps qualitatively) little different from changes affected by more traditional methods of intervention.

The nature of Levenstein's intervention programme has already been summarised by Ian MacFadyen in Chapter 2. Levenstein's research has, however, recently thrown up something which leads one to re-evaluate the whole of her research, and thus the importance attached to it when designing the Lothian Region programme. While her research continues to demonstrate marked short-term gains in IQ on the part of her experimental subjects, it now shows an equally marked short-term gain in the IQs of her control subjects. This reminds one of Weikert's (1978) finding that all three centre-based programmes which he studied produced results of a similar order of magnitude. If all types of intervention—including the visit of a researcher who simply tells one that one is part of an experiment— produce gains of similar magnitude, why have an elaborate Home Visiting Programme?

Lazar (1979) was responsible for summarising the results obtained by the Developmental Continuity Consortium. In 1975 a group of investigators who had been conducting intervention programmes came together to pool their data and consider the long term effects of their efforts. The consortia included such well known authors as Deutsch, Gordon, Gray, Karnes, Levenstein, Palmer, and Weikert. What the consortia results suggest is that, while virtually all programmes result in short term cognitive gains, these tend to "wash out" in *all* cases, whether centre-based or home-based. However, there *are* long term effects. Children who have been involved in such programmes are less likely to be assigned to remedial classes or held back at school, and their standardised achievement scores rise continuously with age when compared with those who have not been involved in such programmes.

As will be argued later, the most probable explanation of these results is that the children have been taught the specific operations required to do well in IQ tests for young children. They have also been taught what to expect of schools, teachers, and other adults. As a result, the children will be better adjusted to school and less rebellious and disruptive. Not being held back, they will be in the right grade to study the curriculum on which they will be assessed and this will result in higher achievement test scores. In our opinion, it is reasonable to expect from the Lothian Region Educational Home Visiting Scheme results similar in all respects.

We cannot conclude our brief review of the American literature without commenting on the small size and short term nature of many of the studies. While the funds available to some of the US researchers were several million times the funds available to us, the US programmes (see Haney, W. 1976) have frequently been characterised by wild expectations as to what can be accomplished both by the intervenors and by the evaluators, by failure to be clear about whether the programmes being evaluated were best thought of as services or as a planned variety of alternative programmes the effects of which were to be compared one with another, by utterly unrealistic fundings and time scales, and by failure to budget time and resources for the development of appropriate instrumentation. Nearly all the evaluation exercises are based on experimental and control groups of less than forty, and most on less than twenty.

BRITISH PROJECTS

Turning now to British Projects, we find the ground covered much more thinly. Aside from the now widely reported Educational Priority Area projects, which mostly involved groups as small as those reported in the American studies, the number of evaluated schemes can almost be counted on the fingers of one hand. Van der Eyken will be reporting on his evaluation of these schemes elsewhere. Here it is appropriate to say a word or two about the EPA schemes.

In the West Riding study (Smith, 1975), a nursery programme supplemented by Home Visiting was shown to have a significant impact on IQ and the children were rated by the Educational Home Visitors as more independent and likely to take initiative after the Visiting. The parents were rated as less likely to make use of verbal or physical punishment. In addition, Poulton and James (1975) have reported that the study had a significant impact on the mother's attitudes and behaviour. Parents became more likely to say that it was more important to use words carefully when talking to children, and more willing to play a more active role in school classrooms. Teachers were, however, slow to accept the value of Home Visiting. The Home Visitors found their own experiences *as mothers* the most relevant "training" for their jobs. They changed their viewpoint on the locus of "the problem" they were trying to deal with and became more committed to the view that schools, rather than parents, needed to change. Like most of the other British projects, the EHVs found themselves drawn into counselling and "therapy" with the mothers in order to help them cope with their unmet social needs.

Another British project—in Deptford—led parents to feel more important as educators of their children, to forge closer links with schools, and to professionals coming to think of themselves as enablers of, rather than providers of, learning. It also led to IQ gains and to the children concerned settling into school more readily (Jayne, 1976).

Van der Eyken comments that this project, like the US projects we have described, caters for the sort of confident, service-seeking family which can make use of knowledge and skills when they are proffered.

Mention must finally be made of some work on pre-school

education carried out in Dublin (Kellaghan, 1977; Kellaghan and Archer, 1973, 1975). Two incredibly carefully thought out schemes were implemented and evaluated. One involved a centre-based programme. This mainly provided means of involving the children concerned in activities which would be likely to promote their cognitive development, although these activities were supported by some home-school link activities. The other programme involved Home Visitors' going into the children's homes over a period of time and encouraging the mothers to engage their children in activities (such as reading) which would be likely to promote their cognitive development.

So far, the evaluation of only the first of these sets of activities has been published. Despite the cognitive emphasis of the programmes and the care taken in designing the intervention, the mean IQ of the participating children increased only from 93 at the start to 99 at the end of the programme. It then declined to 91 three years later. The programme had no effect on a number of personality variables.

Aside from these results of the evaluation, the study is of interest because it shows that, despite the disadvantaged nature of the homes from which the children were drawn, the variance in their IQs is virtually identical to the variance found in the total population. Whatever explanation is advanced for the low mean scores of the children living in the area, that explanation must also account for the fact that the children's abilities are far from uniform. Whatever is responsible for the variance in IQs, it is unlikely to be the home backgrounds from which the children come.

The position of the Lothian Region Educational Home Visiting Scheme in this array of possible strategies will, it is hoped, by now be fairly obvious in a general sort of way. In the next chapters the activities of the EHVs are described in slightly more detail, and some of the issues which the Scheme has raised are discussed in the context of the available literature. In Part IIC we turn to the task of using the literature we have renewed, and the understanding of the issues which we will by then have built up, to assess what the impact of the Scheme is likely to be.

CHAPTER 5

THREE STYLES OF VISITING

As we have seen, the EHVs, working within the general framework outlined earlier by Ian MacFadyen, and in consultation with their Head Teachers, were encouraged to exercise their professional judgment about how best to go about their work and how best to relate the general orientation of the scheme to the needs of the particular families, schools and communities in which they worked. The variation in style that this produced, the pressures which made for it, and its consequences are reported by McCail in a related publication (McCail, 1980). Here it is sufficient to give the reader, as briefly as possible, some inkling of the extent of the variation.

Four styles of Home Visiting may be discerned within the scheme. Only three of these will be discussed here because the fourth is a style which was developed by the Visitor who works with handicapped children.

The styles which are described below are neither "pure" styles nor "ideal types". The descriptions leave many things out, and no one of the EHVs would claim to do all of the things which are included under any one heading. The sketches simply serve to indicate the sort of variation found within the scheme. To avoid any misunderstanding it should be mentioned that, although only six Home Visitors have been at work at any one time, owing to two retirements, eight Home Visitors have in fact been associated with the scheme up to the time at which the evaluation ceased. The number of EHVs at work has subsequently increased to fifteen.

STYLE 1

Style 1 seems to encompass the following components:

(*a*) An emphasis on teaching particular concepts: colours, relationships, names of objects. (Note the implicit theory of "cognitive development". As Bereiter and Engelmann (1966) assert, this view holds that the ability to think clearly is dependent on having relevant constructs available).

(*b*) An emphasis on teaching a "cognitive skill"—such as how to pay attention to shapes, to the lines on bits of jigsaws, etc. The cognitive skill behind these might be described as the skill of observing, reasoning, listening or analysing. This emphasis is, of course, compatible with a theory very different from that of Bereiter and Engelmann. This theory holds that the development of vocabulary, constructs, parts of speech, tenses of verbs, and linguistic structure is dependent on the prior development of the ability to perceive and think clearly, since these abilities are essential to discern the complex structure of language, which no parent or teacher is in a position to teach children explicitly (Spearman, 1927; MacNamara, 1972).

(c)   A "teacherish" style in interaction making extensive use of closed questions with the right or wrong answers.

(d)   An emphasis on encouraging parents to adopt discipline by reasoning, without being able to give any very explicit account of why this is so important.

(e)   Little questioning of the current programme of primary schools or "middle class values".

(f)   Minimal involvement in helping the parent to think about and solve her problems. (Such activities are felt to be a digression which is sometimes necessary in order to get the problems out of the way so that the "real work" of the visit can go ahead).

(g)   Involving parents, in a classroom-like situation, in group activities designed to teach them the received wisdom about how to bring up their children.

STYLE 2

The Home Visitor who best exemplifies this approach takes the view that developmental learning follows interest. It is necessary to follow the child's interest and give him the information he needs to explore them. He will then come to observe and to think. He will pick up concepts in the process, and his need to observe and to think about his interests will lead him to develop these cognitive skills, which he will then use in order to master language. Thus, like Spearman (1927) and MacNamara (1972), she holds that the ability to perceive and think clearly is a prerequisite to the acquisition of language—not the reverse (cf Bereiter and Engelmann, 1966).

Like Bruner (1966, 1967, 1976), Cazden (1975) and White (1976), her view is that the educator's job is to create environments in which children can grow. There is no need to direct their attention or to "stamp in" basic constructs.

Like Kelly (1955), she holds that the child, like herself, is an experimenting, analysing, thoughtful being who is already trying to reflect on, and improve, the effectiveness of his actions, and trying to understand the world. Thus it is not necessary to constrain his actions by rigid rules. Indeed this is to be avoided so that the child can exercise these abilities.

In order to prevent the mother viewing the child as incompetent and ignorant (and therefore as something to be disciplined, trained, and instructed), but rather as competent, thoughtful, interested, and anxious to learn, she is anxious to draw the mother's attention to her child's abilities and to encourage her to develop a great respect for her child's competence.

Because the child is capable of reasoning, it is important to adopt discipline strategies which stress reason. But by reasoning with the child one also promotes the development of the ability to reason, question and analyse. The effect becomes cyclical.

In order to help the mother to become better able to model appropriate cognitive processes in action—for the child to see and copy—she encourages the mother to mull over the goals of the visiting, the success with which they are being achieved, and ways in which they could be attained more effectively.

In order to help them to think about children's behaviour, styles of interaction between parent and child, and educational processes, she encourages parents to visit the nursery school—where they can not only see teachers and children interacting, but also see parents interacting with their own and other children. They can also try out new styles of behaviour with other peoples' children in a situation in which the consequences of a mistake may be less serious than they would be with their own children.

Because of the subtlety of her approach to promoting growth and development she is doubtful about the notion that effective Home Visiting could be carried out by mothers who have only a minimum of training and supervision.

STYLE 3

The third style of visiting is characterised by:

(a) A belief that it is necessary to use language to promote the development of reasoning ability.

(b) A belief that reasoning is impossible without language and concepts and that it is therefore necessary both to teach concepts and teach the analytic styles which are required to evolve concepts.

(c) A belief that an effort to help the mother to cope with her own problems will lead her to use language, get help from other people, make plans, anticipate the future, anticipate obstacles to the achievement of her goals and invent ways of surmounting them, bring to bear and utilise past experience, and increase her confidence in her ability to lead her life effectively. By doing these things more often in her child's presence, the mother will portray cognitive processes in action, and competent behaviour in general, in a way which it is easy for the child to copy. Indeed, the child will have a strong inducement to copy it—because he will see that the behaviour helps the mother to achieve her goals effectively.

(d) A belief that helping the mother to deal with loneliness by reflecting on the nature of the problem and taking effective steps to deal with it in the way which has just been described is an activity which is *directly* relevant to the achievement of the main goals of the project—and not merely a means of getting one's foot in the door or a valuable side-effect of having been involved in the project.

(e) A belief that schools urgently need to change away from their knowledge-communicating function to a growth-promoting function, but that, pending that change, children need to learn to take advantage of schools in exactly the same way as mothers need to learn how to exploit and manipulate bureaucracies in order to achieve their own ends.

Despite the attachment to language, this style veers toward the view of Bronfenbrenner (1975) that it is important to involve parents and children in activities in which the parents use cognitive activities to achieve their goals effectively. Although still some way from it, it also comes closest to the author's view that the language activities (so conspicuous to educational researchers in the past in the parent/child interactions of competent people) are only a small part of the total picture. So far as the child is concerned, the parental model also involves planning, monitoring the effects of one's behaviour and learning new things from the effects of that behaviour, and putting advancing oneself and the effective achievement of one's goals before attending to one's friends. These activities may have an impact on development which is at least as important as the actual language activities which go on between a child and his mother.

Concluding Comment

The objective of this brief chapter was to give the reader a feel for the different orientations adopted by the Educational Home Visitors. It was in no sense to give a complete account of work of the EHVs and the factors which made for differing orientations. This detail will be found in McCail (1980a, 1980b). None of the styles of visiting depicted here tell the reader everything which it is important to know about any one of the Educational Home Visitors and none of the EHVs do *all* the things listed under any one head. Nor are the styles static and discreet. For example, the EHV who most closely exemplifies Style 3 claims to have begun in Style 2, to have been led by the literature to adopt a Style 1 approach, and, finally, as a result of what she learnt as she went along, to have moved into Style 3. The thumbnail sketches which have been given are useful as a means of gaining an impression of the range of orientations represented within the project, but they grade into each other, and change, in endless ways.

PART IIB

SOME THEORETICAL ISSUES OF PRACTICAL IMPORTANCE

THE NEXT FOUR CHAPTERS discuss a few questions which lie at the very heart of the Project. In them an attempt will be made to raise and to clarify a number of issues of theoretical and practical importance. It is hoped that these discussions, incomplete though they necessarily are, will help others to run better programmes in the future. As has been indicated, one of the main functions of any evaluation is to generate suggestions for ways in which programmes can be improved.

These chapters arise out of topics which came up for repeated discussion at the weekly EHVs' meetings or represent areas of ambiguity which our observations led us to think about. Although the first of these chapters consists mainly of an extended quotation from a technical report published by the Stanford Research Institute and authored by Jane Stallings *et al,* it deals so well with a complex and confused area of such great importance to the Project that we could neither reasonably leave the question out nor hope to discuss it so ably or succinctly.

The four chapters represent a selection from a larger set. It is hoped that at least two of these other chapters—which relate to the logistics of running evaluated innovations and the shared understandings which are required to run them effectively (as distinct from running Educational Home Visiting Programmes) will be published as journal articles. Until that happens they can be obtained from the author in a mimeographed form.

CHAPTER 6

LANGUAGE DEVELOPMENT

As we have seen, the EHVs began their work by involving the children they visited, in their parents' presence, in activities in which "language was used to extend the imagination of the child".

The role of language in thought, and the role of the EHVs in developing language, was a matter for almost continuous discussion at the EHVs' meetings. One EHV maintained—and continued to maintain–that she *never* taught language. Another maintained that— although she was not very bothered if the evaluation did not show an improvement in IQ—language was *essential* in order to recall past events, make plans, anticipate obstacles, think of ways of getting round those obstacles, and persuade other people. It was, therefore, a *central* objective of the project to lead the parents to encourage their children to use language in new ways. It might not affect IQ, but it would certainly affect competence.

Since this range of perspectives is likely to be represented in any similar project, it may be helpful to make brief reference to the issues which have been raised in this, at times, fierce and acrimonious, internal debate.

Let us first look back at how Ian MacFadyen saw the situation. "Language is to be *used* to extend the imagination". He does not appear to be saying that language is to be "taught" in the sense in which knowledge is taught, though the fact that teaching seems to be more closely associated in the public mind with teaching concepts and conveying information than with developing new ways of thinking, feeling, and behaving is revealing.

But what of the word imagination? A quotation from Spearman is helpful:

"IMAGINATION . . . can be interpreted in two widely different ways, (1) the ability to form more or less clear and vivid 'images'. The importance of these comes chiefly from the view held by many psychologists, that they constitute the essence even of thinking itself. For any such view, however, but little support is afforded . . .;

the forming of images seems to be just the one ability the correlations of which with those involving 'g' never in any circumstances rises appreciably above zero! (2) inventiveness or creativeness . . . Analysis, however, would appear to demonstrate that *no such special creative power exists.* All three noegenetic processes are generative of new mental content and of new knowledge; and no other cognitive generation can possibly be attained in any other way whatsoever, not though a Shakespeare, a Napoleon, and a Darwin were rolled into one. That which is usually attributed to such a special imaginative or inventive operation can be simply resolved into a correlate—eduction combined with mere reproduction.

From this analytic standpoint, then, we must predict that all creative power—whether or not it be dubbed imagination—will at any rate involve 'g'. And such a prior conclusion seems to be corroborated by all the experimental evidence".

While later research into creativity reveals that Spearman has neglected its crucially important motivational component, and while it suggests that at the upper end of the IQ range convergent and divergent thinking tend to separate out, what he is saying is that imagination is essentially "basic intellectual ability". If this is so, what Ian MacFadyen is asserting is that he wishes to test the hypothesis that language *usage will* develop a child's IQ. While most of the EHV's would initially have accepted that proposition, most would now find it threatening, and not only because they would fear that—as the United States' Headstart and Follow-through investigations have confirmed—a tendency of the evaluators to focus on *this* goal would lead to a de-emphasis of other goals.

It may help us to tease out some of the issues involved in the concept of language development, and the role of language in intellectual development, if we quote extensively from the work of Stallings *et al* (1976).

Language Skills

Language skills encompass mastery of phonology (the sound system of language), syntax (the rules for correct choice and sequencing of words), and semantics, the latter including both knowledge of the meanings of individual words and comprehension and production of meaningful utterances. Language development occurs at an extremely rapid rate between the ages of two, when multiword utterances begin to predominate in the child's speech, and approximately four, when complex syntactic forms close to those of the adult can be found in the child's discourse.

Obviously, language is in part a learned skill; children absorb the language or languages spoken in their social environment. However, current linguistic theory (e.g., Chomsky, 1975) holds that all languages use similar underlying rule systems. Moreover, the sequence of stages of linguistic development and the approximate age at which each stage appears are remarkably uniform across cultures (Brown, 1973). The rapidity and uniformity of linguistic development, together with the universality, complexity, and abstractness of linguistic rules, cast doubt on the adequacy of ordinary learning processes (e.g. reinforcement, modelling) in explaining how the child masters his native tongue. Many workers in the field of developmental psycholinguistics concur, at least in some degree, with Chomsky's claim that important aspects of the capacity to acquire language are innate in the human species. (Note that this claim has nothing to do with genetic effects on individual differences in language ability). Direct neurological evidence has also been brought to bear in support of Chomsky's claim (Lenneberg, 1967). It is clear that language learning builds on complex cognitive skills that are present very early in life, whether these are innate or developed through experience in infancy as some cognitive-developmental psychologists believe (e.g., MacNamara, 1972; Brown, 1973).

Aspects of language that *can* be affected . . . include vocabulary, the surface details of syntax and pronunciation that constitute 'standard' (middle-class) English, the *rate* of acquisition of more fundamental skills, and perhaps the ways in which language is used. These aspects of language development can be tested, and they affect the child's relationship to the school. Vocabulary development requires little comment, but the remaining aspects of linguistic development raise important issues.

The surface variations of syntax and pronunciation that characterize 'nonstandard' dialects such as black American English are often interpreted as 'bad grammar' by middle-class teachers who do not recognize that nonstandard English is as intricate in rules and as rich in communicative power as their own dialects (Labov, 1970). Thus, mastery of the surface details of 'standard' English is a useful skill for the black child, who often becomes bidialectical in order to deal with both his own subculture and the dominant middle-class culture in the school. To ensure that the child makes progress in mastering 'standard' English while retaining respect for his own dialect is part of what it means to promote linguistic development . . . .

There is evidence that the sheer amount of adult linguistic modelling or adult-child linguistic interaction is related to various indices of linguistic maturity (e.g., mean length of utterances, complexity of verb phrases, variety of sentence types) . . . . There is also reason to believe that the rate of acquisition of general linguistic competence and of specific grammatical constructions may depend on the type of frequency of linguistic modelling and interaction that the child experiences . . . .

(There is no evidence, however, that the child's ultimate level of competence is necessarily related to rate of acquisition).

Another important aspect of language development that may be affected . . . is the way in which children use language—as a means of communication, as a tool for thinking, and as a means of expressing and controlling emotions . . . .

As the child reaches the early elementary school years, language becomes a vehicle for manipulating as well as expressing ideas. The gradual development of this use of language as a tool for thought can be observed over the preschool period (Vygotsky, 1962). Whether this use of language is a cause or a consequence of general cognitive development is a controversial point. Piaget (e.g., in Piaget and Inhelder, 1969) has argued that it is purely a consequence, that language skills have no casual relation to reasoning ability. Vygotsky (1962), Bruner *et al* (1966), and others have argued that acquisition of certain language skills can facilitate cognitive development . . . .

A final use of language that may be influenced by the . . . environment is verbal expression of emotions. There is evidence that children who can express frustration and anger verbally are able to reduce their levels of negative affect and avoid aggressive outbursts (Emmerich, 1966; Feshbach, 1969). In this regard, language use is intimately related to self-control and to the regulation of aggression, as already discussed.

Classroom processes likely to affect language skills in the four domains . . .—mastery of 'standard' English, rate of acquisition, use of language as a tool for communication and as a tool for thought, and use of language to express and control feelings—may be either formal or informal. Formal processes include drill, presenting the child with verbal reasoning or memory tasks, and explicit training in grammar or pronunciation. Informal processes include language games, storytelling (by adults or children), reading aloud, and, most crucially, verbal interaction between caregivers and children . . . .

It is likely that use of language to express thoughts and clarify problems can be facilitated if the caregiver intervenes skillfully in the relevant situations, helping the child to discover how his own verbalizations can aid him. As for use of language to express, and thereby control, emotions, the socialization literature reviewed earlier suggests that impulse control is best achieved through use of inductive discipline techniques that stress explicit verbal reasoning and explanation of rules.

Memory Skills

'Memory' refers to the capacity to store information and experience; obviously, the capacity to remember is necessary for all learning. Since babies exhibit learning (at least in the form of acquisition of conditioned responses) in the first weeks of life, it is likely that some primitive type of storage capacity is part of man's innate cognitive equipment. However, the capacity to acquire, store, and retrieve information voluntarily requires the development of mnemonic skills that depend on experience; this is particularly true of memory for verbal materials and of memory for verbal labels attached to objects or pictures.

For example, when educated Western adults are confronted with tasks such as memorizing lists of words or memorizing associations between pairs of symbols, they typically rehearse the words or pairs repeatedly to themselves. Rehearsal transforms the items to be remembered from transient 'short-term memory' into more durable 'long-term memory'. (See Atkinson and Shiffrin, 1968, for a review of much relevant evidence and a theoretical overview of this process). Preschool children are unlikely to rehearse verbal materials spontaneously, and as a consequence their performance on verbal memory tasks is poor. The tendency to rehearse and the ability to recall verbal materials or verbal labels for objects and pictures show significant increases with age from the pre-school period into the elementary school years (Flavell, Beach, and Chinsky, 1966; Flavell, 1970b; Hagen, 1972). Clearly the mnemonic skills in such experimental tasks are useful for some of the learning that occurs in schools and preschools. Memorizing the alphabet or the multiplication table, or learning the pairing between written letters and their names, are but a few examples of school-related rote memory tasks requiring verbal rehearsal skills.

Verbal rehearsal has also been implicated in learning tasks of a somewhat more conceptual nature. For example, preschool children do poorly on tasks requiring them to discriminate relative sizes of objects (Kuenne, 1964) or to shift flexibly between responses based on size and colour of objects (Kendler and Kendler, 1961). Kendler (1963) has offered evidence that older children are able to discover and remember the relevant attributes of objects in part because they name the attributes to themselves when performing the learning task.

Verbal rehearsal is not the only school-related mnemonic skill that children acquire. Other examples of memory strategies employed by educated adults include imposition of meaningful structure on lists of items to be remembered (Bousfield, 1953; Tulving, 1966) and use of visual imagery, rhymes, or narratives to connect lists of items (Bower and Bolton, 1969; Bower, 1972). Unschooled, non-Western adults do not spontaneously use all of the various mnemonic strategies in the same way as do their educated Western counterparts or children from their own cultures who have received a Western education (Cole et al, 1971). Therefore, it can be inferred that some of these strategies are learned and that their acquisition probably depends on discovering their usefulness in the school or preschool situation.

Perhaps the most provocative work on memory development in young children is that of Piaget and his colleagues (see Piaget and Inhelder, 1969). Piaget conceives of memory as a process of active reconstruction rather than retrieval of static mental records of past events. He argues that the child's capacity to reconstruct depends on the cognitive operations available to him. Thus memory improves with age, not only because the child acquires specific task-related strategies such as verbal rehearsal but also because his cognitive capacities undergo major, qualitative, structural reorganization. The changes in memory skills and cognitive organization are especially striking between the preschool and early elementary school years (the transition from 'preoperational' to 'concrete operational' thinking, in Piaget's terms). Piaget has demonstrated that pre-school children can reconstruct simple scenes (e.g., an arrangement of sticks ordered from smallest to largest) more accurately after a delay of many months than after a delay of only a few days, if they have acquired new, relevant cognitive operations (the capacity for "seriation") in the meantime. While these experiments present certain problems of interpretation, they lend credence to the view that memory development in young children is part of a broader process of cognitive growth and is not merely due to acquisition of specific mnemonic tricks.

Finally, a good deal of recent work on children's memory (e.g., Kreutzer, Leonard, and Flavell, 1975) deals with what has been called 'metamemory' skills. Such skills include knowing what one knows or does not know before one searches one's memory for the particular information or knowing what kinds of strategies will help one retrieve information (as opposed to merely using such strategies unthinkingly). Research on such 'metacognitive' skills is in its infancy but promises to be a major new area of developmental psychology.

In sum, the memory literature gives ample reason to believe that specific mnemonic skills are acquired in response to particular school-related tasks. The literature further suggests that memory development may be linked to more fundamental changes in cognitive structure with age. While the literature clearly demonstrates that preschoolers differ dramatically from older children in mnemonic strategies and metamnemonic skills, the literature is somewhat less clear in tracing the development of these skills through the preschool period . . . .

Reasoning Skills and Concept Learning

In their broadest interpretation, reasoning skills and concept learning encompass almost the whole of cognitive development. They constitute not one outcome variable but a massive complex of variables. Reviews of research performed before 1970 (Berlyne, 1970; Flavell, 1970a) demonstrate the volume and intricacy of theoretical and empirical work in the two areas. To do justice to the issues relevant to the two fields would be impossible here; only the briefest of summaries can be attempted.

There are two major approaches to cognitive development, one derived from a European rationalist/structuralist tradition most clearly exemplified in the work of Piaget, the second from an American behaviourist/empiricist tradition associated with Watson, Hull, Skinner, and many others. The latter school views the development of concepts and reasoning abilities as the accumulation of specific experiences; for this school, learning consists of appropriate sequences of stimulation, response, and reinforcement. (In some variants of the approach, modelling is also given a role). The Piagetian tradition views intellectual development as a series of qualitative changes in intellectual structure. Learning is assumed to be intrinsically motivated in children; extrinsic reinforcement is not a condition for its occurrence. Environmental stimulation provides a necessary input, but it does not alone determine mental structure; mental structure is shaped by the mind's activities upon the data of experience. Needless to say, these two views are not the only ones possible; many, perhaps most, developmental psychologists adopt hybrid positions, drawing on both traditions.

Cognitive Style Variables

Whereas cognitive skill variables refer to the child's acquired intellectual abilities and knowledge, cognitive style variables refer to the manner in which the child acquires knowledge and overcomes obstacles . . . . The style variables—reflectivity, task persistence, generation of ideas, problem solving, and curiosity—are less directly tied to the school and to the middle-class culture embodied in the school. In fact, prominent psychologists have argued that some of the characteristics captured by the style variables are part of every child's basic make-up. For example, White (1959) has postulated that man is endowed from birth with 'competence motivation', a desire to understand and master the environment, which is in part reflected in his curiosity, persistence, and problem-solving activities.

With Stallings' review of the literature firmly in our minds we may return to our examination of the EHVs' work in the language area. Those EHVs who encountered children who had language *problems* —whether those problems were to do with phonology, syntax or semantics—found themselves unexpectedly impotent. If the child's programming was somehow defective—for whatever reason—then their formula "talk to the child and encourage him to study relationships" suddenly turned out to be inadequate.

At a less extreme level, some of the EHVs regarded the teaching of the syntax of standard English as somehow unethical, perhaps because it smacks of "imposing middle-class values". Others considered it to be important to do this so that the children concerned would be able "to take advantage of what the school system has to offer".

"Formal" processes to promote the acquisition of syntax and to facilitate the use of language as a tool for thought and communication were favoured by some. "Informal" processes were used by others. Both appear to have advantages and disadvantages.

Some of the EHVs made efforts to develop the ability to memorise and recall, though none made use of the rehearsing techniques which would seem to be indicated by Stallings' review.

As to promoting reasoning and concept learning, some of the EHVs have followed what Stallings calls the American Behaviourist model —of teaching particular bits of information and associations—and others the "European" tradition. Clearly both have their advocates.

Those EHV's who have taken the "European" perspective—that it is necessary to be able to observe and think clearly *in order* to acquire language—have, on occasion, argued that it is necessary to teach "cognitive skills"—like observing, classifying, and looking for relationships. Some have tended to do this with materials they or the mothers have chosen—such as jigsaws—and have encouraged the children to reason about the shape of the piece that is needed, or what is implied by lines etc. which are likely to continue on to the missing piece. Others have tended toward the view that it is important to allow the child to define the problem—so that he is "motivated"—and then to encourage him to think and learn in relation to whatever he happens to be interested in at the time. Those who have adopted this perspective have also been inclined to argue that, by following the child's interests, one may encourage him to develop the habit of concentrating for longer periods of time on particular objects, to individuate specific aspects of his environment from their backgrounds, and to develop the habit of tolerating the frustrations involved in trying to generate new concepts and understanding.

"Cognitive Style" variables have also been frequently discussed by the Educational Home Visitors—and they reached as little consensus as did Stallings in her review of the literature. One of the problems is, of course, that many of the variables which Stallings refers to as "cognitive style" are not in fact correctly described as *cognitive* style variables at all. They involve cognitive activity, but they also involve behaviour and emotions as well. They are complex motivational dispositions which involve finely balanced patterns of cognitive, affective, and motor activities. Yet, complex as they are, these are the qualities which parents are most likely to influence—wittingly or unwittingly. And these are the qualities which the EHV's may be most able to influence. The problem is that, if the author is right (Raven, 1977), these qualities are intimately bound up with values—about influencing which the members of our society are, not without reason, extremely ambivalent.

In the light of Stallings' review it would seem that there are good grounds for the EHVs' feelings of bewilderment. Both the meaning of, and the role of, "language development", both as a dependent and as an independent variable is extremely unclear. Future projects may well like to give priority to trying to establish some consensus on the perspective which was going to be adopted and tested before going into the field. And even if they do not wish to define that perspective, then they may still like to draw the project staff's attention to the enormous variety in viewpoints which is represented within the literature.

The EHV's also stumbled across a number of questions which are not raised in Stallings' review. One of these is whether Stallings is right to assume that the ability to adjust to schools is dependent on familiarity with Standard English Syntax and Semantics—or whether it is more dependent on such things as willingness to answer teachers' questions (which often differ from most of the questions asked by most other people in that they are primarily designed to test, and assess, the person who is questioned by finding out whether he knows something which the questioner already knows, rather than to find out from him something which is of instrumental value to the questioner). Where children are not familiar with such questions, the effect may be to discredit the questioner in the eyes of the child—for if the teacher doesn't know the answer she must be stupid and if she does know the answer she must be equally stupid to ask questions to which she knows the answer! Once his teacher has been discredited in this way the child may not be strongly motivated to pay much attention to her!

Another set of questions not particularly highlighted in Stallings' review came to light with the publication of Donaldson's *Children's Minds* (1978) which challenged many of the EHVs' assumptions and, in particular, their assumption that language was a pre-requisite to the development of reasoning, rather than the reverse. But other fascinating questions which her book poses have as yet barely surfaced. How does one foster "disembedded" thinking whilst avoiding disembedded thinking becoming thinking which is bound by a "pedagogic boundary" because it is never reality-tested? How does one teach, or facilitate the acquisition of, meta-languages for thinking *about* such things as the structure of language, disembedded thinking itself, the strategies one would use to discover principles and how to innovate— how to venture successfully into the unknown?

What the EHVs did feel was that Donaldson's own belief that these processes were primarily to be fostered by reading to children might be a little inadequate. And, as we have already seen, *what* is read to children, the values and behaviour patterns portrayed, the insight that is given by the material into feelings and cognitive processes in action, the feelings and emotions children's parents express while reading the material to their children, and what children "read" and try to make sense of themselves, may have many more implications for their future development than the mere exposure to words and syntax.

The EHVs have also questioned whether in promoting an interest in, and willingness to persist with, intellectual activity, *language* activity is anything like so important as, for example, the behaviour and priorities of the mother. The mother's example may include evidence of her brooding over problems and struggling to make relevant variables explicit, showing an interest in intellectual activity on the part of the child and of others, and using intellectual activity as a means of moving herself toward her own goals.

If it has done nothing else, the project has raised serious questions about the role of language in development in the minds of the participating teachers—and, through this report, hopefully in the minds of others. But, whereas the author would maintain that projects of this sort should enable us to move some way toward answering these questions, some of the EHVs have maintained that, if the evidence for the view that the sorts of language activities in which they believe is not forthcoming, then one should not be running projects of this sort at all. Thus, by leading them to question cherished assumptions, the project has, in some cases, led the EHVs to reject a strategy which would take them a long way toward obtaining the very knowledge they need. A moment's reflection reveals that a line of thought such as theirs undermines the project in a much more fundamental way than is immediately obvious. It rejects the view that one way to seek to solve one's problems is to start trying to do something about them and reflect on what one learns by so doing. It rejects the view that human beings are experimenters who seek to act on their environment in order to develop a cognitive understanding of that environment. It asserts that effective action can only be based on prior knowledge. It therefore asserts that human beings cannot learn for themselves, but have to be taught. By definition, therefore, mothers are incompetent, and have to be taught. The mother, therefore, cannot provide a model of competent effective behaviour for her children to copy. Such a viewpoint, therefore, draws attention to a possible contradiction within the project which strikes at its very heart. Fortunately, the blow may not be lethal—for we have yet to learn how the contradiction is going to be resolved.

CHAPTER 7

DISCIPLINE STRATEGIES AND COGNITIVE DEVELOPMENT

Almost as soon as they began their work, the EHVs found themselves trying to influence the discipline strategies which parents adopted. To begin with this generated a great deal of unease, but, over time, influencing parents' styles of discipline came to be seen as something which was central to the attainment of their objectives. Nevertheless it continued to smack of "imposing middle class values", and, therefore, indoctrination. Some of the EHVs took the view that, provided one believed in something, one was entitled to encourage others to believe in it too. Others sought to make explicit the link between discipline strategies and the achievement of the project's goals.

Here our objective is, once more, not to give a blow by blow account of the development of the project, but to share some of the insights which have emerged, so that others can consider them. No claim is made that the chains of reasoning which are described are necessarily correct, or even that they necessarily correctly reflect the points of view of the EHVs who put them forward. They are simply points of view which deserve to be discussed.

One argument advanced for thinking it is important for parents to adopt strategies of discipline which rely on reasoning if they are to promote the cognitive development of their children is that, if the parent reasons with the child, she will come to realise how competent he is and, as a result, not feel obliged to restrict his questioning and his exploratory behaviour. As a result, he will get an opportunity to exercise a wider range of his abilities. If all decisions are made for him, he will never get an opportunity to do this. Still less will he get an opportunity to realise that he can do things competently on his own. By encouraging the child to reason about this process the mother will encourage him to bring to bear relevant past experiences, to anticipate what the effects of his actions will be, to think about the reactions of others and put himself in their shoes, to make his own observations about how things work, and, if necessary, invent appropriate new concepts in the process.

By listening to the child the parent will be able to decide what information is most relevant to his needs, to discover what the child's interests and concerns are, and to encourage him to think about relevant issues. As a result of discovering what the child's interests are, she will be able to create opportunities for him to pursue those interests in a highly motivated manner, thereby enabling him to acquire necessary information and practise appropriate cognitive skills. In the process of doing this the parent will more than likely discover that the child's complaints are reasonable, and, as a result, seek to take action on his behalf in relation to the wider environment—including the school environment.

Whilst reasoning with the child the mother will give the child insight into her own reasoning process. She will share her own values with the child and her understanding of the goals which are important in life and how they are to be achieved. In the course of doing this she will share with him her understanding of how society operates, and how other people react—including the sorts of reactions that she believes to be worthy of consideration and those which are worthy of only contempt. The child will therefore be likely to develop internalised controls geared to the mother's values. She can therefore afford to encourage him to question and take decisions for himself, knowing that he already shares many of her basic viewpoints. Because he has developed internalised controls she does not need to check up on him: he can be left free to adventure into the unknown and the mother can remain confident that he will be able to deal with new situations, as they arise, in a reasonable way.

In reasoning with his parents—ie authorities—the child will learn that he can apply cognitive processes to think out what should happen and that the authority will listen to the results of his reasoning. In other words he will be rewarded for engaging in cognitive activity because he will see the effects of his actions paying off. He will come to think of himself as someone who is entitled to have his own opinions and as someone who is entitled to interact with, and seek to influence, adults. His strategies for dealing with authority are likely to be open, rather than underhand, and this, in the long run, is likely to make it easier for the society in which he lives to respond to new information and new understanding. The child himself is likely to be open to new ideas because he will not have to refer back to authority to find out what to think about each new piece of information.

Parents' views on discipline seem to be closely related to their views on respect. Parents who favour harsh discipline tend also to stress unquestioning obedience, to de-emphasise inquisitiveness and adventurousness, and to equate the child's respect for his parents with fear of, and deference toward, them. Parents who stress the importance of discipline by reasoning are more likely to think that they should *earn* their children's respect. The connection between such beliefs and cognitive development is worth spelling out.

A parent who is concerned to *earn* respect will obviously try to behave in ways which are deserving of respect. He or she will therefore be inclined to behave in a way which is above reproach. He or she will be more likely to discuss his or her actions, the reasons for them, and their long term consequences with the child. These considerations may involve the future of the child, his family, or the society in which the family lives. To do this he or she not only has to talk to the child but also to make his or her own values clear, to share his or her understanding of human behaviour and the workings of the family and society with the child, to share his or her understanding of cause and effect in human behaviour, and to give the child insight into distant causes of immediate behaviour, whether that distance is in the future or in the past.

If parental behaviour is to be seen by the child as fair and considerate the parent must engage the child in a similarly complex set of cognitive activities. He or she must also make clear his or her value-dilemmas and thereby develop a tolerance for cognitive ambiguity and complexity, she must make clear the ways in which they can be resolved, the sorts of information which it is appropriate to bring to bear to resolve them, the sorts of behaviours which they themselves value and the reasons for valuing them, and the barriers to living up to their ideals and the ways in which, by taking thought, those barriers can be overcome.

An effort to treat the *child* with respect is likely to create opportunities for the child to talk, to reason (with authority), to consider the long term consequences of his actions, and to make explicit and discuss the values, codes, and long term considerations which should guide his actions. Not only will these activities lead the child to practise complex cognitive activities, they will lead him to imagine and anticipate possible long term consequences of his actions with which he may not already be familiar, to imagine barriers to his achieving his goals, to consider a broad range of possibly conflicting consequences and choose between them, to develop confidence in his ability to handle such ideas, to think of himself as someone who is capable of handling such ideas, to think of authority as something which is open to reason and which he is entitled to seek to influence, and, above all, if the parent *does* treat the child with respect and respond to his arguments, to experience the benefits of sound rational argument.

In the course of the sorts of discussions which are implied in such a pattern of interaction between parent and child, the child will obviously be exposed to an extremely wide range of viewpoints and ideas. As a result, he is likely to find any further new idea a great deal less unfamiliar and frightening. He will have more pegs on which to hang it. He will therefore be more open to new ideas and innovations and more likely to explore their relevance to his own behaviour.

In short, as the EHVs, Brandis and Bernstein (1974), Hess and Shipman (1965) and others, have recognised, the mutual respect and discipline issue is central to the cognitive goals of the project, whilst at the same time posing serious value-laden problems for those who wish to implement it.

Yet, despite the apparent logic of this position, that logic may well be wrong. Quite obviously any parent who is to encourage respect and discipline based on reasoning must himself be extremely competent at cognitive activity. It may well be that many of the parents involved in the programme have moved into their present jobs and environments, and come to seek prescriptive moral codes to guide their behaviour, precisely *because* they are less able to reason and cope with complex arguments. This hypothesis finds some support in the data collected by Raven (1976) who found that downwardly mobile pupils, who had, presumably, previously been exposed to the child rearing practices which, as we will see, are more characteristic of High rather than Low Socio-Economic Status parents, were more likely to wish to have prescriptive codes laid down for them and were more anxious that they be firmly enforced. It is therefore of the greatest importance to find out whether the patterns of relationship we have hypothesised here are borne out in practice or whether it is *possible* for people to *change* their perceptions, expectations and behaviour in this area.

CHAPTER 8

TEACHERING VERSUS MOTHERING

"The overall aim of the Project is ... to emphasise the unique and irreplaceable contribution of the mother to the educational development of her children during the critically important formative period before the child begins formal schooling".—IAN MACFADYEN, *in a Paper to a Seminar on Home, School and Community, Glasgow University, June 1977.*

Although there have been several indications throughout the duration of the project that it might be important to distinguish between teachering and mothering, the issue came to a head when a Home Visitor, who had been reading over a transcript of one of her visits, exclaimed "I was *horrified* by that. There I was being a *teacher.* I was doing all sorts of things which I would not do as a *mother*".

Further discussion suggested that the distinction revolved around such things as: the use of closed, "tutorial", questions designed to find out whether the child knew something which the Home Visitor thought the child ought to know, pressure to cover "ground" during the visits, a tendency to push things along, rather than "respond" to the child, and a focus on knowledge to be conveyed rather than encouraging the child's personality to flower and develop. In a discussion revolving around the question of whether it was *possible* to follow the child's interests, and respond to him, the same Home Visitor declared that it was not possible for her to respond to a child's interests during a Home Visit because she was only there for an hour a week and therefore did not have time to become thoroughly familiar with the sorts of things which turned him on.

More food for thought was provided on another occasion by a Home Visitor who remarked that she felt extremely uncomfortable if she just visited people's houses and encouraged the children to play. She was, after all, being paid by the Local Authority to visit the houses in order to assist in the children's development. Although she recognized the basic irrationality of what she was saying, she therefore felt obliged to "teach" rather than just allow growth to happen. Her sentiments were echoed by the group "enabler" who said that in her role as facilitator of community activities, she felt under an obligation to "make things happen" (which she nevertheless tried to resist), when what might be best for the mothers concerned might be a rather slower, and somewhat different, course.

A third indication of the growing realisation of the potential importance of this issue is contained in the paper which the Home Visitors wrote for a Lothian-Strathclyde Meeting on "Teacher in the Year 2000?—Strategies for Change in Education". In that paper the Home Visitors particularly stressed the need for a move from "teaching" to "facilitating children's development".

An Internal Contradiction Within the Project?

It may be that the Project's terms of reference contain an internal contradiction or tension. One must, of course, hasten to add that there is nothing wrong with that. As philosophers and leaders throughout history have emphasized, such contradictions provide starting points for many worthwhile developments in thinking and society. But emphasizing the mothers' "unique and irreplaceable contribution" implies that they are to be encouraged to do something which is, by definition, different from what teachers do in nursery schools. However, the EHVs' professional expertise was in the teaching area, not in the mothering area. Nor did they all necessarily agree that the mothers' contribution was "unique and irreplaceable", for several emphasized the need to get children into nursery schools, particularly if the home was "poor". These reflections suggest that one of our social problems may be that parents know only too well what the "unique and irreplaceable" function of schools is, but that there is no widespread recognition of what the "unique and irreplaceable" function of mothers may be.

Background Literature

The tensions of which we have spoken also pervade the background literature. The fact that some two-thirds of the variance in academic achievement between pupils of any one age can be accounted for by home background is widely cited as a justification for early childhood intervention. Less widely cited are two other facts. Firstly, as Moynihan (1966) and Coleman (1966) were at pains to point out in relation to their work, the lion's share of the variance in school attainment between pupils of different ages is almost entirely a product of the school, not the home. Secondly, if the effect of IQ is partialled out before one assesses the effect of the home, the proportion of the variance in school attainment which can be attributed to home process variables drops to 5% to 10%. Whilst most members of our society would be prepared to agree that it should be relatively easy to encourage parents to treat their children in different ways, far fewer would be optimistic that it would be relatively easy to have a substantial impact on children's intelligence. Confronted with evidence of the statistical equivalence of the statements: "The lion's share of the variance between pupils of any one age in their school attainments can be accounted for by home process variables", and "The lion's share of the variance between pupils' academic attainments at any one age can be accounted for by their intelligence", many people would find their faith in the statement that research by Peaker (1967), Coleman (1966) and others has shown that mothers were their children's most important educators severely threatened.

However, there is another sense in which it may be true that mothers are their children's most important educators. In this sense the focus is not so much on school performance as the criterion of development, but on qualities like initiative, self-confidence, adventurousness, and the ability to make use of one's talents and abilities. It is in this sense that McBeath (1978), for example, suggests that parents are their children's most important educators. It is in this sense that both Coleman (1972) and Bronfenbrenner (1974) suggest that parents were in the past their children's most important educators and that there is now a gap in the socialisation process. It is in this sense that parents vary considerably from one to another in the qualities they think it is important for their children to develop and in relation to which the processes that are used to foster development vary greatly between households. (Further evidence to support this statement will be found in Part III of this Report). Nevertheless, there is evidence to suggest that, even in this area, the belief that parents are their children's most important educators may be ill-founded. As has already been mentioned, the stress which pupils place on developing these qualities is at least as much a product of the destinations pupils see themselves bound for, as of the backgrounds they come from.

The tension which we have suggested exists within the present Project and in the general background literature is also to be found within specific items in the literature on which the Project was based. For example, the extremely influential Plowden Report (1966) on primary education contains Gilbert Peaker's analysis which, as we have seen, purports to show that two-thirds of the variance in school performance at any one age is attributable to home background.

Nevertheless, the educational outcomes with which the Plowden Report itself is most concerned are, not academic performance in the traditional sense at all, but the development of such qualities as initiative, the ability to make one's own observations and learn without instruction, autonomous learning, and the ability to work with others. As Bernstein has emphasized, the most important shift to be discerned within the Plowden Report is from a single, explicit, criterion of performance toward a multiple, implicit, network of criteria. The Report is no more able than were the participants in the present project to say what those multiple goals might be, how they are to be achieved, and how progress toward them is to be assessed. But Peaker's work, carried out within the traditional framework (and, as we have seen, using the device of an apparently impersonal regression equation which stacks the evidence in favour of "environmentalist" position), is somehow used to lend credibility by association to a very different viewpoint, albeit an environmental one.

It is, perhaps, because of our inability to make these new goals explicit that, after the first flush of enthusiasm, there has been something of a swing back toward a concern with a smaller number of explicit criteria of school success. This swing—and it is something our own EHVs were very concerned about—was in fact a product of the evaluators of educational programmes not being able to measure progress toward the wide variety of goals which those directly concerned with the change felt were most important—often not at a fully conscious level. Given a definition of science as "that which is unarguable" the resulting evaluations presented a very lopsided—and anything but "objective"—picture which failed to say anything significant about the programmes' ability to reach their *main* goals. That this swing may, however, have been somewhat premature is suggested by the work of Stallings (1974). In a sentence or two, what Stallings shows is that the more classrooms stress traditional goals like reading and arithmetic the higher are pupils' reading and arithmetic scores. But these same classrooms produce a substantial *decline* in the ability to perceive and think clearly. On the other hand, classrooms which are systematically directed toward the goals of "modern" education—the ability to explore, make one's own observations, evolve one's own concepts, and find one's own information—do in fact produce a substantial increase in the ability to perceive and think clearly. (This was measured by a test which had nothing in common with the activities which were actually taught). Such programmes did however result in a decline—which other, more limited, studies have also reported—in reading and arithmetic scores.

This study therefore provides clear evidence that the multiple goals which parents and teachers can pursue in education are in tension, and cannot necessarily be assumed to be mutually supportive.

The Project's Contribution to Making Explicit the Processes which are to be used to facilitate Growth

The conclusion to which our discussion thus far may be leading us is that the notion that the mother has a unique and irreplaceable contribution to play in promoting her children's development may be a source of confusion in two quite different ways. If she can be taught by a teacher to do what it is necessary to do to promote school success, then her contribution is neither unique nor irreplaceable. Furthermore if her contribution toward achieving other goals can be made explicit, and if she can be helped to develop mothering skills, then the conclusion is again that her contribution is neither unique nor irreplaceable. If goals such as those we have mentioned are made explicit, and if the procedures which are to be used to pursue them are made explicit, then it may be possible for other people to pursue those goals with her children. On the other hand, it may not be. It may be that pursuit of these goals is dependent on such a deep-seated pattern of relationships, extending over such a long period of time, and on such intimate knowledge of the child, that it is impossible to conceive of any way in which the development of such qualities might be fostered except in the context of a close personal relationship. But, if that *is* the case, then it seriously calls into question our current perceptions of what is desirable in educational institutions. And it certainly calls into question the widespread belief that it is desirable for children to attend nursery schools.

In point of fact, of course, neither extreme statement is likely to be true. What is much more likely to be the case is that we need to become clearer about the sorts of qualities which can best be fostered in a parent-child relationship and the sorts of qualities which are best fostered through formal educational processes. These formal educational processes may, of course, look very different from those with which we are familiar in most classrooms today. They may involve, for example, on the one hand, community-oriented, project-based educational programmes in which parents and children work together to solve some of their joint problems with the assistance of other members of their communities, and, on the other, educational exercises designed to enable the participants to experience particular patterns of thinking, feeling and behaving, and try them out in new situations which are not so threatening as normal home situations.

The Project suggests that the quality of family relationships, the ability of the mother to amuse her children and to keep them out of mischief, her relationships with a wider network of friends and relationships, and her opportunity to work jointly with other equally ignorant people in seeking a solution to her problems are all important determinants of the effectiveness of any educational process orientated toward facilitating growth than "teaching". It also suggests that the role of "tutorial questions", in which questions are asked in order to discover whether the "learner" knows something which the person asking the question already knows, deserves to be thoroughly explored. Such questions assume that the person who asks the question knows what it is important for the learner to know. As such, such questions reinforce the notion that "authority knows best what you should be doing", and, as a result, tend toward the acceptance of uniform goals and treatments. They therefore tend to reinforce the notion that it is possible to sove our present social problems through centralised analysis and rigid plans and controls. As Emery (1974), and the author (1973, 1978), have shown, such a way of thinking may be disfunctional in the situation in which our society finds itself. It might (and we will see that many of our HSES mothers also advocate this) be more appropriate to seek a de-centralised solution in which individual members of our society are encouraged to exercise discretion in a responsible way, bearing in mind their own calculations of the long term consequences of particular actions. We may therefore conclude, as we began, by suggesting that mothers may have much to teach teachers. Discipline strategies and attitudes to authority may not only have a great deal to do with cognitive development, but also with the development of other qualities which are of critical importance in the future development of our society. The title of our next Conference should, perhaps, be "*Mothering* in the Year 2000?"

CHAPTER 9

FACILITATING PERSONAL LEARNING

Some people, eg Midwinter, have seen Educational Home Visiting as a route toward the introduction of a new concept of education: a concept of education which is based on people working together to solve their own problems, and growing and developing in the process. We ourselves have been anxious to study the adequacy of the weekly EHVs' meetings as a means of facilitating personal learning—as a means of facilitating people in making their own observations, evolving their own constructs and building up their own understanding of the problem they are trying to tackle. The Home Visitors too, in their paper "Teacher in the Year 2000?—Strategies for Change in Education", predicted that there would be a move away from the teaching of subject content toward the facilitation of personal learning by the end of the century. And, as we have seen, and as we will document more fully later, in their role of "friend", the Home Visitors, by working with the mother to help her tackle her own problems, have led her to feel more strongly motivated to do something about her problems. They have helped her to grow in confidence and competence. The question of what the project has to say about how to facilitate development is therefore of more than personal interest.

When we embarked upon our research we had hoped, from our observation of the EHVs' weekly meetings, to be able to say something about the sorts of activities and structures which facilitated personal learning. Unfortunately, we are not able to do this. All we are able to do is draw attention to one or two of the barriers to implementing such a sysem of education.

We would not wish to give the impression that the weekly meetings have been unsuccessful. On the contrary, everyone concerned has made great strides forward. It is clear that, if a school, or a group of schools, decided to do something to try to tackle some aspect of the current crises in secondary education, it could, by plunging in, and simultaneously setting aside enough time to mull over its activities and catch up with developments elsewhere, be virtually certain of making great inroads into the problem. The structures which the Project has created are, therefore, generaliseable to other school settings, certainly for teachers, and almost certainly for pupils.

As we see it, the chief barriers to the effective implementation of such a system are, firstly, the deeply ingrained desire to have authorities come along and tell one what to think and how to carry out one's tasks. Equally deep-seated is the desire for structure. Even some of the EHVs who did not wish an authority to come along and talk, consistently expressed the view that the meetings should be structured to cover a number of previously planned issues. There was some impatience with wandering discussion, and the idea that one would, through such discussion, stumble across new insights and understandings which no one had previously possessed was an anathema to some. The value of generating a better formal understanding of the processes with which the Home Visitors were trying to grapple as a means of improving their own performance was doubted by some. The task of generating a formal understanding was not regarded as problematical and it was felt that a formal understanding of these processes would not help to improve practice. Linked to the desire for authoritative information and structure was the view that the group leader should act, not as "facilitator", but as someone who took sole responsibility for seeing that group members did not speak out of turn, for identifying group goals, and for ensuring that they were attained. There may therefore be a case for the group to examine its own attitudes towards authority and leadership.

But the most difficult task faced by the group was, perhaps, to come to terms with the anxiety generated by not having a clear job definition, by not knowing who was responsible for setting the criteria against which their work would be judged, by knowing that other people defined the same job in different ways, by knowing that their work was being assessed and evaluated, and by not being certain whether they owed their primary allegiance to their school base or to the central team. In a context like this it may be particularly important for those responsible for an action research project to go out of their way to provide support for whatever it is that the Home Visitors at a particular point in time believe to be important, and to do their best to make clear where the limits of personal responsibility and discretion lie. It may be important for them to insist that the achievements of each Home Visitor will be recognised—even though those achievements may lie outside the area which was originally thought to be important and even though they may lie primarily in the area of helping the group to clarify its goals rather than accomplishing something with the families they visit. There may be a need to recognize the frustrations inherent in doing a job such as this, and to minimize other frustrations—such as bureaucratic niggles over expenses. There may be a need to create a mechanism whereby Home Visitors can pair up with other Home Visitors to try to think through a problem which is bothering them. There may be a need to take great care to ensure that sufficient trust is built up between members of the group to permit open confrontation between conflicting points of view, so that doubts neither continue to gnaw away at their insides nor fail to get expressed because of the fear of hurting others, or because of the fear of recriminations. In short, it may be desirable for the members of a group such as this to participate in an induction programme designed primarily to make use of trust-building exercises, ego-development exercises, exercises designed to help the participants to develop non-threatening ways of expressing differences of opinion, participative leadership, and styles of providing support, warmth, and recognition. More generally, these may be important pre-requisites to the generalization of the styles of learning which have been adopted in this project to other educational settings.

Attention may also be drawn to the parallel between what the EHVs were doing in these sessions and what some of them hoped the mothers would start to do in relation to their own problems and the cognitive styles they hoped the mothers would be able to help their children to develop. To the extent that the EHVs, as individuals or as a member of a group, found it difficult to make the procedures they were using explicit and analyse them explicitly in such a way as to be able to improve their performance, to the extent that they found intuitive intervention more effective than action based on generalised abstract principles, to the extent that they felt themselves to be dependent on the teaching of authorities rather than able to generate and test abstract principles for themselves, to the extent that they did not spontaneously search for relevant literature, constructs, and resources which would help them to tackle the problem they were seeking to tackle, their behaviour paralleled that of the mothers and belied the most basic principles they were trying to teach.

The role of a "facilitator" in a group such as this may parallel the role of the EHVs as facilitators of parent and child growth—whether based on a group or an individual basis—and this in turn may parallel facilitation of children's growth by parents or teachers.

PART IIC

THE PROBABLE AND POSSIBLE EFFECTS OF THE LOTHIAN REGION EDUCATIONAL HOME VISITING SCHEME

OUR OBJECTIVES in this part of our report are to explore the probable and possible effects of the Programme, making use of our understanding of the way it is operating, the experiences, hopes and fears expressed by the Educational Home Visitors, the notes made for us on the progress of their visits by the EHVs, and our open-ended interviews with parents, headmasters, and others. Our aim here is not, and cannot be, to provide "hard" data on the effects of the Programme. Rather it is to make explicit what we might find—with a greater or lesser degree of certainty—if we did in fact mount appropriate studies. In many ways, it would be more appropriate to present this discussion in terms of hypotheses which might be explored, rather than in terms of the "probable effects of the Programme". And this would indeed have been the most appropriate form of presentation had the evaluation been viewed as an exploratory study which was carried out prior to mounting a more statistically-based study. However, despite the fact that the budget allocated to it was of the order of magnitude of a budget typically allocated to such exploratory studies, it was *not* set up in this way. The research proposal laid down that, among other things, the evaluation would assess "what effects, if any, does the programme have on the social, intellectual and emotional development of the children who take part?"

Taken at its face value, that statement might be interpreted to mean that data would be collected to document its impact. However, the proposal goes on to make clear that it is not to be interpreted in this way: "The available research procedures are very weak. There is little, if any, agreement, as to what should be measured, how it should be measured, or how the results should be interpreted". It goes on to suggest that there is a way round that problem. Unfortunately, it does not say what that route is. One can only surmise that it was intended to examine the operation of the Project in order to discern, in the light of the available literature, what its effects were *likely* to be. This conjecture is supported by the fact that considerable stress was placed on the need to thoroughly review the available literature on the impact of similar action projects in the UK and abroad. But, regardless of what was originally envisaged, it is, in fact, extremely important to set down our impression of the effects of the project for, as the quotation from the original contract says, the state of theory building and measurement expertise in this area is so poor that, even with an extremely large project, making use of measures which would take years to develop, we would be unable to document all the processes and effects which it is important to assess. In policy evaluation it is more important to get a rough fix on all relevant variables than to get an exact measure of any one of them.

The material to be presented has deliberately been kept separate from the material derived from our statistical study. It was, after all, derived from an independent source. As we will see, our statistical material on the impact of the programme was derived from two small samples who were interviewed using different interview schedules. By and large, the results support each other. The material to be reported in this section of our Report was derived from the observations made by McCail and the present writer. On the whole, we agree with each other, and, in general, with one important exception, our observations are supported by the statistical data. Thus, small though the samples are, and subjective though our own observations necessarily are, our main conclusions are based on four, relatively separate, sets of observations. There is, therefore, every reason to take them seriously.

CHAPTER 10

THE EFFECTS AND PROBABLE EFFECTS OF
THE PROJECT ON THE CHILDREN INVOLVED

We may consider the impact of the programme on the children
under two headings: the direct effects which the Home Visitors are
likely to have on the children, and the indirect effects they are likely to
have on them via the mothers.

Probable Direct Effects

There is little doubt that, had we tested the children's intelligence,
their scores would have gone up. In some cases this would be because
the EHVs had taught the children the names of colours and shapes,
how to do jigsaw puzzles, and how to cut out shapes. The items in
many intelligence tests measure just such knowledge. The Home
Visitors also help children to develop the knowledge and skills
measured in other tests. In other cases the EHVs encourage the
children they visit to reason about things which interest them. All
encourage the children to sit down and concentrate for longer periods
of time, whether on things which the Home Visitors have selected or
on things of their own choice. Such activities are also likely to affect
test scores. Thus, because the Home Visitors have given the children
they visit practice at the tasks which are set in most intelligence tests
we would expect that this EHV programme, like most others (*see*
Love, 1976; Brown, 1977), would affect IQ test scores.

But, despite its undoubted impact on such scores, the interpretation
to be placed on this finding remains in doubt. One question concerns
the extent to which the abilities that had been fostered would transfer
to other aspects of cognitive functioning. Our own hypothesis is that
those Home Visitors who focus mainly on creating an environment in
which the child can explore and follow his *own* interests will be most
likely to have most effect on the ability to perceive and think clearly in
relation to tasks which have not been directly practised, and that these
Home Visitors will have the greatest impact on the children's

motivation, language development, and long-term IQ scores. This hypothesis is supported by the previously mentioned work of Stallings *et al* (1974), which shows that the greatest effect on the ability to perceive and think clearly, as measured by a test which had nothing in common with the activities which had been taught, was produced by open, exploratory, forms of teaching.

While other Home Visitors will also have an impact on such things as the ability to name colours and cut along lines we would have serious doubts about whether the ability to perform such tasks is a basis on which future IQ is built. In an untutored situation intelligent children may well learn to do these things more quickly than less intelligent children, but improvement in their ability to perform these tasks may still not provide a basis on which to build the rather different abilities which are assessed later in life. Careful study of the immediate and long term impact of these activities is strongly indicated.

Another probable effect which virtually all the Home Visitors will have will be to help the children to adjust to schools. The children will be much more familiar with what to expect of the teacher, and, in particular, much more well disposed toward teachers and "tutorial" questions in which teachers ask questions in order to test the child and find out whether he knows the "right" answer, rather than in order to get some information which she herself wants.

Not only do the Home Visitors familiarize the children with a teacherish style of behaviour, they also orient them toward books. As Wells (1978) has shown, reading ability is greatly influenced by the provision of opportunities for children to become familiar with the rules of print and hardly at all by such things as verbal and exploratory behaviour. While many infants teachers do make an effort to help children who suffer from the disadvantage of not having acquired these basic attitudes and orientations to overcome it, it is more difficult for them to do so in a relatively impersonal group situation than in a warm one-to-one situation like a Home Visit.

These processes, taken together, will undoubtedly have the effect, documented by Lazar (1979), Palmer (1977) and Love (1976) in the States, of markedly reducing the number of children who are allocated to remedial classes, held back for a year, or designated as "problem" children. The children will be less likely to be "in school" but not "with" the classroom curriculum. They will be in classes in which the curriculum is "appropriate to their age and ability", and therefore get higher scores on attainment tests.

Those Home Visitors who encourage children to think for

themselves about their own problems may, however, lead some of the children concerned to be more likely to question what goes on at school. As Keddie (1971) has shown, one important reason for some children's failure at school is, not their lack of intelligence, but their willingness to question what they are told and relate it to their everyday experience and find their teachers' assertions wanting. They break the rule—"the pedagogic boundary"—which asserts that one should not reality-test what one is told. Thus, in the child's eyes, a teacher may not only discredit herself by asking tutorial questions ("If she doesn't know *that,* there is no point in paying any attention to anything else she says!"), but also by not reality-testing her assertions, ie, for living in an academic ivory tower. A child who has been encouraged by a Home Visitor to make his own observations, and think about the things he is dealing with, may, therefore, be pulled in two contradictory directions. On the one hand he may, through this early experience, have become well disposed toward, and developed a great respect for, teachers. On the other hand, he may well find that the teachers he meets in later life do not take kindly to children who check out the statements they make. In an earlier study (Raven, 1975) we found that very few secondary school teachers wanted their pupils to be sceptical about what they were told! A similar conclusion seems to emerge from the study of nursery school teachers' priorities carried out by Taylor, Exon and Holley (1972). We would be most unwilling to even hazard a guess about the way in which this dilemma will be resolved. In a small project such as this so much will depend on the individual schools the pupils attend and on the particular teachers they work with. But, if the project were implemented by a large number of schools and local authorities and a facilitative style of visiting adopted, we would not expect the consequences for the children's adjustment to school to be entirely positive.

Attention should, perhaps, be drawn to the difference between a child who has been encouraged by a teacher to question things he is told and one who has been encouraged to do so by his parents. The latter may be more willing to tolerate the limitations of the teaching situation and adjust to the differing expectations of the home and the school, while the former will find that he has to adjust to discontinuities in teacher behaviour, without the support of the home.

It is also almost certain that the Project will have an impact on the children simply by exposing them to another adult who takes an interest in them, and who brings with her a new set of interests, styles of interaction, and concerns. The children's mothers are not the only people who have commented on this. As Zajonc (1975, 1976) has observed, children's rate of development early in life seems to be influenced by the number of adults with whom they interact. But this effect, again, wears off over time.

Zajonc also draws attention to the probable importance of children having an opportunity to teach other children. As we have seen, some of the Home Visitors seem to go out of their way to allow the children to teach them. These Home Visitors may not merely have an effect on the children's feelings of competence and their confidence that they know something which other people do not know, they may actually, through putting the child in the position of a teacher, lead him to become a great deal more explicit about what it is he wishes to communicate, and thereby develop analytic skills, and the ability to evolve, or find, relevant concepts, and the necessary linguistic skills. He may not only be more willing to answer teachers' questions, he may be better motivated to do so because he thinks he really is teaching his teachers something. (And, of course, if those teachers make use of project-based, enquiry-oriented, methods of teaching he will be quite right—a fact which again underlines the conclusion that the effects of the project will depend as much on the type of school the children enter as on what the EHVs do).

A possibly less desirable effect of the Home Visitors is likely to be that the children will come to rely still more heavily on their *teachers'* assessments of their ability. The Home Visitors often lead the children they visit to do things which are worthy of commendation. As a result, they are often more positive about the children's abilities than are the children's parents. Now, unfortunately, both Stones and Fend have shown (in personal communications) that most teachers give most of their pupils to understand that they are not particularly competent. According to Fend, what typically happens is that LSES children believe their teachers, rather than their parents, and are therefore gradually cooled out of the system. In contrast, the HSES children believe their parents (who have themselves got much better self-images, and are therefore much more confident in their judgment) and this over-rides their teachers' negative assessments, leading the children to persist in school. What the Home Visitors may have done is to lead the children to be still more dependent on, and trusting of, their teachers' assessments, and, when these start to be negative, they could have a much more devastating effect on the children than would otherwise have been the case. This, of course, is a hypothesis which it would be impossible to test without mounting a substantial follow-up study.

Indirect Effects on the Children via the Parents

By and large the parents think that school success is an important determinant of their children's future. This position is not only clear to them as individuals, it is also culturally accepted, and the Home Visitors are walking testimonies to its truth: they carry badges of social approval which many of the parents would like. As a result, it is clear from our own interviews that some of the parents start to do the things which the EHVs do—and do so in sufficiently large numbers for it to be reasonably certain that the effect would show up as a significant result in a statistical study. They seem particularly likely to take up aspects of the EHVs' behaviour which are clear, easily identifiable and imitable, and apparently directly relevant to the child's later school success. They buy books and read them to their children. They insist that the children sit still, pay attention, and use materials in the ways in which the Home Visitors used them. They set about using "play" to teach language. (In at least one case the parents put away the child's nursery rhyme books and bought *Ladybird* books instead). They ask more "tutorial" questions, designed to find out whether their children have learned something which they, the parents, think they should have learned, rather than encourage the children to tell them things which they do not already know. They make more effort to teach their children the names of things, and the names of relationships. They stress the importance of *knowledge;* to know the things which adults know is important in itself. In all of these ways they would be expected to lead their children to adjust to school. The children will be more likely to know what is expected of them by their teachers. They will have been taught the "hidden" curriculum.

The Home Visitors lead some of the parents to think that school success is more important than they did before and convince them that they can do something to ensure that the child succeeds there. The parents pick up the idea that school success can be bought by hard work at the tasks set by teachers. It is therefore virtually certain that some of the parents will be more likely to insist that their children do their homework and attend school regularly.

Those Home Visitors who place emphasis on using language for new purposes—in order to help the children achieve their own goals —may well have the effect of leading the parents to take up this tendency to encourage the child to use language for new purposes, and this, in turn, is likely to promote school success indirectly by leading the child to be able to make his own observations, find his own information, and learn without instruction.

Most of the Home Visitors will also lead the parents to develop more confidence in their children's ability. All go out of their way to draw parents' attention to what children *can* do. For these reasons the parents are more likely to expect their children to do well at school, and therefore to take an interest in how well they are doing in the expectation that they will be told something good, rather than something bad, about them. They will also be more likely to react sharply if the children do not do as well as they now expect and thereafter take steps to help the child to overcome the problem.

All of the Home Visitors also lead most of the parents they visit to be better able to entertain and amuse their children, and keep them out of mischief. The "play" activities they introduce are often perceived as a means of keeping the child interested, and therefore out from under their parents' feet. As a result of parents' being better able to amuse, occupy, and entertain their children, family relationships seem to improve. Parents become less likely to think of the time they spend with their children as a stressful situation in which they are forced, against their own inclinations, to spend the time shouting at and scolding them. In this less strained situation at least some definitely develop more respect for their children's abilities. The long term effect of this may be that they will expect them to do better at school. It seems to us that, as a result of the visiting, at least some of the parents have established a warmer relationship with their children and it seems probable that the children concerned will wish to retain this. They can therefore be expected to strive not to let their parents down by, for example, allowing themselves to do badly at school. As a result of both having developed a greater respect for their children's abilities and having learned that, if the child is unhappy, something can be done about it, the parents are more likely to believe that something is really wrong if their children complain or are seriously disruptive. They are therefore more likely to create a situation which is conducive to growth, and can also be predicted to react more positively if the child complains about something which is wrong at school. They would be expected to be more likely to seek the reason for the child's complaints in the environment than in the child himself—because they *know* that it is possible for the child to be happy and behave in a competent way. They will have learned from experience that, when he complains, there *is* something wrong. And they will be more likely to respect the child's, rather than his teacher's, account of the reasons for his difficulties once he gets to school. Having established a less strained relationship with the child, the parents may relatively automatically move on to activities which satisfy the developmental needs which come higher in Maslow's

(1954) hierarchy—ie they may be able to devote more time to self-actualization since they no longer need to devote all their time to establishing basic co-existence. They may be able to move on to becoming more concerned with their own, and their child's, growth and development.

Most of the Home Visitors have also had an impact on the discipline strategies of the parents. By demonstrating, and explicitly encouraging, discipline based on reasoning, they may produce a large number of effects which we have, as yet, been unable to observe.

In the first place the child may, for the first time, have an opportunity to learn that the requirements and requests of authorities are not arbitrary and capricious, but based on reason. This may encourage him to shift from a tendency to try to learn the rules to trying to understand the reasons for them. He may therefore be more likely to spontaneously study regularities in his environment and seek logical, rather than magical, explanations of events.

Secondly, a cyclical process may be set up. Because the parent encourages the child to reason, she may discover how capable he is and develop more respect for the products of his reasoning and be more willing to do something about the legitimate requests of the child. This may give the child experience of logical reasoning producing effects which he desires, and this may in turn reinforce his tendency to reason about the social situations, and communicate the products of that reasoning to adults. As Piaget has shown, the child's tendency to reason about *social* situations is one of the strongest pressures toward the development of abstract thinking.

But besides encouraging the child to practise thinking for himself, sharing those thinking processes with others, and rewarding him for reasoning, the parents' move toward discipline by reasoning may confer other benefits. The child may develop increasing ability to guide his own behaviour by reference to long term considerations and principles, rather than the dictates of authority. As a result it may be safer for him to adventure and be inquisitive. Adventurousness and inquisitiveness are dangerous if one has not developed the ability to decide for oneself what one should do about situations that have not been previously encountered, and the behaviours for coping with which have not been prescribed.

Those Home Visitors who have established a network of social contacts for the parents they have visited have, in effect, as Van der Eyken (1980) has emphasized, created a sort of safety net enabling the mother to get others to help her with her problems. As a result of being able to cope with her problems more effectively, she can move on from having to spend most of her time gaining a precarious hold on life to the more personally developing activities which come higher in Maslow's Hierarchy (1954). She can spend more time attending to the child's psychological growth and development, rather than just feeding him and keeping him warm. This social network also operates to reduce her loneliness, thereby reducing depression, enabling her to become more vivacious and better able to tackle the problems which beset herself and her children. She can devote more of her time more flexibly and more developmentally to her children. Her whole life style becomes lighter and more growth enhancing. She becomes better able to see her own and her child's problems in perspective. She may also have more energy available to do something about them. The child himself is more likely to be able to devote his whole energy to thinking about the task in hand, rather than worrying about his parents' problems.

Those Home Visitors who have moved on to trying to help the mothers develop the abilities needed to cope with their loneliness and their problems, rather than just provide a safety net for them, will probably confer a whole series of other benefits on the children concerned. As a result of seeing their parents use language to think about how to get control over their lives children are likely to learn how to do these things themselves. They have a greater opportunity to share in their parents' efforts to bring to bear relevant past experiences, anticipate obstacles that are likely to occur in the future, think of ways round them, and share in the joys of success and the frustrations involved in making progress. They have a greater opportunity to participate in clarifying goal and priorities, thinking through the long term consequences of alternative courses of action, and getting help from other people. The mother's increasing confidence, and her more positive self-image, is likely to communicate itself to the child. So is the mother's growing feeling that she has a right to be listened to by those who are responsible to her for the environment in which she lives.

For many of the parents this is their first opportunity to establish a warm relationship with a teacher. It is sometimes their first opportunity to learn that many teachers are not the harsh, authoritarian, judgmental figures they took them to be. For the first time, many of them realise that teachers are human beings, and can be approached on that footing. As a result they will be more likely to approach their children's teachers later in life. Those Home Visitors who go out of their way to stress the parent's *right* to deal with teachers, and have some say in their children's schooling, may well reinforce this indirect effect, and those Home Visitors who have further established groups of parents designed to have this sort of effect may provide a mechanism whereby these desires can be translated into action. It is unlikely that the parents will go overboard on this because, as we will see when we turn to our statistical results, many EHVs have communicated the message: "yes—please come and see us—but we will only convince you that we are already doing the right thing".

From what has been said it is clear that, in one way or another, the Home Visitors, via the parents, are very likely to have a marked impact on the children's future lives. What *is* in doubt is whether they will have a substantial impact on the children's cognitive development as such. Our own view is that the answer to that question is certainly not a foregone conclusion.

Undesirable Effects

One cannot expect the effects of any intervention programme to be entirely beneficial. This is particularly likely to be true in this area, because the nature and variety of competence is poorly understood, the processes which lead to its development are still less well understood, the art of measurement in the area in its infancy, and the existing literature extremely unsatisfactory. Further activity along the lines of this intervention programme, associated with critical evaluation, is one important way in which it would be possible to improve on this state of affairs. In such a context it is important to draw attention to possibly undesired and undesirable side effects which such a programme may have.

As has just been hinted, the growth of competence may involve a great deal more than what normally goes on in educational institutions (Coleman, 1972; Bronfenbrenner, 1974). Most mothering may involve a great deal more than much teaching. Mothers may, in general, be in a much better position to respond sensitively to child-initiated activities, without feeling the pressure of time and the constraints of formal educational evaluation, which are felt by many teachers. The bond between parent and child may make available to them strategies for reward and punishment which are not usually available to teachers. They may be better able to handle values issues directly, because they are less likely to be constrained by our cultural ambivalence about teaching values explicitly and openly in schools. They may be able to give their children insights into the way in which they think and feel, in ways which would not generally be open to teachers. Encouraging parents to adopt a "teacherish" style of interaction involving closed questions, tutorial questions, direct teaching of concepts and time pressure may, therefore, in the end, and on balance, be undesirable.

On the other hand, perhaps more likely, is the possibility that, in many of the families visited, the mothers are at present neither able to behave in such a teacherish manner nor able to behave in the more sensitively responsive manner which is characteristic of some parents (White, 1976) and which might be more likely to facilitate the development of a wide range of personal characteristics. However, the probability that this is the case should not be used to brush the problem aside. There is a real possibility that, at least some of the EHVs, in at least some of their actions, may be encouraging mothers to abdicate their parental role rather than encouraging them to play their unique and irreplaceable part in promoting the educational development of their children.

While it is tempting to assume that many of the mothers who were visited were either unable to do much by way of mothering their children (because of the environment in which they were placed), or did not *know* how to do it, that assumption may be altogether too comfortable. While there is little doubt that, as far as we could judge from our own observations, they were not doing the things which would be most likely to promote the development of independence of thought and behaviour, self-confidence, a questioning scepticism, and the ability to learn without instruction, these qualities may not be particularly important in the environments in which the children are most likely to live, and the parents may be doing just the right things to promote the development of the dependence, unquestioning obedience, and rule-following, conforming, behaviour which, as Kohn (1969) has emphasized, may be required in those environments. Such a statement will, of course, lead many to protest that we seem to be advocating the establishment of a caste society. While rejecting that accusation (*see* Chapter 2) we would like to reiterate that we think that the question we have just raised—which is really about what children are prevented from learning if their parents are encouraged to adopt the activities which the EHVs would like them to adopt—is of the utmost importance. We have no reason to assume that children who are not engaged in the activities modelled by the EHVs are learning nothing at all. The EHVs are not going into a vacuum when they go into the houses. They influence *what* children will learn, not *whether* they learn. Given the ecological relevance of some of the attitudes the EHVs are trying to change there is every reason to suppose that the Scheme may be doing at least some of the children a dis-service.

The possible disbenefits of this process have, of course, to be set against the fact that the Scheme has undoubtedly—and intentionally —had the effect of leading at least some parents to become more articulate about what *they* think schools should be doing and able and willing to set about ensuring that they do it. In the end, the parents may be able to transform schools so that they are more appropriate to what they conceive as their children's needs. They may be able to get them to help their children to develop the qualities they need to transform their communities—rather than the qualities they need to succeed in a competitive academic race and to move away from those communities. They may be better able to get control over their environment in such a way as to be able to transform it so that it is easier to pursue their *own* goals, rather than feel that they will have to give up that which they value in order to avoid the disbenefits of that way of life.

There is another, related, way in which the Project may be doing parents and their children a dis-service. The Project will undoubtedly have a major impact on the children's subsequent adjustment to school, and, to the extent that adjustment to school is associated with school success, on school success itself. However, if it is true that an individual's life success is more dependent on his independence, confidence in dealing with other people and new situations, willingness to adventure and seek information for himself, and willingness to set out into the unknown, confident that he will find a way through the maze in front of him, then the balance sheet may be none too positive. Such qualities may make for school and life success, and yet they are not stressed in the LREHV Scheme. By encouraging the parents to focus on school success, and failing to encourage them to focus on these wider qualities, the Scheme may, in the long run, make for considerable frustration on the part of the children.

At an earlier stage, as has already been hinted, the Scheme, while making for adjustment to school, may not have anything like the same impact on success at school. Those parents who have been led to believe that, by talking to, and reading to, their children, they will assure themselves of their children's success, may be in for a disappointment. If it is not true, as we suspect it is not true, that the Scheme has a major impact on children's level of cognitive development, then it may be important to create situations which will enable parents to adjust to unfulfilled expectations. Their already deep distrust of professionals may otherwise be deepened still further.

Referring again to the existing literature, Stallings (1974) in the US has shown that, at infant school level, classroom emphasis on reading and arithmetic leads to a decline in the ability to perceive and think clearly. Some of the Home Visitors undoubtedly lead parents to place more emphasis on pre-reading and arithmetical skills, and this, while promoting school success, may well lead to a *decline* in the cognitive ability.

Finally, it is possible to argue that, by leading children to accept school, the Home Visitors may have the effect of making still more widespread the undesirable effects of schooling to which some authors point. The children may be less likely to protest at the irrelevance of what they are taught. They may be more likely to accept the "pedagogic boundary" and not question what they are taught. They may be more likely to blame their fellows for not doing well at school rather than question the institutional structures which force at least some people not to do well in the race. They may develop negative self-images, feelings of trained incapacity, and dependence on books and authorities, rather than positive self-images, a feeling that they could tackle other things, and independence in thought and behaviour. They may be still more likely to appeal to authority rather than take direct action in relation to their own problems. We will return to some of these questions when we come to look at the possible long term impact of the EHVs on society.

CHAPTER 11

THE EFFECTS AND PROBABLE EFFECTS
ON THE PARENTS

We have already seen that the Project has had a considerable impact on the parents, and that it will, through them, have a substantial impact, for better or for worse, on the children. The mothers have, more in some places than others, become more confident, outgoing, and able to cope with their own problems. In some cases the Project has contributed to community activity designed to improve the schools for the good of all. There have been many group activities through which the mothers get to know each other and participate in doing something worth-while in their communities, developing new skills and more positive self-images in the process. They have been provided with a network of social contacts which, to some extent, can shield them from the hazards of life. They seem to come to feel better able to cope with their own problems.

However, just as the effects on the children were not entirely beneficial, so some of the effects on the mothers may not have been. Many of the mothers seemed to develop a great respect for the teachers who came to visit them, and came to think that they would never be able to do with their children what the Home Visitors were able to do with them. They felt they lacked the professional's understanding of the processes involved. In other words they became more dependent on the professionals' insights and instructions than they were before. They came to think that schools were more effective than they had previously believed, and this in the face of all the research evidence which points to the inability of schools to have a differential impact on children who come from homes where the mothers do not do the things which the Home Visitors thought it was important for them to do. In this area, at least, the mother's feelings of "trained incapacity" *have* increased as a result of the visiting. As we have mentioned, this effect may override their increased willingness to intervene with the school if their child complains. In some cases the effects were more serious still. Because of their other problems, some mothers have been unable to do the things which the EHVs led them to think they should do—and this seems to have accentuated their already considerable feelings of guilt at not being able to do the things which they know they should be doing with their children.

Another, quite different, question has to do with the possible effects of the mother coming to feel that she has been step by step walked into something into which she only later realises that she did not really want to be walked. While uneasy, she may not have been sufficiently aware of what was going on to call the whole thing off. Besides, as we have seen, the Home Visiting programme may have conferred on her other benefits which she did value. We do not know whether any mothers would have liked the EHVs to have behaved differently and whether they felt unable to influence them. But many of the mothers did make it clear that they regarded the Home Visitors as somehow different from other professionals, including teachers. Such professionals, they often felt, frequently did not understand them, did not consult them, did not allow them to say what they wanted to say, and did not listen to them. The resentment they exuded often seemed to be much stronger than one would assume if one attended only to their words. It was not simply that professionals did not listen. They were frustrated with themselves because they were unable to articulate what they wanted to say. Their *feelings* were strong enough—but they did not have the lingo, the jargon, which would have enabled them to verbalise those feelings. Not only did they not have the necessary words, there would, they thought, have been no point in voicing their opinions anyway—because the professionals would not have a register which would enable them to hear that message. And, even if they heard it, the structures in which they worked would prevent them doing anything about it. The result was seething anger and frustration, not rational argument.

In this context something which happened in one of the Evaluators' meetings may be important. The evaluators asked the EHVs whether they felt that one of the reasons why parents who did not take up the things the EHVs would have liked them to was that some of the parents held basic values which were in conflict with those of the Home Visitors. The EHVs' response was that there was no such difference in values. Perhaps the explanation of the EHVs' failure to notice such differences was that they were not hearing messages which the mothers did not spell out for them. What we are saying is, therefore, that the way the Scheme is operating suggests that—although we have no evidence of it—the Home Visitors, *qua* professionals, may have contributed to the mothers' feelings of frustration and resentment in relation to professionals. If that was so, and if that resentment was communicated to their children, one might expect to find it expressing itself in anti-social, or delinquent, behaviour. Let us repeat, the Home Visitors have encountered ample evidence of this aggressiveness, hostility toward, and resentment of, other professionals, arising from the treatment mothers get from them and from the mothers' inability to influence these professionals from a position of extreme dependence. The Home Visitors themselves have on occasion been furious that mothers' wishes have been ignored and brushed aside and that the mothers have at the same time been in a position of being utterly dependent on the whims of those professionals—which often differed sharply from one professional to another. And, as the Home Visitors have made clear, the professionals to whom these comments apply include not only doctors, welfare workers, health visitors, school psychologists, and physiotherapists, but teachers as well. The possibility that the Scheme itself might be generating precisely these feelings therefore deserves the most careful investigation—although, to repeat, we ourselves have at present no evidence at all that it is doing so.

CHAPTER 12

THE EFFECTS AND PROBABLE EFFECTS
ON THE SCHOOLS

Given the way the Scheme was set up, with close links between the EHVs and the Heads of their schools, it was virtually certain that the Scheme would have a substantial impact on the Heads of the schools, and possibly other teachers. In point of fact there is ample evidence that the schools have been affected by the Scheme, although they all began at very different starting points. At the most basic level, the Home Visitors have conveyed to the Heads of some of the schools, in quite unmistakable terms, the fact that, contrary to what those Heads said to us in the course of their early interviews, the parents do *not* lack interest in the education of their children. They may not want their children to develop some of the qualities which might make for school success, and they may not want some of the consequences of that success, but of the fact that they want their children to pass school examinations if they can do so without spilling too much blood, sweat and tears, there is no doubt, and this fact has been relayed in the clearest possible terms to the Heads of the schools. In some schools the effects have been wider. In some, many members of staff were involved in writing a paper "Teacher in the Year 2000?—Strategies for Change in Education" which the EHVs produced for a Lothian-Strathclyde meeting. There is no doubt that the EHVs had been instrumental in implanting some of the ideas which were expressed.

As a result of the Scheme, virtually all the schools established activities which involved groups of parents. At one school this comprised a library for mothers and children. At another it consisted of the involvement of parents in the actual process of nursery education. At another it involved a whole series of community activities. Although the germ of all these developments may have existed previously, there is no doubt that the Home Visiting programme played a significant role in bringing them into being.

Nevertheless, in all cases, it is clear that the activities which have been established for parents are primarily designed to encourage parents to support what the schools are doing, rather than to give them any significant say in what schools do. Joyce Watt's data, the Dundee EPA study (Watt, 1977), and the general confusion about what is meant by "parental involvement", would hardly lead us to expect anything else. Nevertheless, some of the Home Visitors have been anxious to try to find ways of encouraging schools to be more tuned in to the variety of children's needs. As thinking on ways in which this could be done develops, it is likely that the Home Visitors will have a more substantial impact on patterns of formal education.

At least some of the nursery teachers and nursery nurses have been markedly influenced by the Home Visitors, and have, in some cases, become involved in the Home Visiting itself. At least some of these have now moved on to other positions from which it is their declared intent to implement something of what they have learned as a result of being involved in, and with, the Home Visiting Scheme.

The Scheme may also have effects on schools in another way. The interventionist, open-ended, nature of the Scheme led the Advisory Committee on the Evaluation to discuss some wider issues. The Advisory Committee very quickly became aware that the Scheme raised some very general issues about the educational system. What are we about in education? How are we going to cater more adequately for the variety of pupils' needs? How are we going to bring about change in education? What methods are to be used to facilitate the growth of pupils? What is the role of different types of parental involvement? How satisfactory is the professional basis for educational activity? How satisfactory are the theories on which educational activities are based? How are we going to measure outcomes in such a way as to give credit for the genuine benefits and assess the disbenefits? One view was that discussion of these issues should not form part of the evaluation. However, another view was that, without discussion of these wider issues, the Project was worthless. The evaluators' view was that, although, in theory, it would be possible for a committee which was not involved in the Scheme to discuss these issues, in practice such a committee would be much less likely to do so, the fact of having an on-going Scheme which raised these issues providing an invaluable stimulus to thought. As a result, we have, in this Report, attempted to share with others our attempt to set down some of the issues which many people kept raising in relating to the Scheme. In some ways, the Scheme provides an exemplar of project-based education: *do* something and see what you learn in the process!

CHAPTER 13

THE POSSIBLE AND PROBABLE LONG TERM PERSONAL AND SOCIAL EFFECTS OF THE SCHEME

We turn now to one of our most difficult and most delicate tasks. Very many people—even before the Scheme began (*see* Ian MacFadyen in Chaper 2)—had expressed doubts about the Scheme's morality. Ian MacFadyen hoped that the evaluation, by making *facts* available, would help to resolve some of these doubts. We share his hopes, and we believe that he was right. But, although we believe that the questions which have been asked are basically factual, these questions have to do with the *long term social* effects of the Scheme. While it would not, in principle, be difficult to collect the necessary information, and while the funds required to do so would be trivial in comparison with funds currently being invested in Home Visiting Projects, it is the case that we had to push the minimal resources available to this Project to their limit in attempting to come to terms with these important issues. We shall be speculating about what the effects of the Scheme *may* be in the light of the understanding we have built up of the operation of the Scheme itself, our own observations and interviews whilst working with the Scheme, and our knowledge of, and assumptions about, other social processes.

One possible effect of the Lothian Region Educational Home Visiting Scheme is that mothering skills may be further de-valued and undermined. Although, in the end, it may turn out to be the case that "mothering" skills are no more characteristic of mothers than teachers (and that mothers vary as much from one to another as do teachers) it may also be that the styles of caretaker behaviour which promote the development of different qualities in children have not yet been made explicit. Certainly, both Bronfenbrenner (1974, 1979) and Coleman (1972, 1974) believe that mothering skills are both important and neglected. And the demographic data which both produced strongly suggest that both mothers and father don't wish to be uninvolved in the socialisation of their children. Rather, their withdrawal from such activities seems to be a product of wider social changes. Now the Lothian Scheme, despite its avowed aim of encouraging the mothers to play their unique and irreplaceable part in promoting the educational development of their children may, as we have seen, lead some of the mothers concerned to feel that they should adopt a more directive "teaching" stance rather than a more facilitative and responsive "mothering" stance, that they are less adequate at the task than teachers, and that teaching is best done in nursery schools. However, as we have seen, mothers may be in a better position than teachers to facilitate the development of a much wider range of qualities and it may also be argued that mothers would be likely to lead their children to develop a much wider range of alternative qualities (all of which may be necessary to our society) since they, between them, may include representatives of a much wider range of motivational dispositions than are represented within the teaching profession. Society may, in the long run, be the loser if it is deprived of a wide variety of human concerns and abilities, and deprived, in particular, of qualities like initiative, the ability to make one's own observations, and confidence in one's ability to turn a risk to advantage, which it may be easier for mothers than teachers to foster.

As we saw when we discussed possible undesired and undesirable effects on the mothers, the way the Project operates may also lead some of the parents to feel that they are pawns, rather than origins, and this feeling of being a pawn may be communicated to their children in such a way that their children react in socially deviant ways. How much choice do the parents in fact have about whether to enter, remain involved in, or drop out of the Project? At one level, of course, the question is trite: they should clearly throw the Home Visitors out on their ears at any time. But at another level the question is by no means so easily dismissed.

Many parents become involved in the Scheme because they are told that it is something new which might possibly benefit their children. They remain involved, not because it helps them to play their unique and irreplaceable part in promoting the educational development of their children, but because they see that their children enjoy it and look forward to the visits, because it alleviates their own feelings of isolation and depression, shows them new ways in which they can entertain and amuse their children, because the Home Visitor occupies their children so that they can get on with the housework, or because it holds out—free—the promise of helping to ensure that their children are able to compete effectively in the critically important business of schooling.

So there are good reasons for admitting the Home Visitors to their homes: once they have admitted the EHV because she confers one set of genuine benefits or another, they may have less choice about whether they take up the values and styles of caretaker-child interaction which are modelled by the EHV. The EHV is a successful, prestigeful person who has an articulate values position. The mothers' value positions may be much less articulate, and certainly much less prestigeful. The EHV displays many of the badges of social approval which the mothers themselves would like. It is therefore likely that the mothers will come to believe that, by doing the things which the EHV does, they themselves will be able to acquire these badges. The EHV holds out the promise that, by doing the things which she does, the mothers will be able to ensure that their children are successful in the scramble for the spoils available in society.

So the mothers may, in effect, have very little choice about whether to let the Home Visitor in, and once in about whether to take up the things which the Home Visitor advertises. The mothers' values position is less articulate, less prestigeful, and, possibly, not even recognisable as a position by the Educational Home Visitor. Certainly none of the Home Visitors were able to articulate a legitimate values position which differed significantly from their own and which might be held by the mothers. (They *did* recognise that some mothers valued dependence and obedience rather than an enquiring mind, but thought that such a values position was not legitimate and that they should set about broadening the mothers' horizons. Indeed, in a sense, some of the EHVs saw this as their very *raison d'être*). So any feeling the mothers have of being manipulated may remain unexpressed, and, possibly, unexpressable—at least in words which would be understood by anyone who did not share their feelings and experiences. And it is entirely possible that those feelings of having been hood-winked and manipulated may simmer away and find expression in displaced, aggressive, anti-social behaviour.

Whatever the validity of the argument put forward in the last paragraph (which relates to this particular scheme) there is no doubt at all that the Scheme was set up in the context of a general climate of professional opinion which asserted that experts knew better than did some mothers about how to bring up children. For many years, the problems to be tackled by teachers were thought to be within the child. In due course the "problem" came to be defined as the child-in-his social-context—in his family. One had to tackle the "whole family". And this in turn was widened to include the child-in-his-community. Clearly, the implicit assumption here is that professionals know, better than the child, his mother, and his community, what is good for him and them. A substantial number of professionals had in fact come to think of themselves as responsible *for* their clients, rather than responsible *to* their clients. This process is part of a wider picture in which, it is asserted, many members of our society are ignorant, uninformed, and lacking in the abilities which are required to tackle their own problems. The long term effects of such a set of perceptions and expectations may well be, as Emery (1974) and the author have observed elsewhere, to make it increasingly difficult for society to adapt to a non-stable environment. They imply that only senior members of Government and our bureaucracies can take important decisions, and that the rest must do as they are told and be checked up on to ensure that they are doing as they are told. This climate occasionally finds expression in this Scheme. One frequently hears that the parents do not know *how* to play with their children or that they do not recognise the importance of talking to them and reading them books. They must therefore be taught to accept the professional's view-point on these issues. Less frequently one hears that it is important to convince the parents that obedience, conformity, dependence, and toughness (the ability to stick up for oneself) are not really desirable qualities for their children to develop. And one occasionally hears that, where the families are completely unresponsive to the EHV's message, the only thing that can be done is to take the child away from the family and into nursery school as soon as possible, thereby taking the decisions about what should be done with the children completely away from the parents.

This is a one-sided picture, of course, for one also hears, for example, that one of the primary objectives of the Scheme is to break down social barriers so that professionals can realise how competent the mothers really are if they are given an opportunity to express their competence, or that the real objective is to give them more choice about the sort of person their child will become. Nevertheless, it is hard to avoid the conclusion that the scheme was based on the belief that, in at least many ways, the professionals involved in it did know more about certain aspects of child-rearing than did some of the parents. The effect of this, however well-intentioned it may be, is to diminish parents' opportunity to build on their own knowledge and take their own decisions. An alternative way of proceeding might have ameliorated such effects—for example, by strengthening the elements of the Scheme which emphasize the need to create growth-enhancing environments in which parents learn to do new things and become more willing and able to take explicit decisions which might differ from those of the EHVs.

From this discussion it would seem that there is little doubt that both the climate of opinion in which the scheme was conceived and the framework of beliefs in which it has operated are likely to have produced the feelings of anger and resentment which commonly arise when one is treated as less than competent, responsible and intelligent, and to have led, firstly, to the dependence and demand for more instruction which teaching commonly produces, and, secondly, to the decline of initiative, responsibility, and decision-taking ability which one so often notices among those who are forced to be dependent on welfare services. It therefore seems *probable*—although we have no evidence of it—that, despite the good intentions and indeed the acute awareness of the problem, which so many of the EHVs have voiced, the scheme will, by the way it operates, contribute to the very problems which those involved so badly wanted to avoid. Whether it does do this, is, therefore, a question which demands serious, and urgent, investigation.

The Scheme may also contribute to the growing cynicism about rational planning in our society. Although this cynicism may sometimes be based more on feelings than on explicit considerations, data in Stevens (1960) shows that many schoolchildren state explicit, logical, reasons for being sceptical and cynical about statements made by their teachers and headmasters. This scepticism strikes at the heart of education, for the statements they question have to do with the developmental "benefits" of schooling. The pupils say that schools do not contribute to growth and development. On the contrary, they say, they operate only to provide a proportion of the pupils with passports to high status jobs. In this context many argue that it is legitimate to be deceitful in order to gain certificates, because nothing of importance is lost by evading the supposedly educational exercises to the satisfactory completion of which the certificates are often taken to testify. Nor do they object to hoodwinking examiners by pretending to be familiar with things they do not know, because they believe that the knowledge that their teachers tell them is so important is not, in fact, in itself, going to be of any great use to them. As we will see later, many of the parents interviewed in the present study believe that schools are much more about getting jobs than about developing talents and abilities. Thus, if EHVs, headmasters, and others talk about "the educational benefits of the programme" when the real benefit lies only in the scheme's ability to confer on some a head start in a scramble for qualifications, it may serve to discredit not only the Home Visitors themselves but the legitimacy of any attempt to base the management of our society on rational decision-taking instead of the law of the jungle or the unfettered workings of a competitive market place.

Whatever the answer to the question of whether the Lothian Region EHV Scheme *does* tend to foster cynicism about rational planning, there is no doubt that the discussion in the last two paragraphs raises the question of how unverbalised, and often hard to verbalise, feelings are to be handled in a socialised economy. A market economy, with all its warts, does at least allow some people to vote with their feet on the basis of their feelings without having to go through the time-consuming and difficult process of translating those feelings into words, giving them social legitimacy (for they are often unacceptable at first), and getting decision-takers to do something about them. How are such feelings to be given due weight when someone in authority has decided to offer a particular (free) service which, while conferring undoubted benefits, has a number of unwanted, undesirable, and hard to articulate side effects?

This question in turn raises another. We have seen that the Scheme was initiated in the context of an assumption that public servants (who are, interestingly enough, more often known as "the authorities") sometimes knew more about what was good for their clients than did the clients themselves. We have seen that it was often extremely difficult for the mothers concerned to argue with such (if not these particular) professional public servants (authorities) because they were so dependent on them, because these public servants conferred undoubted benefits which they did not wish to have withdrawn, because their own viewpoint was less articulate and less culturally acceptable than that of the authorities, because they found it hard to put their feelings into words because, by the time they came to put these feelings into words a confrontation situation had arisen which was accompanied by feelings of anger, and because the professionals (and researchers) concerned did not have a register which would have enabled them to hear what the mothers were saying or a brief which would allow them to act upon it if they did hear. The question which arises is whether, instead of, or as well as, setting up the scheme in such a way as to tend to lead the mothers, and society as a whole, to see the problem in the way in which it was explicitly and implicitly defined by professionals, those concerned might have funded an "advocate" whose task it would have been to make explicit a counter-viewpoint and an alternative solution. What is most interesting about this suggestion is that, clearly essential to rational decision-taking though it is, it tends to create alarm among administrators (authorities, public servants). In this context it is relevant to note that *failure* to make explicit provision to fund someone whose task it is to help those involved to formulate a counter viewpoint strikes at the heart of the EHV scheme in a very basic way—because it deprives the participants of the very opportunity to gain access to any alternative viewpoint which is as articulate and well worked out as that of the EHVs. It therefore deprives them of the opportunity to make the meaningful decisions which are so often said to lie at the heart of the project and reinforces the trend toward the centralisation of decision-taking in the hands of senior public "servants". Furthermore, it creates a self-fulfilling situation which legitimises such centralisation of decision-taking. For, in the absence of an alternative viewpoint, all a citizen can do is vote for the policy, or display apathy—not suggest an alternative. Inevitably he is cast in a role of being ignorant and lacking in understanding. Thus, by setting up a "research-based" project of this sort one may unwittingly contribute to the development of a society which is divided into the informed and the ignorant, the rule-generators and rule-followers, in which the citizenry is unable to exercise decision-taking skills, intiative and responsibility in anything other than a negative manner.

It may be useful to conclude this discussion of the possible long-term effects of the scheme by drawing attention to one more of the implicit assumptions which seems to run through much (but by no means all) of the thinking associated with it. This is that it is important to help parents and children to develop the ability to succeed in a competitive situation. Despite the undoubted "realism" of this viewpoint, the long-term social consequences of reinforcing it may not be entirely desirable. One is likely to find that, over time, even more children strive to get the better of their fellows by doing well at school instead of joining them in order to improve the community for the good of all. One is likely to find that one has set working class children against each other for, as Hope (1976) puts it, the effect of "enrichment" programmes in Scotland can only be to advance one subset of "deprived" children at the expense of another subset of the same children. It will not advance those children at the expense of children from other sectors of society. Thus, one is likely to find that one has reinforced the already widespread belief that "if the poor are poor it is their own fault—because they did not put in enough effort to do well at school". (And it should be noted that the "environmentalist" orientation of the scheme specifically encourages this belief). And one is likely to find that one has reinforced the myth that if everyone does better at school, everyone will get jobs. Acceptance of this myth inevitably leads to qualification-inflation as it becomes necessary to demand higher and higher qualifications to justify refusing jobs to many (Berg, 1971). This in turn leads to the diversion of more and more of society's resources into "education" and, specifically, into Educational Home Visiting programmes which hold out the promise of increasing some people's chances of success in the scramble for qualifications. Nothing could better illustrate the difficulty of interpreting what lies behind the demand for a service—expecially a *free* service—particularly in a socialised economy, and the importance of putting in hand the social research which is needed if we are to understand the social processes involved and work toward more appropriate provision.

Conclusion

It would appear from what has been said that there are good grounds for unease about the long-term social implications of the Scheme. How serious these are we cannot tell without further research, but it is clear that that research is of the greatest possible importance for our society, both in a short term in relation to this Scheme, and, in the longer term, from the point of view of developing more effective ways of running our society. However, in raising the questions we have raised we do not wish to discredit the Scheme. On the contrary, it is the very existence of the Scheme in the context of an evaluation study which has led us to ask these questions. As a stimulus to understanding and thought, the Scheme has been of outstanding value. While, therefore, it is hard to arrive at a conclusion which is both succinct and balanced, it is extremely important to attempt to do so. Such an attempt might read as follows: while our results fall short of justifying introducing Educational Home Visiting Programmes as part of routine educational provision, the Lothian Scheme has shown itself to have such potentiality that further action-research programmes should be carried out with a view to evaluating a wide range of alternative strategies for tackling the extremely important problems in this area and to providing a better understanding of the processes involved and a better knowledge of both short and long term outcomes.

PART IIIA

THE STATISTICAL STUDY: INTRODUCTION

DEVELOPMENT OF THE STATISTICAL STUDY, SAMPLING, SAMPLE SIZES AND STATISTICAL SIGNIFICANCE

The way in which the statistical study evolved was described in Chapter 1. It began as an attempt to develop relevant measures and collect background data, and was only later, under pressure, extended to involve collecting some data on the impact of the current Educational Home Visiting Programme. For this reason the number of Home Visited families who were interviewed was relatively small. This stepwise, evolutionary, rather than planned, growth also in part accounts for some of the other limitations of the study.

One of these is that we are unable to make use of a before-and-after design. As a result, when, in the chapters which follow, we speak of "changes" induced by the EHVs, we are in fact *inferring* such changes from differences between the responses of the Home Visited mothers and other mothers from the catchment areas of the same schools (to which the Home Visitors were attached). As will be shown, there is every reason to believe that this inference is justified. Nevertheless, a before-and-after design would have permitted us to be more confident that the differences we will report reflect genuine changes.

Why did we not make use of such a design? There are a number of reasons. Firstly, we did not, at the start of the Project, have an adequate understanding of the effects which it was important to measure. This developed only as we went along. Secondly, even after we had become clearer about what *should* be measured, we still had to *develop* appropriate measures of these qualities. Thirdly, in many cases, the Home Visitors' initial link with the families they visited was so fragile that it would have been jeopardised by the intrusion of a researcher asking searching personal questions. Many of the parents would have felt threatened by questions about topics—such as discipline strategies—which, at that point, they would, despite the close connection between cognitive development and such strategies stressed by writers like Hess and Shipman (1965), have thought irrelevant to the Project. Fourthly, the EHVs and the Heads of the schools all saw the Project in different ways, and the questions which one Head of EHV believed to be pertinent were likely be thought irrelevant by another. Questions which the evaluators, because of their theoretical perspective on the Project, believed to be crucial were liable to be rejected by Home Visitors, teachers and parents alike.

So a before-and-after design was not feasible. But neither, given the level of funding and the limitations of the available evaluation instruments, was a design which sought to contrast a control group with an experimental group. After we had developed our interview schedules we did not have time to interview a large enough sample of Home Visited mothers, let alone to interview a matched control goup. But, again, this was not the only problem: as some of the Home Visitors visited all the families who were recommended to them, there was no pool from which to draw a matched control group. Even in other cases, the ways in which the families were selected were such that those chosen for visiting would differ in many ways from those who were not visited. Fortunately, these very processes, and the demographic data we collected, suggest that the Home Visited group were, in many ways, disadvantaged even in relation to our Low Socio-Economic Status (LSES) bench-mark group— who lived in the same catchment areas of the same schools. If one assumes a continuum in attitudes from LSES through to High Socio-Economic Status (HSES) parents, then the attitudes of the Home Visited group prior to visiting would be expected to have differed even more from those of our High Socio-Economic Status bench-mark group than did those of our LSES group. In point of fact their answers to questions which related to the operation of the Project—and only such questions—usually fell *between* those of the two bench-mark groups, thus strongly suggesting that the EHVs were responsible for the observed differences from the LSES group.

The way in which the Evaluation Project evolved—obtaining, uncertainly, and only with difficulty, funds for one small accretion after another—also accounts for the fact that the number of Home Visited parents who were interviewed was only 41, the fact that it was not possible to modify the questionnaires in order to collect data on the mothers' perceptions of the Home Visitors and the benefits of visiting, and the fact that, whereas the bench-mark samples had been interviewed in the winter and spring, the Home Visited mothers were interviewed in early summer, thus, to a degree, invalidating comparisons between the way the Home Visited parents and children and those in the two bench-mark groups spent their time.

Development of the Inverview Schedules

The study went through three phases: exploratory, pilot, and main. At the end of the exploratory and pilot phases the data were examined and discussed, and the questions reviewed and amended. At the end of the pilot stage an interim report was produced and discussed with a number of interested people, including the Home Visitors and Advisory Committee on the Evaluation of the Lothian Region Educational Home Visiting Scheme.

Sources of Questions

The questions which were asked in the structured interviews were selected because they were felt to be important in relation to the evaluation of the Educational Home Visiting Project, because they related to tentative hypotheses which were being formulated in the author's mind about the impact of the Educational Home Visiting Project, because the literature which had been reviewed had emphasised their potential relevance, because it was felt that they would produce data which was of importance when designing educational programmes, or because they were of value in seeking to establish the relative importance to be attached to extending Educational Home Visiting projects in comparison with other possible types of adult education programme which might make competing demands for the same funds. Thus they were selected as much because it was thought that they would produce useful background data as because they would be valuable from the point of view of assessing the impact of the Educational Home Visiting programme. As has been explained it was, at the time, intended to use the results of this study to develop interview schedules tailored to the task of assessing the impact of the EHV programme. It was not intended to use them as they stood for that purpose. The way in which the questions were selected and developed through the exploratory and pilot phases of the enquiry is described in Appendix D, which is available from SCRE.

In that appendix we also present some important results which were obtained by using a "Personality Images" technique in the Pilot Phase of the enquiry. We were unfortunately unable to carry this section of the interview through into the Main Study owing to pressures of time.

The Final Interview Schedules

The questions we had developed and piloted were finally boiled down to the two interview schedules which are reproduced in special

Appendix C, which is available from SCRE. These enabled us to cover most of the issues which seemed to be important and to tackle the same research questions using a number of different types of question. The two interview schedules (termed "A" and "B") were administered to alternate mothers.

Sampling

In order that the data collected should be of maximum value as background to the EHV Project, it was planned from the start that the main study should be conducted in the catchment areas of the schools in which the Home Visitors were based. However, in order not to limit the number of parents available for the main survey, the exploratory and pilot stages of the study were carried out in housing areas similar to, but not including, these areas. In what follows, areas in which Educational Home Visiting took place are referred to collectively as Low Socio-Economic Status (LSES) areas, although, as we will see, they did contain a proportion of High Socio-Economic Status families.

In order that the contrast between what different people said would draw our attention to previously unnoticed topics, a sample of parents of children of similar age, drawn from contrasting areas of the city, were also interviewed. In these areas the families were, on the whole, more affluent. The houses were larger and owner occupied, and all had gardens. These areas are referred to as High Socio-Economic Status (HSES) areas, although they did contain some low income households.

It was anticipated that fuller documentation of the differences in attitudes, behaviours, beliefs and expectations of parents from these two types of area would yield insights into previously unnoticed factors which might be responsible for the differential growth and development—and particularly the differential school performance—of children who come from these two types of background. This has proved to be the case and the HSES sample provides an important second bench-mark against which to view the data collected from the Home Visited sample.

Samples for the Main Study

To select our final sample, lists of pre-school children in each of the selected areas were made available to us by Lothian Region. From each area a completely random sample was taken, allowing extra numbers to compensate for any families who had moved out of the area (as a high turnover of tenants was common in some areas), and for deletion of the names of any families which had been, or were being, visited by the Educational Home Visitors.

It had already been decided that we would draw our sample from the five areas involved in Lothian Region's Educational Home Visiting Scheme. These areas were Craigmillar, Niddrie, Gorebridge, Wester Hailes and Broxburn. On certain tables the names of these areas have been abbreviated as follows:

Greendykes (Craigmillar)	— D
Niddrie Mains (Niddrie)	— N
Gorebridge	— G
Clovenstone (Wester Hailes)	— C
Kirkhill (Broxburn)	— B

As a contrast to these areas, two other areas were selected, both areas of private housing. One was in the Fairmilehead area of the city, and the other was a fairly large area on the South West side of the city. This we have described as Spylaw. Abbreviations are as follows:

Fairmilehead	— F
Spylaw area	— S

In each of the seven areas, forty families were visited; half were interviewed using the "A" questionnaire, and half with the "B" questionnaire. Therefore, for most questions we have twenty responses for each area, and a total of 140 responses to each question, though there are exceptions which will be discussed as they arise. The total number of people interviewed was 280.

Greendykes, Niddrie Mains, Gorebridge, Clovenstone and Broxburn are all areas where, with only the occasional exception, the houses are rented from the local authority, are all similar in appearance and are unlikely to have gardens (although families in Broxburn and Gorebridge were more likely to have gardens than those living in the other areas within the city boundaries). Most are flats, many multi-storey. There are high levels of unemployment and many families have low incomes.

These areas are known in the report, from now on, as Low Socio-Economic Status areas, abbreviated to LSES areas, or, in tables where space is limited, to L. In the other two areas (Fairmilehead and Spylaw), where families own their own houses which have gardens and garages, most fathers, and many mothers, are professionally qualified people with much higher average incomes than those who live in our LSES areas. These areas will be known as High Socio-Economic Status areas, abbreviated to HSES areas or H.

The Sample of Mothers who had had Home Visits

Each of the Home Visitors gave us a list of about a dozen parents who had been, but were no longer being, visited by them. Originally it was envisaged that all of these would be interviewed. However, it proved to be more difficult to contact these mothers than the mothers in the background samples, and, in order to complete the work in time, we had to settle for eight interviews in each area, although, before this decision was taken, nine people had been interviewed in one area. As we again used both interview schedules, that gave a sample of twenty on one schedule and twenty-one on the other.

Demographic Characteristics of the Samples

Non-contact rates and demographic characteristics of the samples are given in Appendix B. Very few of the families who were contacted refused to be interviewed. The following special characteristics have to be noted:

(1) The households in the LSES samples were more likely than those in the HSES samples to have larger families: 22% had four or more children.

(2) Mothers in the samples from LSES areas were more likely to have someone at home during the day to help with the children. 30% had. These were mainly unemployed husbands or husbands working shifts. (Many mothers said that they didn't help very much!)

(3) More mothers in the samples from the LSES areas lived on their own, and more were single, widowed, divorced or separated. (Indeed we only found one such person in our HSES sample).

(4) Few of either group appear to have been isolated. Most mothers in both areas, saw relatives or close friends regularly, though mothers living in LSES areas were five times as likely as those living in HSES areas to see relatives or friends daily. Only just over one fifth of mothers living in HSES areas saw relatives or friends daily. Most nearby relatives or friends were in fact *relatives* for both groups, although friends came a close second in the HSES area.

(5) The majority of breadwinners in the samples from HSES areas were in the Professionally Qualified and High Administrative class, whereas most breadwinners in the samples from LSES areas were in the skilled or semi-skilled manual group. For both groups, the mothers, on average, had left school earlier than the

fathers, and the LSES parents had left school or full time education much earlier than the HSES parents.

(6) The majority of parents in the HSES areas lived on over £70 per week, whereas the majority in the LSES areas lived on less than £50, and almost a third on less than £35.

The Home Visited Mothers

It will be recalled that families were selected for Home Visiting because it was thought that they would "benefit" in some way from the programme. In practice this meant that they were felt to have some particular problem or disadvantage. However, it does not appear from the demographic data that they were seriously dis-advantaged in Socio-Economic terms compared with other people living in the areas from which they were drawn although, as we will see later (Chapter 22), it seems from the Quality of Life data we collected that they did have more problems with their families and in relation to the wider society.

The only difference visible in the demographic data seems to be that, compared with the rest of the LSES group, the Home Visited mothers had slightly less contact with other people outside their immediate family. In this respect they are rather more like the HSES group. We do not, of course, know whether the EHV group were still more isolated before the Home Visits began, or whether the Home Visitors have led them to become more isolated—like the HSES group—in this respect. As we shall see later, the Home Visitors do seem to have led them to become more like the HSES group in many other ways.

The families had similar age structures. However, whereas 97% of the Home Visited families had children aged three or four (or both), only 87% of the LSES bench-mark families had children of this age. The LSES group contained rather more families with slightly younger children. The LSES group were the most likely to have children at every age from ten onwards.

Because of what is to follow it is most important to emphasise that the EHV group was *definitely* not better off than the LSES bench-mark group and, because of the way in which the families were selected for visiting, could be expected to be more likely to be plagued by social problems of one sort or another.

Sample Sizes and Statistical Significance

In survey work statistical significance has proved to be something of a red herring. This issue is discussed in the note below.

Note

Experience suggests that carefully drawn samples of about thirty people give fairly reliable estimates of total population descriptive statistics. This reliability increases with the homogeneity of the sampled population on demographic variables which are predictive of responses. Furthermore, the overall, *interpreted pattern* of results one obtains over several related items tends to be highly reliable, provided there are no serious sampling errors. The profile of any substantial interpreted differences between sub-populations, each composed of thirty or more individuals, also tends to be reasonably stable. Percentage differences of fifteen or more *on single items* tend to be reproduced when larger samples are interviewed, but, as part of an interpreted difference, smaller differences can be both revealing and stable. In contrast to such stability of meaningful differences, factor structures obtained from groups of less than about 500 are highly unstable—in contrast to the highly stable factor structures obtained from larger groups (Raven, Ritchie and Baxter, 1971).

In the present study, the numbers in each background group exceed thirty on all but a few subsidiary questions. On single items a difference of about 15% and 20% is required for statistical significance at the 5% level respectively for the HSES/LSES and LSES/EHV comparisons. However, when presenting the results, we have tended to focus on clusters of items rather than on individual items, and these were often drawn not only from different interview schedules, but also from questions which made use of differing approaches to obtaining similar data. Had the answers obtained by using these different approaches been contradictory, it would have been difficult to arrive at a meaningful interpretation of the results. Not only were the same research questions approached in different ways on different interview schedules, the groups which were compared were, as we shall see, relatively homogeneous with respect to variables which are associated with variance in response to the questions we asked.

The material which follows therefore deserves to be taken seriously. There is no doubt at all that the data base should be improved conceptually, methodologically and numerically. But the one thing we do *not* need is more "sophistication" (eg significance testing) in the analyses of *this* data. What is needed in this area is more data-based research.

PART IIIB

THE IMPACT OF THE LOTHIAN REGION EDUCATIONAL HOME VISITING PROGRAMME

IN THIS SECTION of our Report we are going to see what can be learned about the impact of the Lothian Region Educational Home Visiting Scheme on parents' attitudes and behaviours by comparing the responses of our sample of Home Visited parents with the responses of our LSES and HSES bench-mark samples. As will appear, those bench-mark samples give evidence of two very different value systems and sets of perceptions and expectations in relation to child rearing. The responses from the Home Visited parents to many of the questions tended to occupy a position intermediate between the two. We shall illuminate these differences from the LSES group's responses by reference to the responses of the HSES group. In doing so we will, on the whole, attribute the differences between the LSES and EHV parents' responses to the impact of the Home Visitors. This inference that the differences between the two groups reflect an *effect* of the Visiting is, of course, a hypothesis rather than a demonstrated fact. To the extent that the LSES bench-mark group was not typical of the EHV group prior to visiting (which it was not), and to the extent that the samples were unrepresentative, this inference is unjustified.

Attention should, however, be drawn to a number of reasons for believing that the results we obtained *were* due to the Visiting and not due to sampling errors. Firstly, as we have seen, the Home Visited group was, if anything, "worse" off than the LSES group. One would therefore expect the Home Visited mothers' responses to be further removed from those of the HSES group than were those of the LSES group. As has been indicated, this is rarely the case. Time after time, their responses fall *between* the two groups. Secondly, the EHV groups' answers to questions about issues which would be *unlikely* to be affected by the EHVs are extremely similar to those of the LSES group. The *pattern* of the results is, on the whole, consistent with the hypothesis that the *differences* which are reported are a result of the Visiting (and we will draw attention to those differences which do not seem to reflect an effect of the Visiting as we go along). Thirdly, the statistically documented "effects" of the scheme, with one important exception, support the impressions we formed in the course of our own interviews with parents, the changes noted by the EHVs, and the hypotheses we generated by studying the *operation* of the programme. Fourthly, almost all the LSES/HSES differences found in the pilot study from interviews with much smaller samples of parents in different areas of the city are confirmed in the main study. The response pattern we are dealing with is generally stable and not greatly influenced by sampling errors within HSES and LSES areas. The differences we have found between our LSES and Home Visited mothers are therefore *unlikely* to be due to sampling errors.

To report the differences between the LSES and EHV parents' responses *without* suggesting that the differences were an *effect* of the programme would, therefore, be over-cautious. But, equally, we would be failing our readers if we did not draw attention to the need to increase the size of the sample of, particularly, Home Visited mothers, and to relate those responses to the style of Visiting.

We will look first at the apparent impact of the programme on mothers' feelings about their ability to influence their children, the importance they attach to developing certain qualities in their children and to certain child-rearing practices and activities. Next we will discuss the impact of the Home Visiting on why mothers consider certain activities to be important and unimportant and on what they think can be done to foster certain qualities. Next again we shall discuss its impact on the qualities parents feel that their children learn from them and on what they actually do with their children. Since parents' child rearing activities are often influenced by what they will expect will happen in the future, we next discuss the impact of the Home Visiting on the problems parents anticipate as their children grow older. Parents' problems, and their feelings of confidence and competence to cope with them, may have an important impact on the way their children develop. Accordingly, the impact of the Home Visiting programme on these perceptions and expectations is discussed before we finally turn to its impact on parents' views of their own role in the formal educational system.

This step-wise presentation of the data will be followed by a general summary and discussion in which we attempt to tie together data relevant to particular themes, but which has been separated in the step-wise discussion in order to make a rather different set of points.

Owing to the cost of printing them, most of the Tables on which the discussion which follows is based have been omitted from this volume. This applies to all Tables prefixed "A". Appendices containing these Tables, data on the demographic characteristics of the samples, the questionnaires, and an account of the development and piloting of the questionnaires are available from the Scottish Council for Research in Education, 15 John Street, Edinburgh.

CHAPTER 15

DO PARENTS FEEL THEY CAN HAVE AN IMPACT ON THEIR CHILDREN'S DEVELOPMENT?

Figure 1* shows that most parents feel that it is at least fairly possible to influence the sort of person their child will grow up to be. The effect of the Home Visiting has apparently been to increase the proportion of parents from LSES backgrounds who feel that it is "very possible" to do so, although they are still much less confident about this than the HSES group.

This effect has been greatest in the intellectual area, which is most central to the Home Visitors' activities. The proportion of parents who feel that it is possible to influence the development of their children's intelligence is 81% in the EHV group in comparison with 45% in the LSES bench-mark group. The proportion of Home Visited parents who believe this even exceeds that found in the HSES group. The Visiting also appears to have had a major impact on the proportion who feel that it is possible to influence their child's friendliness. While more Home Visited than LSES parents feel that it is possible to influence their child's character, the proportion who think so still does not equal that of the HSES group. The programme appears to have had little, if any, impact on the proportion who feel that it is possible to influence their child's interests, values and beliefs.

In the light of what is to come later it is, perhaps, important to comment on the fact that, although *this* evidence shows that the Home Visited parents feel that it is *possible* to influence the development of these qualities, it does not necessarily imply that they think that they themselves could influence them. Whether they think that they themselves have either the will or the ability to influence their children is another question, to which we will return.

*Figures 1-3 correspond to Tables A1-A3, which are available from SCRE in an Appendix of Tables to this Report.

FIGURE 1

How possible do you think it is to influence the sort of person your child will grow up to be?

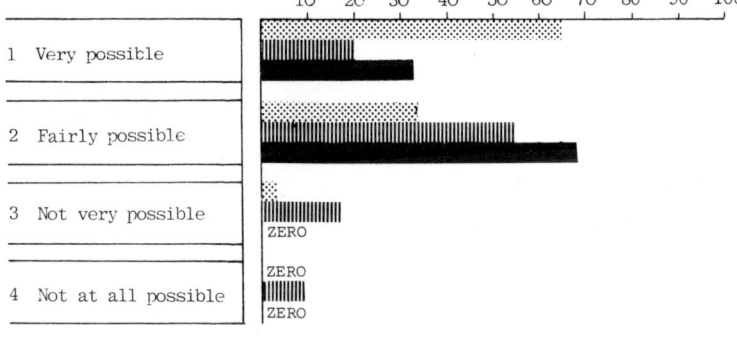

1 Very possible

2 Fairly possible

3 Not very possible

ZERO

4 Not at all possible

ZERO

ZERO

KEY

HSES
LSES
EHV

FIGURE 2

% Saying it is possible to influence:-

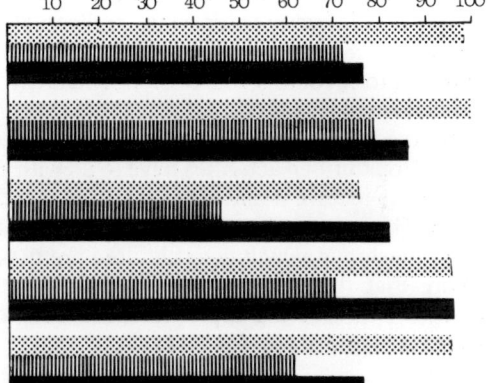

1 His interests

2 His values and beliefs

3 His intelligence

4 His friendliness

5 His character

KEY

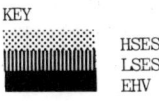

HSES
LSES
EHV

THE IMPORTANCE ATTACHED TO CHILDREN'S DEVELOPING CERTAIN QUALITIES OF CHARACTER, AND TO PARENTS' ENGAGING IN CERTAIN ACTIVITIES AND PRACTICES WITH THEIR CHILDREN

We asked parents to rate, on a 5-point scale, how important they thought it was to do various things with their children and how important it was to them for their children to develop certain qualities. The proportion who rated each item "very important" is given in Figure 3. Since it is difficult to digest this Table as a whole, we will look at it in several different ways. Let us first compare the items which were considered most important by the EHV group, the LSES group, and the HSES group. These are shown in Table 1.

Attention may first be drawn to the dramatic differences between the LSES and the HSES groups. Top priority for the HSES group is, quite clearly, intellectual activity. Only two of their top thirteen items do *not* have directly to do with intellectual activity, and these two ("For your child to know how you feel when he does something well", "For you to encourage him to be independent") are at least supportive of intellectual activity.

For the LSES group, however, things are very different. Only three of their top thirteen activities have to do with intellectual activity, and even these receive a much lower rating than they do from the HSES group. They are much more inclined to say that it is important to foster a relationship in which their children are dependent on them, and to ensure that their children respect property and can stick up for themselves. Fostering appropriate attitudes toward authority figures is also a high priority for them.

One of the striking things about this Table is that there are only three items which more than 60% of the LSES group rate "very important", compared with twelve for the HSES group. What this is saying is that, despite the work which went into the development of the questionnaires used in this project, and despite the author's considerable amount of previous work in the values area (Raven,

TABLE 1

TOP PRIORITIES IN CHILD REARING FOR LSES, HSES, AND EHV PARENTS

(% rating each item "Very Important")

	EHV Group		LSES Group		HSES Group	
1	That your children need you.	90%	That your child develops respect for his parents.	81%	For your child to be read to.	93%
2	For your child to be read to.	85%	That your children need you.	75%	For you to talk to your child a lot.	90%
3	For you to ask him about pictures in books and things he has seen.	75%	For you to teach him to respect property.	63%	For your child to have books at home.	88%
4	To teach your child to respect property.	75%	For your child to learn to stick up for himself.	55%	For you to ask him about pictures in books and things he has seen.	73%
5	That your child develops respect for his parents.	75%	For your child to be read to.	54%	To encourage your child to be willing to use books to find information for himself.	73%
6	To teach your child to think for himself.	72%	For your child to develop the ability to work with others.	53%	For your child to know how you feel when he does something well.	70%
7	To encourage your child to talk to you about what he is doing.	70%	For your child to have plenty of time to play with other children.	50%	To encourage your child to talk to you about what he is doing.	68%
8	For your child to have books at home.	67%	To talk to your child a lot.	50%	To teach your child to think for himself.	68%
9	For you to talk to your child a lot.	67%	For you to ask him about pictures in books and things he has seen.	49%	For you to treat him with respect as an individual in his own right, who is entitled to pursue his own interests and ideas.	63%
10	For your child to be given educational toys.	62%	To teach your child to respect figures in authority.	49%	For you to encourage him to be independent.	60%
11	To encourage your child to ask questions.	57%	For your child to develop the ability to mix easily with others.	47%	To encourage your child to ask questions.	60%
12	To encourage him to work and read on his own a lot when he's older.	55%	To teach your child you don't get anything you want without working for it.	46%	That your child develops respect for his parents.	60%
13	For you to continue the work of the school at home.	55%	For your child to know how you feel when he does something well.	46%	For you to encourage your child to question and seek reasons for things he is told.	58%
	For your child to do well at school.	55%				
	To encourage your child to question and seek reasons for things he is told.	55%				
	That your child develops the ability to work with others.	55%				

FIGURE 3

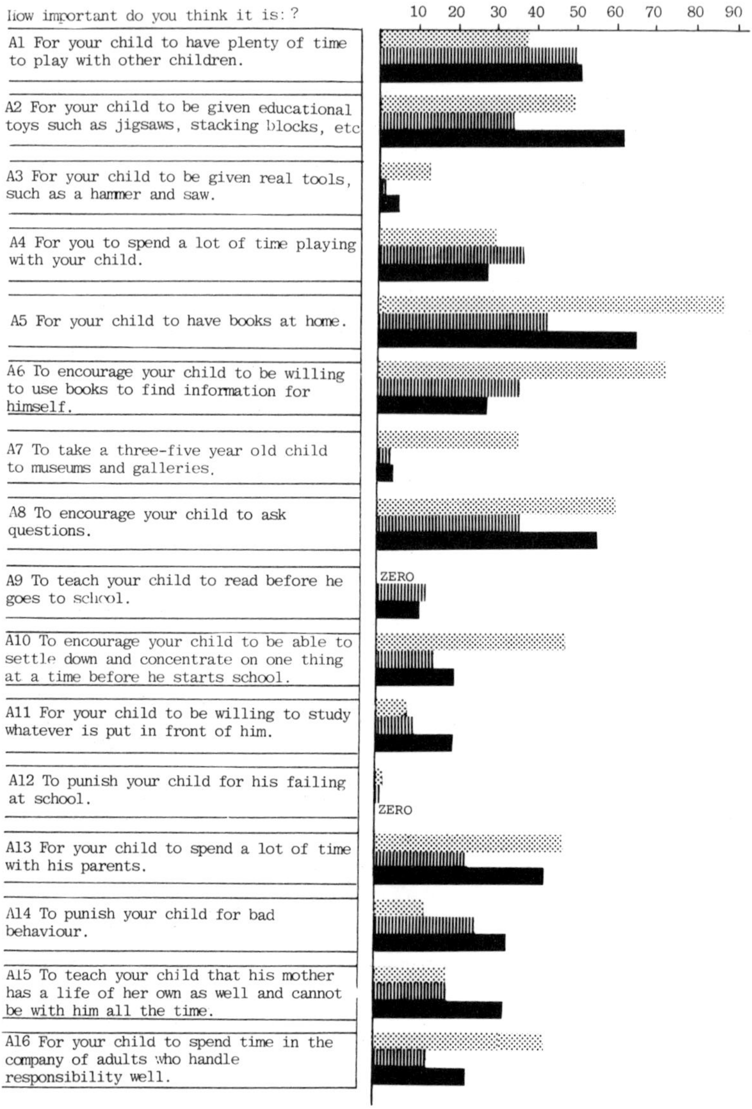

% answering "very important"
How important do you think it is: ?
10 20 30 40 50 60 70 80 90
A1 For your child to have plenty of time to play with other children.
A2 For your child to be given educational toys such as jigsaws, stacking blocks, etc
A3 For your child to be given real tools, such as a hammer and saw.
A4 For you to spend a lot of time playing with your child.
A5 For your child to have books at home.
A6 To encourage your child to be willing to use books to find information for himself.
A7 To take a three-five year old child to museums and galleries.
A8 To encourage your child to ask questions.
A9 To teach your child to read before he goes to school.
ZERO
A10 To encourage your child to be able to settle down and concentrate on one thing at a time before he starts school.
A11 For your child to be willing to study whatever is put in front of him.
A12 To punish your child for his failing at school.
ZERO
A13 For your child to spend a lot of time with his parents.
A14 To punish your child for bad behaviour.
A15 To teach your child that his mother has a life of her own as well and cannot be with him all the time.
A16 For your child to spend time in the company of adults who handle responsibility well.

FIGURE 3 (cont)

% answering "very important"

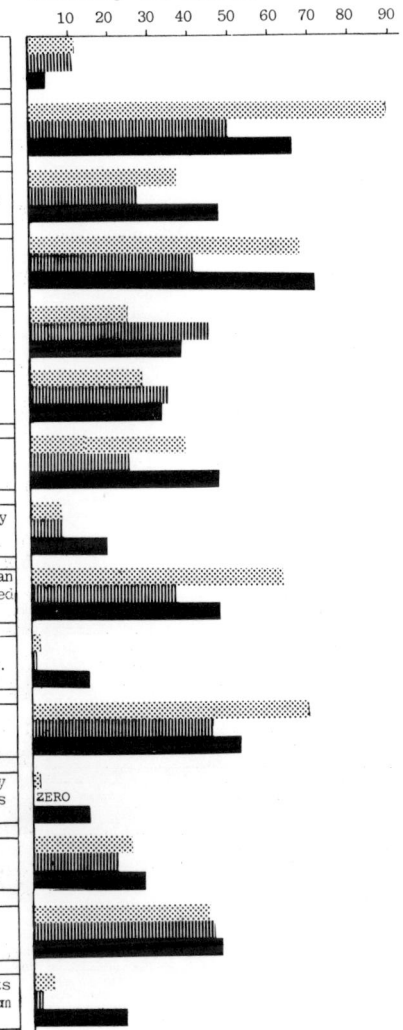

A17 For your child to learn how to get people in authority to do what he wants them to do.

A18 For you to talk to your child a lot.

A19 To spend time talking to your child about what his interests are and what he wants out of life.

A20 To teach your child to think for himself.

A21 To teach your child that you don't get anything you want without working for it.

A22 To teach your child not to do just what's good for him but what's good for everybody.

A23 To help your child to think clearly about what he's trying to do.

A24 For you to help him only occasionally when help was really needed.

A25 For you to treat him with respect as an individual in his own right who is entitled to pursue his own interests and ideas.

A26 For him to start thinking it is important to do better than other people.

A27 For your child to know how you feel when he does something well.

A28 For your child to develop the ability to get other people to do things he wants them to do.

A29 For your child to stand up for what he thinks is right even though it makes him unpopular.

A30/1 For your child to develop the ability to mix easily with others.

A30/2 For your child to develop interests and tastes which are quite different from those of other people.

FIGURE 3 (cont)   % answering "very important"

A30/3 For your child to develop a vivid imagination.

A30/4 For your child to develop competitiveness.

ZERO

A30/5 For your child to develop toughness.

A30/6 For your child to develop inventiveness.

B1 For your child to have ample time to play with sand and water.

B2 For your child to have the opportunity to play on waste ground, (eg scrapyards, building sites).

ZERO
ZERO

B3 Not to iterrupt your child when he is playing.

B4 For your child to be read to.

B5 For you to ask him about pictures in books and things he has seen.

B6 To encourage your child to work and read on his own a lot when he's older.

B7 To take a 3-5 year old child to the public library.

B8 To teach your child to count before he goes to school.

B9 For you to continue the work of the school at home.

B10 For your child to do well at school.

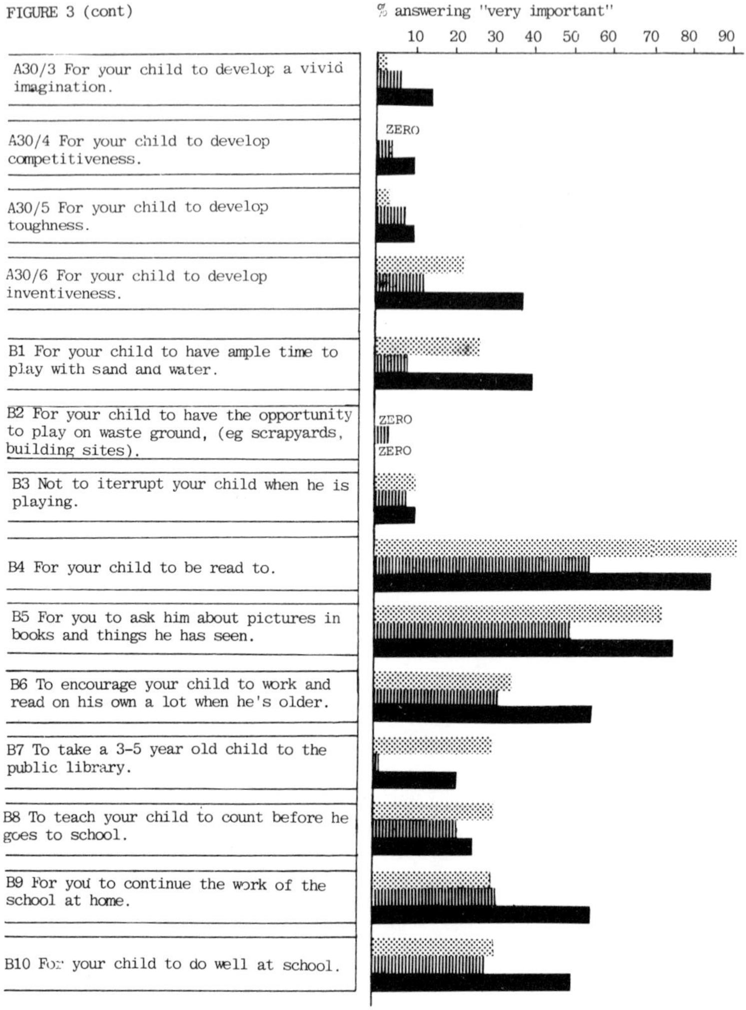

FIGURE 3 (cont)

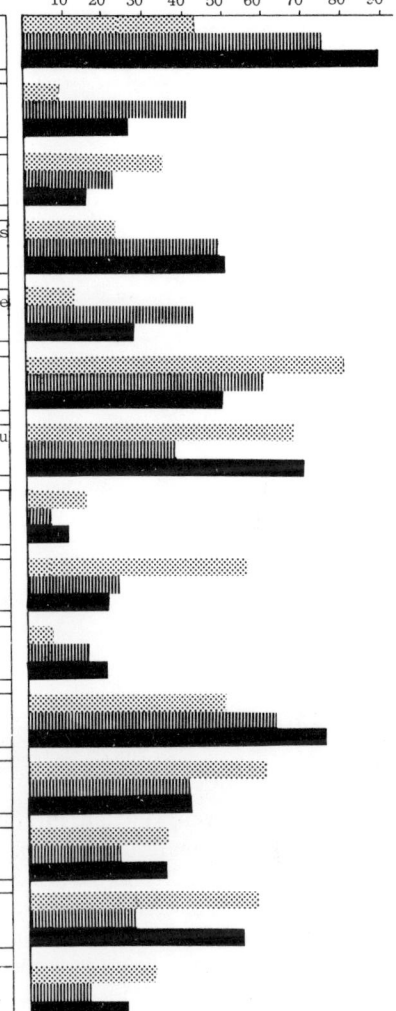

% answering "very important"

B11 That your children need you.

B12 For your child to learn to obey his parents without question.

B13 For your child to see his parents as hardworking resourceful people.

B14 To teach your child to respect figures of authority.

B15 To teach your child to learn his place and know who's boss.

B16 How important is what a child learns from his parents to his future.

B17 To encourage your child to talk to you about what he is doing.

B18 To talk to your child about the sort of person you like and admire.

B19 To teach your child to be confident with people, situations and things he hasn't met before.

B20 To teach your child to be thrusting and determined to get on.

B21 To teach your child to respect property.

B22 For you to encourage him to be independent.

B23 For your child to make his own decisions and experience the consequences for himself..

B24 For you to encourage your child to question and seek reasons for things he is told.

B25 For your child to value doing things better than he has done them in the past.

FIGURE 3 (cont)

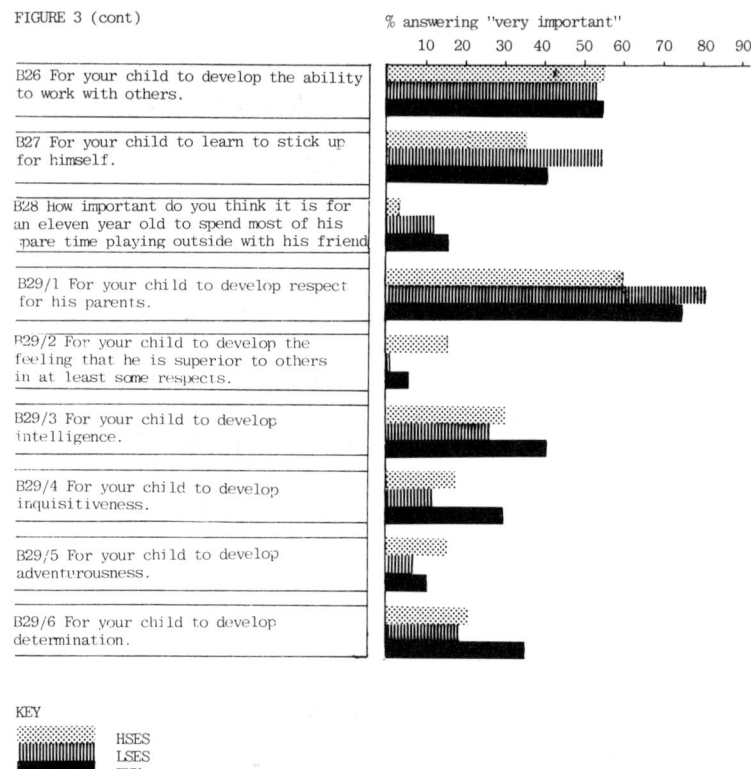

% answering "very important"

B26 For your child to develop the ability to work with others.

B27 For your child to learn to stick up for himself.

B28 How important do you think it is for an eleven year old to spend most of his spare time playing outside with his friend

B29/1 For your child to develop respect for his parents.

B29/2 For your child to develop the feeling that he is superior to others in at least some respects.

B29/3 For your child to develop intelligence.

B29/4 For your child to develop inquisitiveness.

B29/5 For your child to develop adventurousness.

B29/6 For your child to develop determination.

KEY

HSES
LSES
EHV

1973, 1975; Raven, Whelan, Pfretzschner and Borock, 1976; Raven, 1977) it is extremely difficult for HSES researchers to formulate items which correctly express LSES parents' feelings. This is an intriguing problem. On occasion, as one works in this area, one feels that one's informants just don't have any positive values. But somehow one can't accept that conclusion. Perhaps the problem has more to do with our inability to hear what our fellow human beings are saying. Evidence to support this conjecture has emerged in this survey—for the author's colleagues have cross-questioned him at length about what on earth LSES parents can *mean* when they say that they think it is very important for their children to *need* them. The result has been to discredit the item and to make the author wish he had never asked the question—despite the fact that three-quarters of the LSES sample think it is "very important". This mechanism may well explain why we know so little about LSES parents' values. And, as we shall see later, *that* may explain why it is that LSES parents often do not seem to engage in activities which would give their children insight into the components of competent behaviour, for they may well display their competence only in relation to goals the legitimacy—or even existence—of which we are not prepared to admit.

On turning to the Home Visited group, it is clear that their top priority, like that of the LSES group, is for dependence rather than independence in their children. Their top thirteen items (which had to be extended to fifteen to allow for ties in the thirteenth place) do, however, include more intellectual activities. They include more references to the child's doing intellectual things for himself: thinking for himself, talking to parents about what he is doing, and asking questions. None of these things is among the top thirteen items for the LSES bench-mark group. Nevertheless, although the proportions who think that these intellectual activities are important is higher in the EHV than in the LSES group, the proportion who think it is very important for their children to learn to respect property is no lower. Indeed, the proportion who say that this is very important is actually higher. The proportion saying that it is very important for their children to learn to speak up for themselves is, however, noticeably lower for the EHV group. The proportion who said it is very important for their children to learn to respect figures in authority is not as low as that in the HSES group, but this item is not among their top thirteen priorities. Educational toys is a newcomer to the list, not being among the top items of either the HSES or LSES group. Finally it may be observed that, whatever else the Home Visitors may have done, they appear to have raised the mothers' consciousness of a number of issues, for many *more* of the items are rated "very important" by the EHV than by the LSES mothers.

If we look at Figure 3, we see that it would be difficult to argue that the Home Visitors have had a particularly great effect on any one belief or expectation. Rather it seems that they have had a major impact on a whole series of inter-related beliefs. They appear to have led the Home Visited mothers to be more likely to believe that it is important for their child to spend a lot of time with his parents, talk to his parents about what he is doing, have books in the home, have educational toys, question and seek reasons for things he is told, play with sand and water, develop inventiveness, inquisitiveness, and interest and tastes which are different from those of others, and do well at school. They have led them to be more likely to believe that they themselves should read to their child, ask him questions about books and things he has seen, teach him to think for himself, talk to him a lot, encourage him to ask questions, continue the work of the school in the home, help him to think clearly about what he is trying to do, and take him to public libraries.

Attention may now be drawn to a number of items on which the Home Visited mothers' responses differ from those of the HSES group although the LSES group's responses do not do so. This applies to the importance attached to children reading and studying on their own when they are older, to the parents continuing the work of the school in the home, and to the child doing well at school.

There are a number of items for which the EHV group's responses do not differ from those of the LSES group, although the activities they deal with may be important from the point of view of promoting the development of the children. The Home Visitors have apparently had no impact on the importance the parents attach to encouraging their child to be independent, to use books to find information for himself, to settle down and concentrate, to the child's being confident with people and situations he has not met before, or to letting the child know how one feels when he does something well. They also appear to have had relatively little impact on the parents' views on whether it is important to treat the child with respect, as an individual in his own right who is entitled to have interests and ideas of his own. The absence of differences on these items, which ask about behaviours which may well be crucial to the development of autonomous learning—by which we mean the ability to make one's own observations and learn without instruction—is striking.

Finally, there are a number of ways in which the Home Visitors' activities may well have been counter-productive. The most striking of these is that the Home Visited mothers are actually less likely to feel that what the child learns from his parents is important to his future than are the mothers in the LSES bench-mark sample (Figure 3, item B16). Whereas the Home Visitors set out to convince them that their role in bringing up their children is of crucial importance, it may well be that, temporarily or permanently, they have actually made them feel less adequate than previously to introduce their children to all the things to which they now feel they ought to introduce them. They are also slightly more likely to say that it is very important to punish the child for bad behaviour.

At the other end of the scale, the proportion of parents who feel that they should not punish their children for failure at school and the proportion who feel that a child should not learn to obey his parents without question is markedly higher in the EHV than LSES group, and the proportion who say that he should not be given real tools such as hammers and saws is lower (Figure 3 and Table A4).

Discussion

One possible interpretation of the results so far presented is that the Home Visitors have had a marked impact on the importance attached to school-related activities. They have, however, left unchanged the importance attached to a number of activities which would make for autonomous learning on the part of the child. These activities may be of particular importance from the point of view of enabling the child to develop confidence in his ability to cope with new situations and new people. The relatively small difference in the proportion of EHV and LSES mothers who say it is very important to treat the child with respect, as an individual in his own right who is entitled to pursue his own interests and ideas, may be of particular significance. Unless parents do this they may fail to recognise the abilities their children actually possess and, as a result, fail to create situations in which these abilities can be exercised and developed. They may well not *expect* the child to reason since they may not have evidence that he is *capable* of reasoning. They may be prescriptive and directive. The child may be deprived of many opportunities to reason and express himself. If the results of whatever reasoning he does do are ignored he may not come to think of reasoning and intellectual activity as a means of solving his problems. He may not find that he is able to attain his goals in this way and his tendency to reason may not be reinforced. Instead, the development of his self-confidence and his feelings of worth—his right to *have* opinions and ideas of his own and his beliefs about his right to be listened to—may be stunted. With such a negative self-image—as someone who has little to contribute, no right to ideas, and no right to be listened to—and a lack of experience of intellectual activity and reasoning producing effects which he wants, it is unlikely that he will be strongly motivated toward intellectual activity.

In such a context it may be particularly important to note that the mothers' own feelings of worth—of having something important to contribute to the development of their child—appear to have actually gone down, and we shall see later that this tentative indication that this might have happened is supported by other data. This finding may, however, be more hopeful than it seems. It is common experience that, as one plunges into something important, something which one feels that one should and can do, one feels inadequate; one feels that one will never be able to do it as well as the "experts". There is no doubt at all that the Home Visited parents now feel that there are many more important things that they should be doing with their children: their perception of their role in educating their children has, in some important sense, greatly expanded. If they have not yet learned to cope easily with this new role it would not be surprising if they felt that they were less competent at it. But, if that *is* the explanation of our results, it may indicate a need for further support, possibly through continued Home Visiting, until they master their new role.

CHAPTER 17

WHY ARE CERTAIN ACTIVITIES BELIEVED
TO BE IMPORTANT OR UNIMPORTANT?

We now examine the apparent impact of the Home Visitors on the reasons parents give for thinking that certain activities are important or unimportant.

Parents were asked open-ended questions about why they thought it was important, or unimportant, to ask the child questions about pictures in books and things he had seen. Table A5 shows that the Home Visitors have probably had a major impact on the mothers they visited by making them less likely than other LSES mothers to say that this is a means of teaching the child and encouraging him to recognise things around him. The proportion who give answers of this sort is well below even that of the HSES group. In contrast, they appear to have led the parents more frequently to give answers which fall into the category of trying to find out what the child is learning and find out whether he is paying attention (this category includes all mentions of tutorial questions designed to find out if the child has picked up things or he ought to have learned). It should be noted that the LSES group is more likely than the HSES group to think that the function of questions is to test the child's understanding in this way and that it therefore looks as if one of the effects the Visitors have is, in this instance, to lead the mothers to move away from, rather than toward, the HSES group. The proportion who give answers which fall into the category of encouraging the child to understand, find out, and take an interest in things is slightly higher in the EHV than LSES group. This type of answer is much more often given by HSES than LSES parents, but, while the frequency with which HSES parents mention it is supportive of their tendency to attach more importance to helping the child to learn to use books to find information for himself, and their general tendency to be more likely to encourage a pro-active, rather than a re-active, learning style, this is not true for the EHV group. Although the Home Visited parents are more likely than other LSES mothers to say that they should ask children questions about pictures in books and things they have seen in order to develop intelligence, they are, like their LSES counterparts, less likely than HSES parents to say that one asks children questions in order to encourage the children to talk or to show that one is interested in them and what they are doing (and thereby provide further encouragement?).

Similar results were obtained when parents were asked what were the main benefits of looking at books with children (Table A6). The proportion who said that looking at books is interesting and enjoyable is dramatically higher in the EHV than LSES group and far exceeds that found in the HSES group. Although the proportion who say that it helps to develop language is higher in the EHV than LSES group, the proportion is still well below that found in the HSES group. The same applies to the proportion who say that it helps to develop imagination and creativity. The proportion who say that such activities prepare the child for school is markedly lower in the EHV group.

The proportion of Home Visited parents who say that teaching the child language is a very important reason for reading to the child is more than twice that found in the LSES group and exceeds that found in HSES group (Table A7). The proportion who say that one important reason for doing so is to establish a warm relationship between the parent and child is also almost twice as great as in either bench-mark group. The proportion who say that an important reason for doing so is to please the child is about twice that found among other LSES parents, and about the same as that found in the HSES group.

A closed question on what would happen if they did not talk to their children a lot (Table A8) shows that the major effect of the Home Visitors appears to have been to increase the proportion who say that parent and child would not get to know each other very well from 46% to 95%. This brings the responses of the EHV group into line with those of the HSES bench-mark sample. The EHVs also appear to have had a major impact by leading the parents to be more likely to think that the child will feel rejected if they do not talk to him a lot. The impact on the belief that failure to talk to the child would lead to failure of the child's language to develop fully does not appear to have been so marked. An apparent effect of similar magnitude can be observed in relation to the perceived connection between talking to children and the development of intelligence.

The main impact of the Home Visiting on what parents think will happen if they do not give their children educational toys seems to have been to lead the parents to feel that they will not get to know their children so well (Table A8). The Home Visited parents are even less likely than the LSES parents to associate such toys with the development of intelligence and school success.

Encouraging the child to ask questions and seek reasons for things he is told is much more often associated with the development of responsibility and independence (Table A9) in the EHV than the LSES group, and this may in part account for the fact that the Home Visited mothers think it is more important for the child to question and seek reasons for things he is told. Another factor which may have contributed to the importance they attached to the child questioning might have been that mothers in this group are more likely to think that the child will do well at school if he questions and seeks reasons for things he is told. The proportion who say that husbands, teachers, and relatives will find the child more difficult if he is encouraged to ask questions is lower in the EHV group than in the HSES and LSES groups. They are also less likely than the LSES group to say that husbands and relatives will disapprove of encouraging him to ask questions.

In addition the Home Visitors have, to some degree, apparently been successful in leading the parents they visit to view treating the child with more respect—as an individual with his own interests and tastes—more positively—although they still do not consider it to be very important (Table A9). The Home Visited parents are more likely than other LSES parents to say that it will: promote responsibility, language development, general development, working things out for himself, and school success.

The Home Visitors have had no impact on whether the parents think that the main value of engaging in rough and tumble with the child is to toughen him up (Table A10). (The belief that this *is* its main value sharply differentiates the HSES and LSES groups). The Home Visited mothers are more likely than other LSES mothers to say that such activity helps to get rid of energy and aggression and, again, that it helps to promote a good relationship between parent and child.

Discussion

There are, perhaps, two common threads running through this data. One is that the Home Visited parents have come to think that many of the activities we asked them about will improve their relationships with their children. As we will see later, LSES parents much more often find it difficult to establish satisfactory relationships with their children than do HSES parents. It may therefore be that many of the activities which the EHVs encourage come to be thought important, not primarily because they are thought to promote the cognitive development of children, but mainly because they are seen by the parents as a means of solving one of their more immediate and pressing problems. Although the assumptions behind the typical HSES response might be that creating a relationship in which more reasoned discussion can take place, or a relationship in which the parent develops more respect for the child's abilities and therefore "feeds" those abilities more, will in the long run have the effect of enhancing intellectual development, the fact that the EHVs have had such an enormous impact on the parents' feeling that looking at books with the child, reading him stories and talking to him will be enjoyable, enable parent and child to get to know each other, strengthen the bond between parent and child and improve their relationship with the child, and rather less impact on their feeling that such activities will promote the development of language, imagination, creativity, and intelligence, suggests that this connection may be less likely to be perceived. The data on the HSES sample suggests that High Status parents may well perceive a casual connection between satisfactory family relationships and intellectual and moral development. On the other hand, it may well be that they see a *direct* connection between development of these characteristics and looking at books with the child, reading stories to him and talking to him. In contrast it is *unlikely* that the EHVs have led the mothers they visited to associate such things as looking at books with their children, reading stories to them, and talking to them, with intellectual development through the intermediate stage of establishing better family relationships. Low status mothers may not see beyond the immediate gain (in improved relationships) to be derived from these activities.

Perhaps one of the lessons to be drawn from this data is that LSES parents are inclined to focus on relatively direct and immediate connections between the activities they undertake with their children and the qualities they think their children will develop, whereas the HSES group have a much broader and more long-term view. It may, therefore, be that one of the main difficulties the EHVs have had has been to encourage the parents to shift from a narrower to a broader concept of development.

The failure of many LSES parents to see a connection between these activities and what many people would take to be synonyms for intelligence—imagination, creativity, understanding, finding out, taking an interest in things—has already been remarked upon. But whereas the Home Visitors have been able to lead parents to realise that reading stories to their children promotes the development of language, they have not had such a marked effect on parents' perceptions of the cognitive benefits of looking at books with their children or asking them questions about books and things they have seen. Equally, it is remarkable that, after all the Visiting, the proportion of parents who feel that their children's language will fail to develop fully even if they do not talk to them a lot is still only 75%. Perhaps the reason why *reading* stories comes to be imbued with such potency is that it more clearly resembles formal educational activity and may, in addition, both introduce the child to new words which his parents would not normally use and introduce him to turns of phrase which (*pace* Bullock (1975)) are associated with received forms of expression.

One conclusion we can draw is that we cannot assume that the greater importance that many Home Visited parents attach to some of the items rated in the "importance" section of the interview is due to the reasons which we would tend to assume. In the case of at least some of the sub-group of items we have studied in detail, the reasons which lay behind the Home Visited parents' responses were unexpected, and in some ways foreign to us.

From the data we have presented it seems likely that parents desperately want to enjoy their relationship with their children, and have seized upon many of the activities encouraged by the Home Visitors as potential ways of helping them to enjoy that relationship. Unfortunately, as we shall see later (Table A41), either because they are not able more frequently to engage in these activities, or for some other reason, they do not actually seem to enjoy their relationship with their children any more. Data from informal interviews suggest that the reason for this is that though they find that they do indeed come to enjoy the activities which the EHVs demonstrate, and discover that their children enjoy them a great deal more than they thought, they just do not have the time to spend with their children in these activities. They seem to be too pre-occupied with coping with the demands of daily life. As we shall see, there are recurrent indications (though admittedly no clear proof) that this is so: it emerges when they are asked about the quality of their lives, the problems they expect their children to encounter as they get older, and the ways in which they could help their children to do better at school. By giving the mothers a taste for something which they cannot obtain, the Home Visitors may, therefore, have led the parents they visited to feel increasingly frustrated. (This, however, is a hypothesis which we cannot test from the present data). Nevertheless, if family relationships do improve, that may indeed give the children a greater opportunity to flower and develop. Their parents may come to realise how competent they are and, as a result, come to rely on them more and stretch them more and, by taking their children's complaints seriously and doing something about them, they may reinforce their children's tendency to make logical requests and express them in a reasoned and linguistically coherent form. What we may be observing in the Home Visited parents' responses is a gut reaction to the effect that the first priority is to improve family relationships without a clear understanding of why it is so important to improve those relationships or what would follow from so doing. If it is the case that this is what is happening, and if improving family relationships is a more important way of promoting cognitive development than promoting early intellectual activity, the implications for the design of Home Visiting programmes, and the priorities of the Home Visitors, could be considerable. However, even if this is the correct way to construe the problem, it is, as the EHVs have observed, often easier to gain access to family relationships by focussing on the children, their play and their education, than by focussing directly on the interpersonal inadequacies of the parents. As we have seen, this is one of the great advantages which the EHVs feel they have over social workers.

CHAPTER 18

WHAT CAN BE DONE TO FOSTER
CERTAIN QUALITIES?

We have now looked at the importance parents attach to children's developing certain qualities, and, to some extent, examined the reasons they have for considering these qualities important. We now consider what they think can be done to foster some of them, and the impact of the Educational Home Visitors on these beliefs.

After parents had rated how important it was to them that their children developed certain qualities, they were asked to say how they would foster three of those which they believed to be important. (For this reason the base on which the percentages in Tables A12 to A23 was calculated varies from Table to Table. For some of the items too few people were asked the question to make an analysis meaningful).

Figure 4* shows that the Home Visitors seem to have led significant proportions of those parents who thought that it was important for their children to develop their intelligence, to think that a parent could do this by reading to the child, talking to him, discussing things with him, answering his questions, giving him plenty of attention, taking an interest in him, and playing with him. They appear to have actually led the Home Visited mothers to place more emphasis on reading to the child than do the HSES mothers and the Home Visited group, in contrast to the LSES group, are as likely as the HSES group to mention talking to the child and discussing things with him. However, the enormous difference between the proportion of the HSES and LSES groups who think that intelligence is to be fostered by giving the child plenty of attention, taking an interest in him, and playing with him has not disappeared. Nor is the proportion who think it is important to provide and encourage the child to use books for himself the same for the HSES and EHV groups. We will see later that HSES parents were much more likely than LSES parents to say that most of the child's activities were joint activities in which both parent and

* Figure 4 corresponds to Table A12.

FIGURE 4

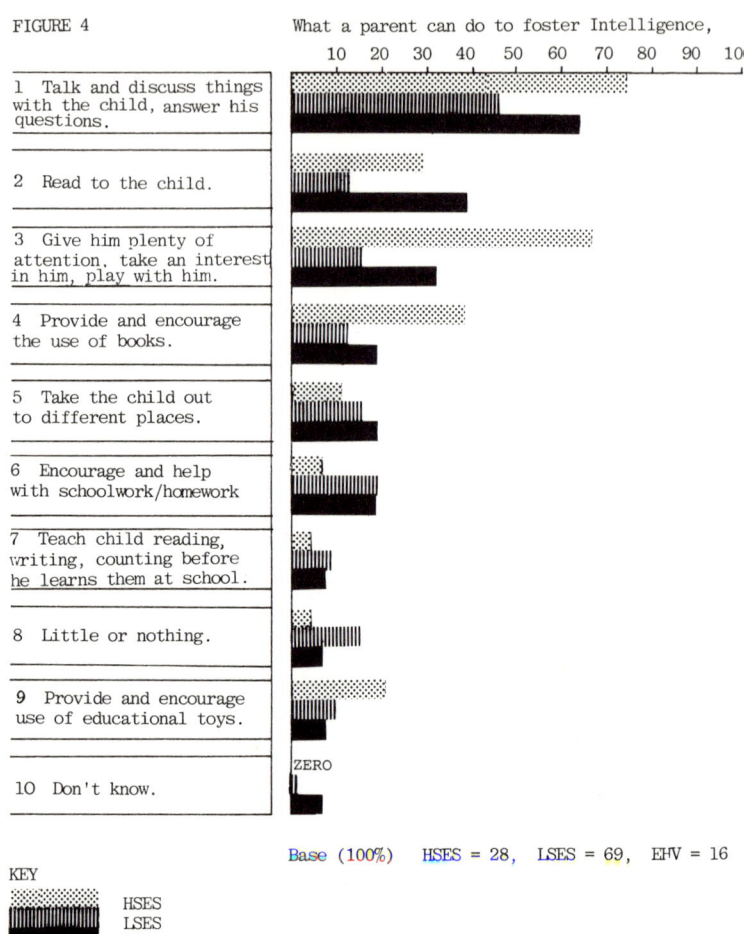

What a parent can do to foster Intelligence,

KEY

HSES
LSES
EHV

Base (100%)   HSES = 28,   LSES = 69,   EHV = 16

child participated. In that context, it may be conjectured that, not only are the HSES parents much more inclined to encourage pro-active rather than reactive behaviour on the part of the child, they are also much more likely to be sensitively responsive to the child's needs. Whereas the LSES group seem to make a sharp distinction between activities the child initiates—which encompass most of his activities —and their own teaching, (ie telling) activities, the HSES group seem to be more facilitative of development, and sensitively responsive to child-initiated activities. The Home Visitors seem to have had more difficulty in leading the Home Visited group to adopt such a transactional viewpoint. Once again this is a conjecture which seems to be emerging from the data, rather than a finding which has been fully substantiated.

Inventiveness (Table A13) seems to be primarily associated with practical activities and using construction materials. The Home Visitors seem to have reinforced this sort of conception of inventiveness and virtually eliminated a motivational conception in which inventive activity is thought to be released by sparking off the child's interests.

The proportion of Home Visited parents who think that inquisitiveness is to be encouraged by leading the child to think and question is higher than that found in the LSES bench-mark group (Table A14). The view that answering questions will lead to question asking is less common in the EHV group—and it may be that the Home Visited parents feel that they should throw the child's questions back at him and encourage him to answer them himself. Once again, the failure of the EHV group to proffer the response "Do not repress his natural inquisitiveness" suggests that the Home Visitors have reinforced their (low status) clients' notion that teaching means telling rather than "Creating an environment conducive to natural growth".

Figure 5, on imagination, leaves the author feeling profoundly uneasy. We have already seen that most parents, HSES and LSES, are none too keen on their children developing a vivid imagination. The remarks made to the interviewers in the course of their work made it clear that the parents thought that the problem was to prevent the children's imagination getting out of hand, rather than to encourage it. Under these circumstances it is perhaps not surprising that the Home Visitors, by talking about the importance of imagination, appear to have increased the proportion of mothers who said there was little or nothing one could do to develop it! Likewise, it would seem that the most satisfactory interpretation of the data presented in Figure 5 is that, in order to find a way of handling the cognitive dissonance produced by the Home Visitors' apparent espousal of "imagination", the mothers have reacted by adopting a more constricted definition of what is meant by imagination itself. It now has much more to do with such things as books, reading stories, and looking at pictures. It has, specifically, less to do with making up stories. As many mothers made clear to the interviewers, stories that their children have made up but presented as true, are the bane of their lives. Nevertheless, it is significant that 27% of the HSES mothers did encourage their children to make up stories, presumably with the intention of fostering the sorts of abilities required to generate disembedded imaginative products—such as school compositions—in which the objective is not to solve problems or deceive others but to generate a fictional product of merit.

The data suggest that the Home Visitors may have been suggesting to parents that children's interests are universal, rather than idiosyncratic (Table A16). All children can be expected to be interested in the sorts of activity they encourage. This would explain why the proportion of parents who said that interests and tastes which are different from those of other people are to be promoted by encouraging the child's special interests is so much lower in the EHV than LSES group and why more of the EHV group say that they don't know how it is to be done. It would also explain why none said that it was important to do it by encouraging their children to experience different situations and activities, although this answer was given by almost half the HSES sample.

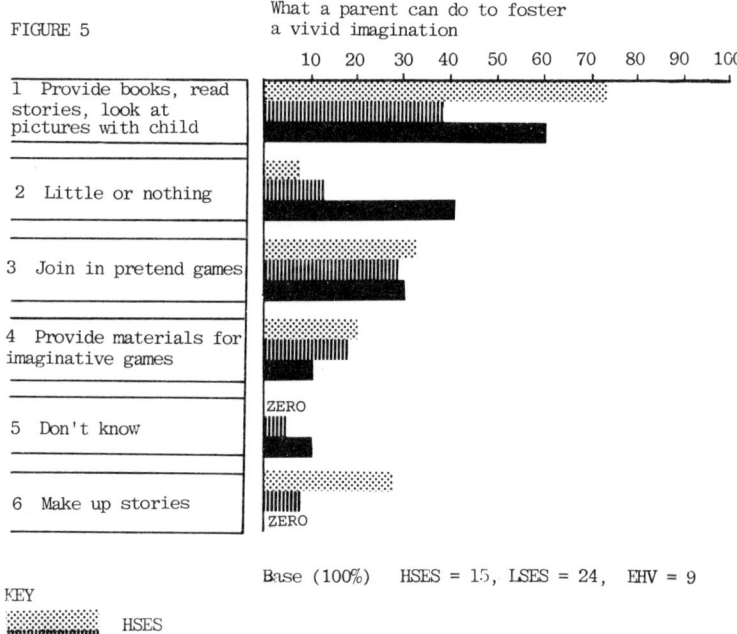

FIGURE 5

What a parent can do to foster a vivid imagination

1 Provide books, read stories, look at pictures with child

2 Little or nothing

3 Join in pretend games

4 Provide materials for imaginative games

5 Don't know

6 Make up stories

Base (100%)   HSES = 15, LSES = 24,   EHV = 9

KEY

HSES
LSES
EHV

The data also suggest that the Home Visitors have led the mothers to feel that determination is to be encouraged by gritting one's teeth and keeping on trying (Table A17). They do not appear to have led the mothers to be more likely to adopt the strategies most often advocated by the HSES group, namely demonstrating the benefits of persistence and effort to the child, helping only when help is really needed, creating an expectation that anything one starts has to be finished, or praising and rewarding successful efforts. Once again, what we seem to see here is the strengthening of a somewhat unsubtle and undifferentiated attempt to foster characteristics like "determination" (which may well be known to be important determinants of school and life success). The differences between the way HSES and LSES parents attempt to set about fostering such characteristics may well be more important than *that* they seek to foster them, and Home Visitors may find it difficult to lead the parents they work with to adopt the approaches more often used by the HSES parents. They may well find that their actions are assimilated into the conceptual framework already used by the LSES parents—and transformed out of all recognition in the process.

The data further suggest that the Home Visitors have reinforced the LSES mothers' abhorrence of competitiveness (Table A18). The Home Visitors may therefore have led them to articulate their value for co-operative (rather than competitive) activity, and encouraged them to stand up for what they believe to be good and right. Unfortunately the rest of the data do not really lead us to believe that this is what has happened. A more likely explanation seems to be that the Home Visitors avoided this problem altogether, and that this has led to a marked increase in the proportion who say that they do not know how competitiveness is to be fostered.

It is remarkable that the Home Visitors seem to have had very little impact on leading the mothers to believe that the ability to mix easily with others is to be fostered by taking the child to a nursery or playgroup (Table A19). Nor do they appear to have led the mothers to be more likely to say that it is to be fostered by creating supervised play activities in the home. On the contrary, for some unknown reason (possibly the better weather at the time the EHV sample was interviewed) the proportion who say that it is to be fostered by encouraging the child to go outside to play is much higher in the EHV than LSES group.

Figure 6 suggests that the Home Visitors have had relatively little effect on the strategies which parents think they could adopt in order to engender respect. The Home Visited group, like the LSES group, are more likely to say that respect is to be fostered by firmness, discipline, insisting on respect, and insisting on obedience. The High Status group is much more likely to say that respect is to be fostered by setting a good example, fairness and consistency, and by treating the child with respect. Given that the Home Visitors felt that it was of considerable importance to encourage the mothers to change their

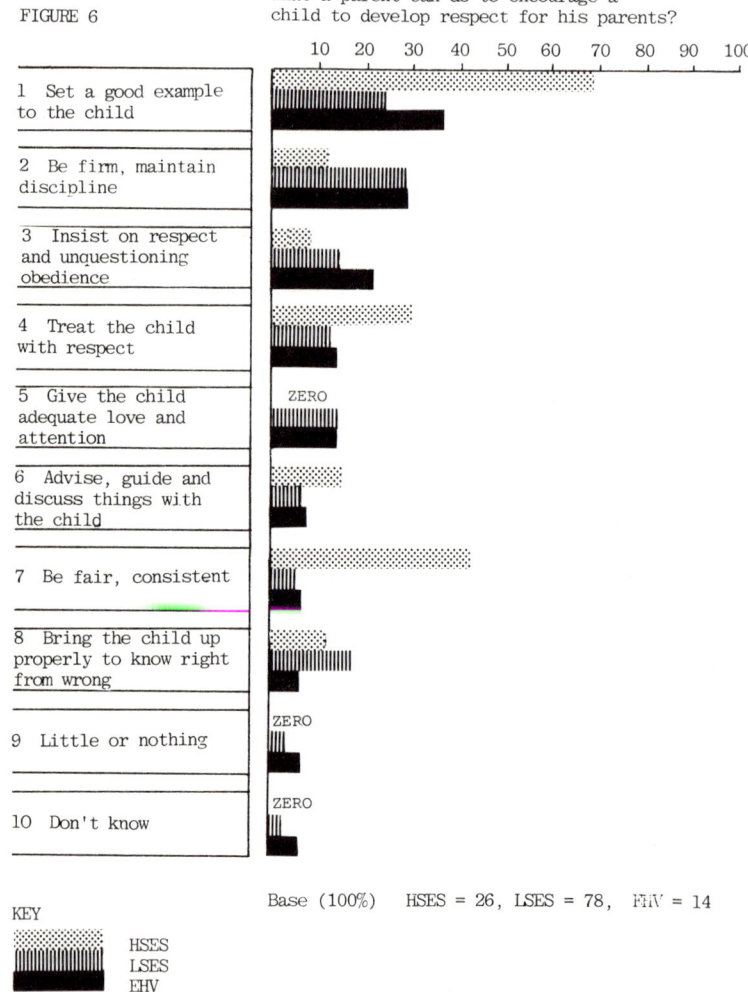

FIGURE 6

What a parent can do to encourage a child to develop respect for his parents?

1 Set a good example to the child

2 Be firm, maintain discipline

3 Insist on respect and unquestioning obedience

4 Treat the child with respect

5 Give the child adequate love and attention

6 Advise, guide and discuss things with the child

7 Be fair, consistent

8 Bring the child up properly to know right from wrong

9 Little or nothing

10 Don't know

Base (100%)   HSES = 26, LSES = 78, EHV = 14

KEY
HSES
LSES
EHV

discipline strategies and to lead them to treat their children with respect—perhaps in order to encourage the child to reason about the long term consequences of his actions, perhaps in order to improve family relationships (so that the parent would be more likely to take the child's complaints seriously and act upon them) and perhaps in order to create an opportunity for the parent to recognise, and therefore be willing to feed, the child's ability—these results cannot be interpreted as anything but discouraging, although the EHV group are, indeed, more likely than the LSES group to mention setting a good example.

The bases for the Home Visited sample in the remaining tables in this section (Tables A21 to A23) are too small to support even tentative discussion, although we will, in Part IV, draw attention to some of the possible implications of the data obtained from the HSES and LSES samples for the design of Home Visiting programmes.

General Discussion

The EHVs again appear to have had a major impact on the *ways* in which the parents they visited think that qualities of intellect, character, and personality are to be fostered. Many of these are precisely what the Home Visitors set out to teach them. Nevertheless, as is often the case, it seems that at least some of the Home Visitors' messages have, in the course of transmission, been translated into the *recipients'* frame of reference and heard as reinforcing views they already held. The Educational Home Visitors seem to have had particular difficulty getting across the notion that growth is to be facilitated by transactional activity in which the parent *responds* sensitively to child-initiated activity. Rather, the EHVs' message in fact—if not in intention—seems to have been that the parent should do more formal teaching. Yet while HSES parents *do* do more formal teaching than LSES parents, this is not the only way in which the two groups differ in their approach. The remaining differences have to do with the difference between "mothering" and "teaching". This difference itself may be a product of the differing constraints under which the mothers lead their lives. We have already seen that time pressures led some of the Home Visitors to feel that they had to do more programmed teaching, rather than wait, as they would have done as mothers, for the right moment to respond to the child. It may therefore be suggested that the Home Visited mothers may be particularly prone to pick up *this* aspect of the EHVs' behaviour because they themselves may be working under considerable time constraints.

Perhaps the Educational Home Visitors should not set out directly to transmit such a complex message. Perhaps they should *begin* by attempting to extend parents' understanding of the ways in which development is to be facilitated to more often include modelling or demonstrating the desired behaviour to the child, personal example, and creating opportunities for the child to experience the effectiveness of cognitive activity as a means of solving his own problems. We might even go so far as to suggest that the EHVs might set aside some time in which to think about ways in which these broader conceptions of the ways in which growth might be facilitated could be communicated to parents. That would, however, raise basic questions about the methods to be adopted by the EHVs. If the EHVs are to *model* mothering behaviour involving sensitive, transactional, reactivity they may require more than *time*. They may need to know the child extremely well—to be aware of the implications of apparently minor things that the child says and does—including his facial expressions and other expressive movements. Unfortunately as one of the Home Visitors said at one of their meetings—and the others concurred—it may just not be possible for anyone who is not the child's *mother* to do this. Thus, the notion of modelling *mothering* skills may be a contradiction in terms. If it is, and if mothering really does contribute in important and irreplaceable ways to child growth, then the implications are serious. And not only for the EHVs—but also for the whole teaching profession. For it would follow that there is no way in which a person who is not a sensitive *mother* can help a child to develop his most important qualities. Put like that, in a *reductio-ad-absurdum* argument, the hypothesis is obviously false. But it does raise questions about the extent to which, and the manner in which, mothers can be helped to acquire what are, perhaps, their most important competencies and, as a corollary, the extent to which school systems can help children to develop their most important competencies.

CHAPTER 19

WHICH OF THE QUALITIES THAT A CHILD LEARNS FROM HIS PARENTS ARE MOST IMPORTANT FOR HIS FUTURE?

We have already seen that the parents who have had Home Visits are even less inclined than their LSES counterparts to think that what a child learns from his parents is important to his future success (Figure 3, Item B16). Elsewhere in the interview, parents were asked *which* of the qualities that a child learns from his parents are most important to his future.

The Home Visitors appear to have led the parents they visited to give answers which are somewhat more like those given by the HSES group (Table A24). The frequency with which most categories of answer is given has moved in the direction of the HSES group. The impact seems to have been greatest for honesty and hard work, which the LSES sample mention less often than the HSES group, but the EHV group mention more often. However, despite the apparent effect of the EHVs, there is still a substantial discrepancy between Home Visited and HSES mothers in the proportions who gave answers falling into the categories dealing with respect for authority, considerateness, obedience, being a good citizen and fitting into society, being sociable and friendly, having initiative, and being clean and tidy. If considerateness, initiative, and concern with the wider society are indeed important qualities which HSES children learn from their parents, then the EHVs have some way to go in leading parents to view the parent-based educational process in a way which will make good the deficiency.

CHAPTER 20

WHAT DO PARENTS ACTUALLY DO
WITH THEIR CHILDREN?

We have seen that the Home Visitors have had a dramatic effect on parents' attitudes. Let us now look at the effect they have had on their behaviour.

Actually, we are not able to do quite that: we are only able to look at the effect that they have had on the parents' *reported* behaviour.

We approached this question in two ways. We asked the parents how often they did various things with their child, and we also asked them how much time they and/or their child spent on a number of selected activities on the previous day. By asking about the previous day we hoped to minimise memory effects.

We have just seen that the Home Visitors seem to have led the parents they visited to be less likely to think that what a child learns from his parents is very important to his future success, but that they also appear to have led them to mention more, and different, things when asked what are the important things that a child learns from his parents. It is evident that the Home Visited parents are more likely than the LSES parents to say that their children learnt a lot from them, although they still do not say this as often as do the HSES parents (Table A25). Figure 7 reinforces the apparent paradox that, despite the fact that the HSES group are more likely to feel that their children learn a lot from them, they actually set out to teach them less and are more likely to say that the child learns himself. As we have several times commented, this paradox is, perhaps, to be resolved by saying that what the HSES parents are saying is that, while the child learns himself, the parent "teaches" by responding in a sensitive manner to his needs. It seems that, if this is the case, the EHVs have had some success in leading the parents they visited to behave like the HSES group.

The proportion of parents who say that, when they set out to teach their children things, they teach them intellectual skills is dramatically higher in the EHV than LSES group (Table A27). The proportion who say that they set out to teach them social skills and behaviour is

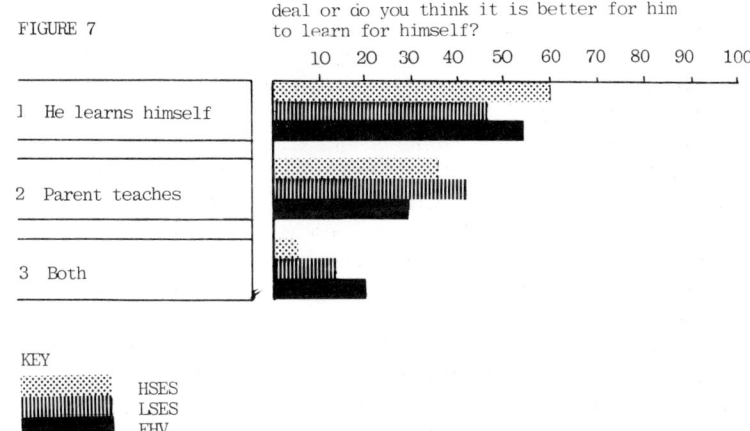

FIGURE 7

Do you set out to teach your child a great deal or do you think it is better for him to learn for himself?

1 He learns himself

2 Parent teaches

3 Both

KEY

HSES
LSES
EHV

somewhat lower, as is the proportion who set out to teach moral values. The proportion who set out to teach physical skills and independence is only slightly higher. However, in all respects, the Home Visitors seem to have led the parents to move in the direction of the HSES group, and, in the case of intellectual skills, they seem to have led them to be even more likely than the HSES group to endorse the item.

They appear to have had much less effect on *how* parents teach their children than on *what* they teach them (Table A28). Although the proportion who say they teach by punishing failures is markedly lower in the EHV group, there has been no increase in the proportion who say they teach by example, though this is the dominant mode of teaching for the HSES group. The proportions who say that they teach by providing a stimulating environment, and that they teach by giving reasons and explanations, are higher in the EHV than in the LSES group, although they are not so high as in the HSES group. The proportion who teach by giving constant reminders (ie nagging) is no lower in the EHV than in the LSES group. And none of the Home Visited parents yet teach by positive reinforcement of desired behaviour. As we have already seen, the parents who have had home visits are no more likely than other LSES parents to create situations in which the child finds intellectual activity positively satisfying because it brings him increasing control over his environment. These data therefore raise the question of whether more effort should be made to influence such perceptions and expectations.

Although the great majority of Home Visited parents, like all other parents, said they would teach counting by using easily available things in the child's environment (Table A30), the Home Visitors seem to have had a significant impact on the proportion who say they would use special teaching equipment such as books. In the case of reading (Table A29) the Home Visitors appear to have led the mothers they visited to be still more likely to use formal methods, although this was already much more common in the LSES than EHV group. The difference in the proportion who would do this now amounts to 40%. The EHV group is also more likely than the LSES group to teach individual letters and sounds and still less likely to say that they would not teach reading.

We now turn to the question of the parents' response to the child's questions, a topic which the Home Visitors believed to be of considerable importance from the point of view of developing an enquiring mind. First it may be noted that the Home Visited parents are more confident than other LSES parents that they will in fact be able to answer the child's questions (Table A31). Second, the Home Visitors seem to have led the parents they visited to be more likely to say they never find their children's questions a nuisance (Table A32), but only slightly less likely to make up an answer when they don't know the answer (Table A33). (They are only slightly more likely to look up the answer in a book under these circumstances). These data, taken together with our finding that the Home Visited parents are no more likely than other LSES mothers to think that it is any more important to teach the child to use books to find information for himself, suggest that it may be that books are seen either as things which have to do with school work or as entertainment. They are not seen as having instrumental value. Alternatively, it may be argued that the data suggest that the parents do not have relevant reference books in their homes. If this is the case it is difficult to see how they can lead their children to believe that the information available in books will help them to solve their own problems. We may conclude, therefore, that, although the EHVs appear to influence the ways in which parents use books, they do not seem to lead them to view books as an aid to that type of cognitive activity which helps one to lead one's life more effectively.

We have already commented several times on the possibility that one of the major differences between the HSES and the LSES groups, which the EHVs seem to have difficulty influencing, is the parents' sensitivity to the child and their willingness to respond to him. Table A34 makes the same point. While the Home Visited parents are a little more inclined than other LSES parents to think it is very important to "study the things the child wants to know and then help him to find out", the Home Visited group is the one which believes most strongly that it is important to make sure that the child learns what the parent thinks he should learn.

Figure 8 shows that, contrary to what one might believe if one reads only the writings of psychologists (apart from a few of the most recent), very few parents think that most of a child's activities are initiated by parents, although there is a dramatic difference between the HSES and LSES group in the proportion who say that they end up by being joint activities. These data strongly support our conjecture that one of the major differences between the HSES and the LSES groups is the willingness of the mother to engage with their children in joint activities. It is clear that the LSES and EHV children tend to play on their own, and that the child *begins* the activity. We cannot tell from these data whether the mother joins in later, but the general tenor of our findings make us suspect that she does not. In contrast it is clear that the HSES group are much more likely to find themselves engaged with their children in activities which neither can claim to have initiated. The impression is one of sensitive transactional activity in which the parent creates an appropriate environment and then responds to the child's interests, inclinations and feelings. White (1976), in particular, has drawn attention to the importance of such behaviour. The EHVs seem to have had difficulty communicating the subtlety of this style of interaction to the parents. Indeed, as we shall see later, those Home Visitors who have tried hardest to model the

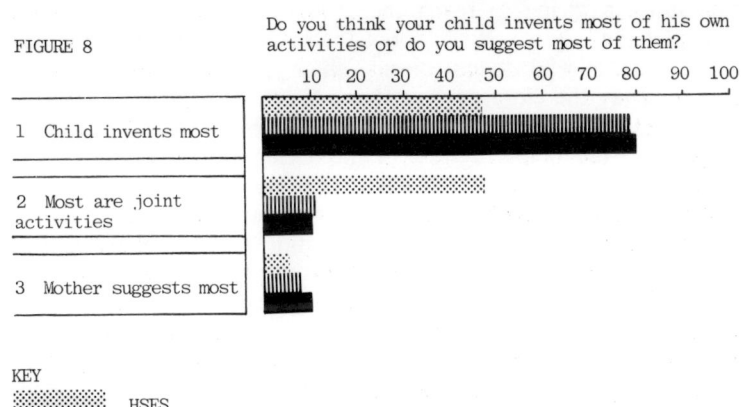

FIGURE 8

Do you think your child invents most of his own activities or do you suggest most of them?

KEY

HSES
LSES
EHV

interactive style for the parents seemed to have led those parents to believe that they are less capable of carrying it out, and less able to understand it. Nevertheless, the Home Visited parents are more likely to say that they often do things that the child wants to do rather than things which they want to do (Table A36). It may be that what these data are telling us is that the EHVs have led the parents to feel that it is important to respond to the child's explicit demands, but that they have not led them to be more sensitive to the growth potential inherent in a wide variety of children's activities.

That their sensitivity *has* been increased is, however, also clear (Table A36). They appear, at least, to be more likely to think about what their child is learning as he plays, and this may be a basis on which future developments can be built.

Asked what sort of things they talk about while the child is engaged on activities such as playing with jig-saws and painting, the Home Visited group are even more likely than the LSES group to issue warnings and instructions (Figure 9). In contrast to what Levenstein's video tapes would have us believe, their activities are more constrictive and directive. But they are also more likely to explain or teach things to the child: ie they turn such activities into formal "teaching" situations. They are even less likely than the LSES group to use them as situations in which they discuss the activity. It is the HSES group that much more frequently mentions this.

In discussing activities in which they are engaged, parents may talk about the goals they would like to reach, the strategies which are likely to enable them to reach those goals, the obstacles they might encounter in trying to reach them, ways of getting round these obstacles, and their feelings about the activity itself and about the goals. Parents who do not discuss their joint activities with their children may therefore deprive them of an opportunity to observe cognitive, connative, and affective processes in action and learn their value from the point of view of improving current activity. The infrequency with which EHV and LSES mothers report discussing past and future events likewise suggests that they may, at least to some extent, deprive their children of opportunities to develop a long time perspective, and diminish any tendency to plan and initiate action with a view to achieving a goal and monitor its effectiveness, any tendency to study spontaneously the causes of events or the effects of their actions, and any tendency to search spontaneously in their memory for past experiences which are relevant to improving current performance and bring this learning to bear on the present. In this context the frequency with which EHV mothers report questioning their child about their activities is reminiscent of the pedagogue's tendency to question a child in order to *test* him—to find out if he knows something they already know, rather than to learn from the child—and it will be recalled that one of the effects of the Home Visitors on the things parents thought it was important to do with their children seemed to be to strengthen their tendency to ask such questions.

FIGURE 9

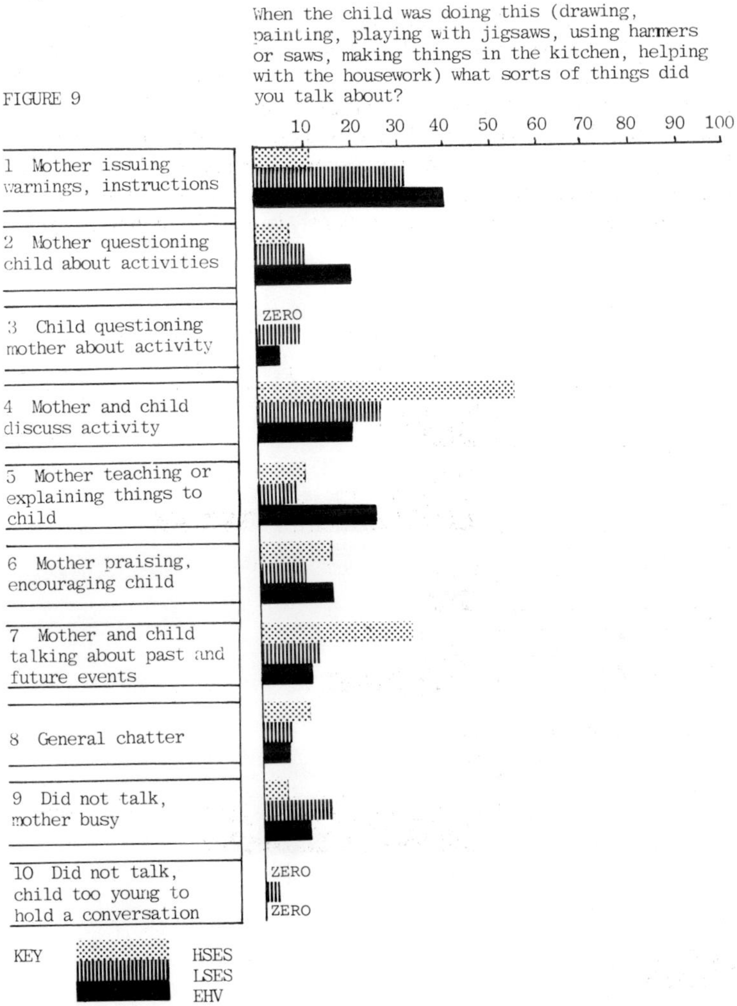
When the child was doing this (drawing, painting, playing with jigsaws, using hammers or saws, making things in the kitchen, helping with the housework) what sorts of things did you talk about?
10 20 30 40 50 60 70 80 90 100
1 Mother issuing warnings, instructions
2 Mother questioning child about activities
3 Child questioning mother about activity
ZERO
4 Mother and child discuss activity
5 Mother teaching or explaining things to child
6 Mother praising, encouraging child
7 Mother and child talking about past and future events
8 General chatter
9 Did not talk, mother busy
10 Did not talk, child too young to hold a conversation
ZERO
ZERO
KEY
HSES
LSES
EHV

Despite the increased importance which the Home Visitors seem to have led the mothers they visited to attach to educational toys, the proportion who say that they often think about what a toy will teach their children before they buy it is slightly lower in the EHV than in the LSES group (Table A36). This takes them even further away from the HSES group who, it seems, almost always consider this. It may be that the interpretation of this finding is that, for the HSES group, almost all toys have educational value, and the question is *what* they will teach the child, rather than *whether* they will teach him anything.

With respect to discipline practices, Figure 10 suggests that the Home Visitors have had some success in leading the parents to be more likely to try to distract their children on to something else, rather than smack them. However, the parents do not seem to have become less punitive in any comprehensive sense, because the Home Visited parents are even more likely than our other LSES mothers to give their children a row. There has apparently been a slight increase in the

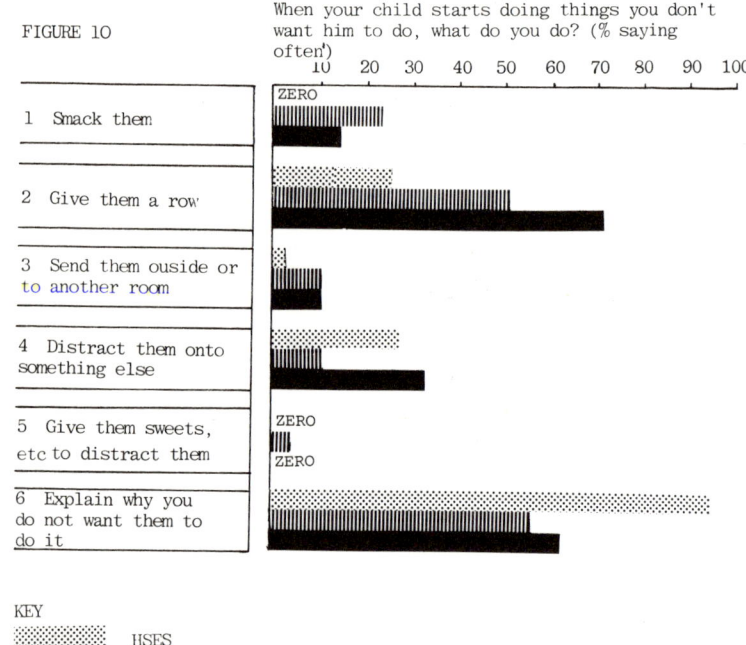

FIGURE 10

When your child starts doing things you don't want him to do, what do you do? (% saying often')

1 Smack them

2 Give them a row

3 Send them ouside or to another room

4 Distract them onto something else

5 Give them sweets, etc to distract them

6 Explain why you do not want them to do it

KEY

HSES
LSES
EHV

proportion who say that they seek to explain to the children why they don't want them to do things, but this has not resulted in bringing their responses into line with the HSES group.

As has already been mentioned, parents were asked how much *time* they, or their children, spent on various activities on the previous day. Their answers were precoded and, in order that the scales should not be too long, the categories were of unequal size. This has made for some difficulty in processing the data since it was not possible to calculate the mean length of time spent on the various activities because the end categŏry consisted of "more than thirty minutes" or, in some cases, "over an hour". Since this category has no upper limit its mid-point is not known (Table A39).

Unfortunately, there is also another problem in interpreting the data, for the effects of Home Visiting are contaminated by the fact that the weather improved between the time the bench-mark samples were interviewed and the time the Home Visited samples were interviewed. The change in the weather would seem to be the most likely explanation of the large increase in the time the children spent playing outside with their friends and going to parks, and the decrease in the time they spent watching television, drawing and painting, and playing with Lego. From our point of view, particular interest centres on questions like the amount of time the parent spent answering the child's questions, looking at books with him, talking about things they had done in the past or would do in the future, talking about what they were doing when they went shopping, teaching the names of colours, etc, teaching him to read and count, helping him to build with bricks and Lego, doing jig-saws with him, and playing with sand and water with him.

On many of these items there are significant differences between the HSES and the LSES groups. In almost every case the Home Visited group also differs from the HSES group. Although the size of the gap is smaller on some of the items, it is larger on others. It would therefore seem that the Home Visitors have had relatively little impact on the parents' actual behaviour with their children. Whereas, as we have seen, they had a dramatic impact on bringing the statements the Home Visited mothers made in an interview situation into line with those made by HSES mothers, this has not been generalised to their reported behaviour toward their children to anything like the same extent. The only exception to that statement is that the Home Visited mothers spent more time than LSES mothers, or even HSES mothers, in taking their children to nursery or play group. This supports our tentative conclusion that one of the effects of the Home Visitors has been to strengthen the parents' emphasis on formal schooling.

The absence of a significant impact on virtually any other single aspect of behaviour may possibly be explained by the constraints which the environment places on the parents' activities.

On the other hand, the apparent inability of the EHVs to influence many of the behaviours they set out to influence, and which do indeed differentiate the HSES from the LSES group, may *not* be due to constraints in the environment. Although parents may, as a result of the Visiting, believe some things to be more important than they did previously, these things may still be much lower down in their *order* of priority. As we have seen, the LSES group attach much more importance than do the HSES group to the child's learning to stick up for himself, becoming strong and tough, and to the child's having time to play with other children. This constellation of values may well account for the major differences between the HSES and LSES children in the time they spent playing outside with their friends. And while the EHVs seem to have led the parents to become more like the HSES group in the value they place on intellectual activity, they had relatively little impact on the value the parents place on the constellation of values we have just mentioned.

CHAPTER 21

THE PROBLEMS PARENTS EXPECTED AS
THEIR CHILDREN GOT OLDER

Although the Home Visited parents were *more* likely than other parents from the same areas to expect that there would be problems with rebellion, with indiscipline, and with school as their children got older, there was no difference, however, in the proportion who did not expect any problems and in this respect they still differ markedly from the HSES parents (Table A40).

As the Newsons (1968, 1978) have shown, parents' actions at any point in time are markedly influenced by what they expect the long term consequences of those actions to be. Thus, although, as we have seen, the Home Visitors appear to have led the parents they visited to be less likely to think that encouraging their children to ask questions and generally think for themselves would lead them to be disruptive or to get above themselves, a possible explanation of their failure to actually do the things which would be likely to promote the development of thinking, questioning, reasoning behaviour may be that they still believe that, in the long run, such qualities will lead to their children getting beyond their control. (We have already seen just how important it is to them that this should not happen). In other words, the EHVs may, in effect, have told the parents not to be so silly as to think that questioning and reasoning will lead to unruliness and insubordination in the short run, but this may have led to the parents' displacing the same fears to the *distant* future, and the anticipated long term consequences may thus have had an impact on their immediate behaviour. What we may be seeing is the result of *not* accepting that reasoning leads to internalised controls. (And who is to say that, despite Kohlberg's (1971) work, they may not be right—particularly if they fail to change their behaviour in a way which will make it possible for their children to engage in high level moral reasoning).

Another, possibly somewhat simpler, explanation of the results (shown in Table A40) is that they do not represent *effects* of the Home

Visiting at all, but rather tell us something about the sort of family that was selected for visiting. This seems an altogether more parsimonious explanation: we have no evidence that the EHVs did, or said, anything which would lead parents to become more aware of these potential problems, but we *do* have evidence that one of the reasons why it was suggested to the EHVs that they should visit certain families was that there were more behaviour problems in the home. However, if this *is* the explanation, the whole question of the EHVs' attitudes to behaviour control comes very much more to the foreground.

CHAPTER 22

PARENTS' PERCEPTIONS OF THEIR PROBLEMS AND THEIR CONFIDENCE IN THEIR ABILITY TO COPE WITH THEM

We have seen that the EHVs have moved increasingly toward the view that it is important to help parents to develop the abilities needed to cope with their own problems if they are to have an impact on their children's development. And we have ourselves suggested that the quality of the mother's whole life style may have a direct bearing on her ability to spend time in psychologically developing activities with her children.

Have the EHVs in fact been able to help the parents cope with some of the dissatisfying aspects of their environment, so that they may now be able to spend more time with their children? Have the parents themselves come to feel more confident and competent to cope with their environment so that that confidence and competence can rub off on their children?

To answer these questions we developed a block of questions which first asked parents to say how important a number of features of their environment were to them, and then to say how satisfied they were with these aspects of their environment. Finally they were asked to say what they thought the consequences would be if they set about tackling one of the "problems" which was revealed by a large discrepancy between their "importance" and "satisfaction" ratings.

Table 2 shows the aspects of their environment which were rated "very important".

It is immediately obvious that there are major differences between the HSES and the LSES groups. For the HSES group, the most important things are to get on well with their children, to get on well with their close family such as husbands and relatives, to have schools which offer a wide variety of courses, to have teachers, planners and officials who take their views seriously, to be able to communicate well with other people, to be on good terms with their children's

TABLE 2: *QUALITY OF LIFE*

	% saying "very important"			% saying "very satisfied"			% saying "dissatisfied"		
	HSES	LSES	EHV	HSES	LSES	EHV	HSES	LSES	EHV
SCHOOL									
A 1. To have a choice of school for your children.	45	25	35	5	4	5	40	34	25
2. To have a school system which can meet your own personal wishes, even if these are different from other people's.	15	3	10	8	4	10	30	19	15
3. To be on good terms with your children's teachers.	63	16	35	38	7	20	0	5	0
FAMILY									
4. To be able to get on well with your children.	88	58	50	58	23	20	0	6	5
5. To be able to learn more about bringing up children.	10	9	15	20	6	5	0	3	10
6. To be on good terms with your neighbours.	28	9	20	33	5	5	0	7	10
WIDER COMMUNITY									
7. To have a doctor who really listens to you.	70	39	35	35	8	10	10	18	35
8. To work in a place where people are encouraged to develop whatever talents they have.	45	16	10	20	5	10	10	13	20
9. To be able to cope with day to day activities more effectively.	8	11	15	25	10	5	0	10	5
10. To have a government which can meet your own personal needs even if these are different from other people's.	15	3	20	0	0	0	28	15	30
11. To feel that you are involved in the affairs of your community.	5	3	5	0	1	0	8	5	10
12. To be able to get a fair share of what society has to offer.	10	20	10	8	0	0	0	36	20
13. To live in a community which is well organised and run.	18	11	10	13	1	0	3	26	45

QUALITY OF LIFE (cont.)

	HSES LSES EHV % saying "very important"			HSES LSES EHV % saying "very satisfied"			HSES LSES EHV % saying "dissatisfied"		
SCHOOL									
B 1. To have schools which offer a wide variety of courses.	73	45	30	3	4	5	20	14	5
2. To have teachers who take your views seriously.	60	38	10	13	8	5	3	5	0
FAMILY									
3. To be able to learn to cope with your children.	58	49	45	25	10	15	0	10	0
4. To be able to get on with your close family (eg husband, relatives).	78	62	25	53	17	15	0	11	0
5. To be able to communicate well with others.	65	26	30	25	10	5	0	11	0
COMMUNITY									
6. To have planners and officials who take your views seriously.	60	24	20	3	0	0	28	31	30
7. To have a wide variety of jobs open to you.	45	26	15	3	2	5	20	53	45
8. To have opportunities to develop your mind and learn new things.	55	9	15	25	1	0	8	14	25
9. To live in a society which makes an effort to make best use of everyone's different abilities.	55	24	25	5	1	0	35	31	40
10. To be able to influence what happens in your country.	53	14	15	5	3	0	40	28	45
11. To have access to a community centre where there are many things going on which you can join in.	13	18	15	8	11	10	18	15	15
12. To live in a community in which everyone plays a part in curbing vandalism.	60	40	40	5	1	0	15	50	75

teachers, to have a doctor who really listens to them, and to live in a society which makes an effort to make the best use of everyone's talents and abilities. For the LSES group, things are very different. Although they do indeed attach importance to being able to get on with their children and their close family, these things are very quickly followed by a felt need to be able to learn how to cope with their children (notice the relevance to our assertion that they seem to have more difficulty coping with their children), and to live in a community in which everyone plays their part in curbing vandalism.

Attention may be drawn to the fact that, while the HSES group appears to be preoccupied with relationships and services—relationships with husbands, doctors, planners, teachers and the wider society in general—the LSES group seems to be preoccupied with getting a firmer grip on life in the here and now. They need to get control over their children and to get control over the vandals who plague them. This precarious nature of their hold on life emerges in their answers to many other questions—their children are more likely to be led into deviant behaviour; it is more important to ensure that they are fed; it is more important to find a way of ensuring that there is someone at home to look after them. Put in one way the data suggest that the LSES parents in general are trying to get a grip on satisfactions at a lower level in Maslow's hierarchy of needs (Maslow, 1954)—and therefore have less *time*, whatever their inclinations, for the niceties of child-rearing. Thus the first task of a Home Visiting programme may be to help them to handle this basic problem. If this were done, the parents might then progress naturally to the wider concerns evident in the responses of the HSES group.

Viewed in another way, the data may be interpreted as supporting Van der Eyken's belief that the individuals concerned are under stress. If this is so, the resulting anxiety may lead to their even being unable to take up such support services as are offered.

But, whichever interpretation is correct, it is important to note that, logical though it may be to argue that body and soul could best be kept together by establishing more effective relationships with the wider framework of society which so much determines the course of their lives, the pressing need to keep body and soul together may prevent the mothers concerned seeing this wider structure and force them to spend most of their time struggling to cope with what they see as more immediate problems.

Having briefly examined the differences between the responses of the HSES and LSES groups, we may now return to an examination of the responses of the Home Visited group. They do, indeed, differ from both the other groups. Learning how to cope with their children has moved up in their priorities at the expense of being on good terms with their close families, such as their husbands and relatives. Having teachers who take their views seriously is dramatically lower in their priorities.

It seems unlikely that the Home Visitors would have led the mothers they visited to feel that it was less important to get on well with their husbands. One can only assume that their tendency to de-emphasise it reflects one of the basic differences between the Home Visited and non Home Visited samples in the LSES areas. The families selected for visiting included a high proportion of families with problems, often with poor relationships between the mother and her husband or children. The data seem to lend support to the view that problem parents don't *care* so much about their relationships with their husbands as do other families.

It seems more plausible that the EHVs were responsible for the fact that the parents who had been visited think it is less important to have teachers who take their views seriously, and to have schools which offer a wide variety of courses. They may also have been responsible for the larger proportion who say it is very important to them to be on good terms with their children's teachers.

But perhaps the most striking lesson to be drawn from Table 2 is that the Home Visitors have, in no way, been able to lead the parents they visited to share the priorities of the HSES parents. If getting on well with husbands and relatives is an important precursor to good pyschological development on the part of children, then the Visited parents have a long way to go. The same applies if children's psychological development is associated with their parents' attaching importance to being able to communicate well with other people, or believing that it is important for their school system and society to develop and utilise people with a wide variety of talents. Likewise, if "self-esteem" is taken to involve thinking that one has a right to be listened to, then the parents' responses to the items which ask whether they think it is important to have doctors, teachers, planners and officials who take their views seriously suggest that the parents' self images still leave something to be desired. They appear to be self-depreciating, and their replies almost suggest that they do not think that their views are *worthy* of consideration. Furthermore, if one does not think that it is important to have doctors, teachers, planners and officials who listen to one and take one's views seriously, there is really very little point in developing initiative, self confidence, the ability to think for oneself or the ability to communicate, or concern with the wider community. The same is true if one does not feel that it is important to be able to influence what happens in one's country. And, if one does not think it is important to have opportunities to develop one's mind and learn new things as an adult, can one really be expected to place great store in the intrinsic value of educational activity at school level?

Such reflections again remind one of Maslow's hierarchy of needs and lead one to ponder its validity. If people are spending time—are forced to spend time—satisfying needs low in his hierarchy, *can* they simultaneously be concerned with needs higher up in the hierarchy? Or is the explanation of the hierarchy, not that the higher level needs cannot be pursued until lower level needs have been satisfied, but that some people are constitutionally incapable of pursuing, or are uninterested in, the supposedly higher level needs? If their low-level needs are satisfied, *do* they move on to a concern with the so-called higher level needs? Quite clearly, from the data we have presented, the way in which one would design a Home Visiting programme is dependent on the way in which one answers these questions. And evaluation of the differential consequences of Home Visiting programmes predicated on these alternative answers would yield the basic data which is needed to answer them.

The dramatically smaller proportion of Home Visited parents, in comparison with the LSES group, who feel that it is important to have teachers who take their views seriously deserves further comment. It almost looks as if the EHVs have led the parents they visited to be even more likely to think that their own views on education are worthless. Having been exposed to such a competent and capable educator, they have come to realise just how incompetent, ignorant and uninformed they really are.

This data does not, however, stand on its own. As we shall see, Home Visited parents are more likely to think that they should complain about things with which they were not satisfied and that they should try to ensure that their child's teacher stretches him to the full (Table A47). But they are also more likely than HSES parents to say that education should be left to the school. It is difficult to reconcile such apparently conflicting answers. Perhaps they represent an interim stage in the parents' struggle to come to terms with changed expectations. Perhaps they once believed that education should be left to the school (with the proviso that the school should do what they wanted it to do!) but have now realised that there is a great deal more to this business of education than they previously thought—and that teachers know more than they suspected. But these same teachers have told them that they should seek to *influence* the school (which they previously did not expect to do). So they should complain about things that are wrong and try to ensure that teachers stretch their children to the full—but the teachers should not really take their views seriously because they are, after all, so much more competent and capable than they are themselves!

Taken as a whole it may be argued that these data suggest that parents' overall self-images and their feelings of worth have actually declined. Exposed to a confident and competent Home Visitor, who clearly knows what she is doing and understands educational processes far better than the mother does, the mother comes to feel insignificant and incompetent. The data lend support to the argument that the expert portrayal of knowledge is incompatible with growth of confidence. An educational system which is based on a teacher-taught model breeds dependence and a lack of confidence. A model based on co-tutoring—on the blind leading the blind—may be better able to promote the growth of confidence and feelings of personal worth. It may also be better able to promote the evolution of new ways of thinking about things. Unfortunately, it may not be the best way of plugging those concerned into the knowledge that is available. In this context it would seem to be of the utmost importance to collect parallel data from a sample of the mothers who have had Educational Home Visits, not from "experts", but from other mothers.*

Levels of Satisfaction with the Environment

The second set of columns on Table 2 show that, by and large, the EHVs do not appear to have led the mothers they visited to be any more satisfied with any aspect of their environment except being on good terms with their children's teachers. They are still a great deal less likely than are HSES mothers to be satisfied with their relationships with their children, and the same goes for their relationships with their husbands, doctors, and neighbours, their ability to cope with their day to day activities, and their ability to communicate with other people.

The third set of columns show the opposite end of the distribution. It would seem that the Home Visitors have led some of their parents to become even more dissatisfied with various aspects of their environment than were other LSES parents living in the same

*An account of the "Mother Home Visitors", who form part of the Lothian Educational Home Visiting Scheme, has been omitted from this report. A discussion will be found in McCail (1980).

FIGURE 11

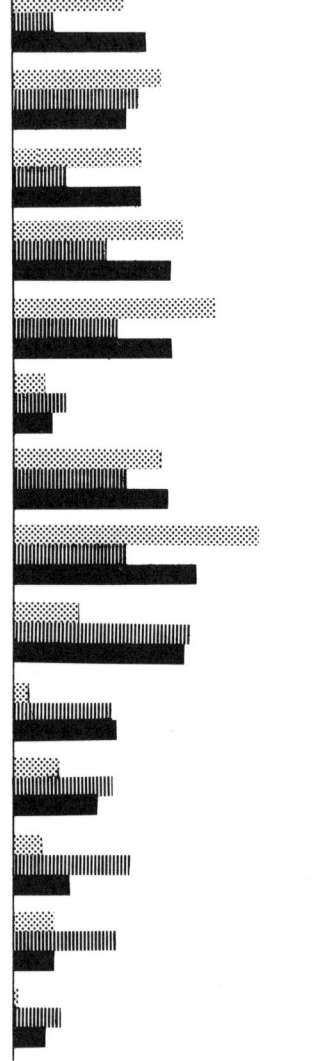

Incentives/Disincentives to
doing something about a complaint.

```
    10   20   30   40   50   60   70
```

1 I'd enjoy seeing that I was
having an impact.

2 I'd be pleased when it was done,
but would not enjoy doing it.

3 I'd enjoy planning what was to
be done.

4 I'd enjoy learning what needed to
be learned in order to do it.

5 I'd enjoy the company of others
whilst doing it.

6 I'd enjoy making other people (eg
people in authority) uncomfortable.

7 I'd be doing something I should
do.

8 I'd be doing something for the
long term good of the society.

9 I wouldn't know where to begin.

10 I wouldn't be able to persuade
other people to support me.

11 I'd lack the ability to make my
point well to those concerned.

12 Those responsible wouldn't
listen to someone like me.

13 I'd be labelled as a troublemaker

14 Other people would ridicule
what I was doing.

FIG 11 (cont)

| 15 Other people would think I was doing it for some hidden motive. |
| 16 I'd be left to do all the work myself. |
| 17 I would be victimised. |
| 18 People in authority would obstruct me and make things more difficult. |
| 19 If I was to be successful I'd have to be more outspoken and aggressive than I'd like to be. |
| 20 If I was to be successful I'd have to be more underhand and man-ipulative than I'd like to be. |
| 21 I'd have to spend time that I'd prefer to spend doing other things on this activity. |
| 22 I'd have to neglect my family and friends. |
| 23 It would increase the stress in my life. |
| 24 Others would take the credit for it if I was successful. |
| 25 There would be a lot of difficulties I'd have trouble getting round. |
| 26 I'd be unable to get the necessary information. |
| 27 I would not be able to make the right contacts and get the right help. |

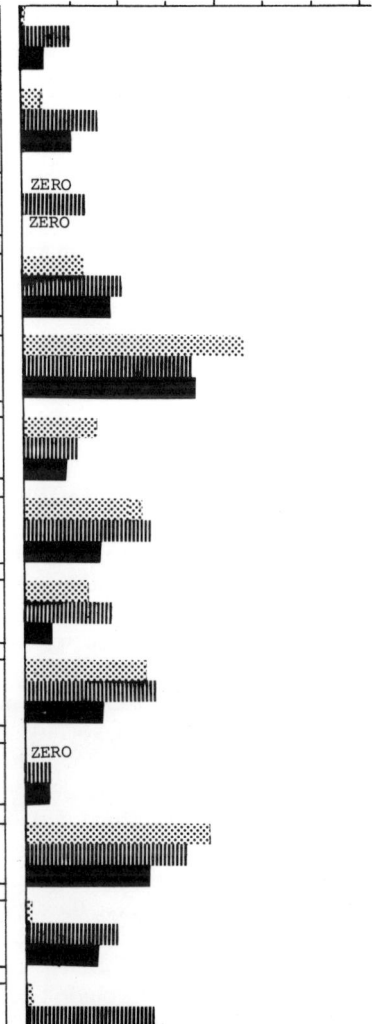

KEY

 HSES
                      LSES
                      EHV

neighbourhoods. They have become more dissatisfied with the part played by members of their communities in curbing vandalism, the general organisation and running of their community, the extent to which their doctors listen to them, and their opportunities to develop their minds and learn new things. While increased levels of dissatisfaction may be a pre-requisite to taking action to do something about them, one can hardly believe that an environment in which there are high levels of dissatisfaction among parents can be beneficial to the psychological development of their children.

Willingness to Tackle their Problems

From the mothers' responses to questions about whether they were the sort of persons who should do something about the problem highlighted by a discrepancy between their ratings of importance and satisfaction, it would seem that the Home Visitors have led more of the people they have visited to say that it was up to someone like themselves to do something about the problem. They are less likely to say that they are prepared only to grumble, and are more prepared to join in if other people start trying to do something about it (Figure 11 and Tables A41 and A42).

Before discussing the impact of the Home Visiting programme on parents' expectations of the consequences of trying to do something about their problems, it is worth commenting on the significance of some of the differences between the HSES and LSES groups.

The LSES group is, in general, less likely than the HSES group to say that, in trying to tackle their problems, they would be working for the long term good of society, enjoy learning what needed to be learned in order to do it, enjoy the company of others whilst doing it, enjoy seeing that they were having an impact on society, enjoy the planning activity involved in doing it, and doing something they felt they should do (ie something moral). On the other hand they were more likely to say that they wouldn't know where to begin, that they wouldn't be able to make the right contacts or get the right help, that they wouldn't be able to persuade other people to support them, that they would lack the ability to make their points well to those concerned, that they wouldn't be able to get the necessary information, that those responsible wouldn't listen to them, and that they would be labelled as troublemakers.

All of these differences suggest that LSES parents would be much less likely than HSES parents to do anything about their problems. They feel they lack abilities which they would need, they are less likely to enjoy the intellectual and social activities involved, other people are less likely to support them, and, in particular, they are less likely to feel that they would be engaged in moral activity which would be in the long term interest of society. They are clearly a great deal less well motivated to do anything about their problems.

The Home Visitors have changed some of these perceptions and expectations. The parents who have had Home Visits are more likely than other LSES parents to feel that they would be working for the long term good of society and that they would enjoy both the intellectual and social activity involved in trying to do something about their problems. However, they don't feel any more *able* to do the things which would need to be done.

Thus, although they are, in some respects, better *motivated* to do something about their problems, in other respects their confidence in their *ability* to do something about them is no greater. Notice that what we have here is both a measure of the strength of their motivation to do something about their problems and a fairly detailed indication of what their educational needs are. What we do not have is an indication of the relative weight to be assigned to such things as the pleasure which is expected to come from the activity and such things as self-perceived ability.

Nevertheless, the indications are that the Home Visited parents are more likely to try to do something about their problems. They are more likely to feel that they are in control of their destinies rather than pawns of fate. The role models they provide for their children may well be different.

Unfortunately, as we have seen, they have not, in fact, been able to do anything about the quality of the environments in which they bring up their children. This may be because they have not yet had time to do so. But it may also be because these environments are extremely difficult to change. The parents may get a rude awakening if they do in fact try to do something about them. As we shall shortly see, the Home Visitors have, in some other respects, led parents to develop levels of confidence that they can influence the school system which, in the context of the HSES sample's feelings about the same issues, can only be regarded as over-optimistic.

Let us now dwell for a moment on what could have been responsible for the mothers' apparently improved motivation. As we have seen, the EHVs did not confine themselves to working with children. They sought to involve the parents in a number of wider activities like "mothers matter" courses, making contacts with the schools, and visiting other mothers. In these they sought to encourage the mothers to become more outgoing, more confident that they could meet other people, and more confident that they could deal with the schools, the Local Authority, the housing department, and the South of Scotland Electricity Board. Some of the Home Visitors reasoned that encouraging the mothers' cognitive activity in these areas would lead them to *value* cognitive activity more highly, lead them to be more likely to use logical thinking as a means of solving their own problems, and lead them to have more confidence in their own abilities and their ability to deal with others. They reasoned, with Bronfenbrenner (1978) and Raven (1977) that, by portraying such patterns of thinking, feeling and behaving in front of their children, they would promote the development of their children's confidence and competence. With Van der Eyken (1980) they sensed that the mothers' isolation and loneliness was a serious barrier, not only to coping with their problems, but also to the growth and development of their children.

As we have seen, the Visitors *did* lead the mothers to become more confident and more strongly motivated (if not to feel more able) to do something about these problems. But through what *process?* Is Van der Eyken right to believe that befriending the mother and helping her to establish social contacts is the active ingredient in the process? Or are we right in thinking that the effect we have demonstrated was due to mother and EHV working together to solve the mothers' problems?

We have no data on the programme's impact on the mothers' feelings of isolation and loneliness. Nevertheless, what was most striking when we discussed the Home Visiting itself with a number of mothers was the strength of the bond they had established with the Home Visitors. (We had planned to include questions on topics such as this in the interview schedules we had hoped to develop to assess parents' perceptions of, and reactions to, the Home Visiting itself). An earlier study (Raven and Haynes, 1966) also throws light on this issue. The only types of social contact which significantly reduced loneliness among the older people involved in that study were regular visits by relatives in their own homes. The EHVs obviously come regularly, and come into the mothers' homes. But they are not *relatives*. However, if we ask ourselves what distinguishes the visiting of a relative from that of a friend, one notices that some of the differences include the commitment to continue through thick and thin—despite the ups and downs of mood and the sense of moral outrage which is liable to terminate the visiting of a friend. One also notices the sense of duty or responsibility to visit irrespective of "need" or "enjoyment of contact". And one notes that the relative has an excuse for visiting which is not linked directly to isolation and loneliness—and the provision of an excuse was something which Raven and Haynes believed to be central to finding a solution to the problems posed by loneliness.

In short, it seems highly likely, both from our own interviews with Home Visited parents, and from our previous work, that the Home Visitors *do* reduce the loneliness of the mothers. But, although it may be a necessary condition for it, is it responsible for the growth in confidence and motivation which was documented (in Figure 11)? It seems to us that most likely it is not. More important would seem to be a process which goes on in parallel with the process of befriending the mother and extending her range of social contacts. This involves the EHV working jointly with the mother to find ways of solving the mother's particular problems. This is not a teacher-taught, or expert-novice relationship because—in this respect—the Home Visitor is as ignorant as the mother. Rather it is a joint problem-solving task. The same is even more true in the Leicester Homestart project, where the Visitor may well come from a similar social and educational background to the mother who is visited. Such joint problem-solving activity, in which two equally ignorant people struggle to find a solution to a common problem, seems much more likely to promote the development of feelings of confidence and competence—and the ability to make one's own observations, evolve new constructs, study cause and effect, and generally think for oneself—than a teacher-taught relationship, although it may well be "less efficient" than instruction from an expert. Indeed, as every day experience, and Van der Eyken's evaluation of Leicester Homestart (1980) in particular, suggests, the experts are only too often wrong—because they know too little about the constraints which operate in a particular situation.

So, at last, the dilemma is becoming clearer. One interpretation of our data is that, in their expert role as promoters of child development, the EHVs may be leading the parents they visit to feel less confident and competent. They influence the parents' attitudes and beliefs — but the parents do not take up the activities modelled by these experts. In their extra-professional role—in an area in which they are as ignorant as the mothers—they lead the mothers to feel more confident and better motivated, if not more competent. Unfortunately, another interpretation is that, just as the EHVs have influenced parents' beliefs about what it is important to do in child rearing, but had little impact on their self-perceived ability to do so, so they may have increased the mothers' feelings that they should tackle their problems and would enjoy doing so, but have not led them to feel any more *able* to do so.

Despite the need to separate the loneliness issue from the competence issue, nothing we have said should be construed to mean that we think the question of social isolation is unimportant. Quite the contrary. One of the problems which has not been solved to anyone's satisfaction is that of finding a way in which the Educational Home Visitors can help the parents they visit to establish a social network so that they can cease to be so dependent on the Home Visitors themselves and so that they have a continuing support network after Visiting ceases. It is clear that the solutions currently being tried out — which involve the mother becoming a "Mother Home Visitor", joining a parents' group, or visiting the nursery, may help, but that these solutions have not yet been fully exploited.

CHAPTER 23

THE PARENTS' ROLE IN THE FORMAL EDUCATIONAL SYSTEM

We have already seen that the Home Visitors seem to have led the parents to be more likely to think that school success is important and that it is important for them to continue the work of the school in the home. The Home Visitors seem to have led the parents to be more likely to think that their children would be unhappy, bored, and feel rejected if they did not do well at school (Table A45). The Home Visited parents are also more likely to think that their children's intelligence will fail to develop fully. Finally, the proportion of Home Visited parents who feel that their children will be difficult later on if they do not do well at school is lower than that found in the LSES group.

It is also clear (from Table A43) that school success is most frequently associated with getting a good job—although the Home Visitors seem to have cast some doubt on this assumption. However, the Home Visitors have apparently led the parents to attach more importance to school success quite independently of examinations (Table A44). Thus these parents would be expected to support their children in their educational activities even though it became apparent that working hard at school was not going to get them through examinations and thereby into a better job. They have also led the parents to re-value their own education. The Home Visited parents are much more likely than other parents from the same areas to say that their own education had been of value to them in enabling them to do their job well, even though it had not enabled them to get a good job (Table A46). Thus they may be more likely to point out the benefits of education to their children even though they are still not as able as are the HSES group to point to evidence of its benefits.

All in all, the data which we have presented suggest that the parents have come to be more favourably disposed towards education.

Additionally the Home Visitors have had some quite dramatic effects on parents' perceptions of the role they think a parent should play in a primary school child's education (Table A47). The proportion of the EHV group who feel that they should find out exactly what happens in school, complain about anything with which they are not satisfied. talk about school as much as possible, make sure that the teacher stretches the child to the full, visit the school regularly, and insist that the child does his best, equals or surpasses that found among the HSES parents. The idea of arranging private lessons for their children in weak subjects is not so unacceptable to them as it is to other LSES parents. However, in line with what we have all already learned about the EHVs' effects in encouraging parents to give formal instruction to their children, 75% of the Home Visited group say that they should teach their children things before they learn them at school, compared with only 23% of the HSES group. This is, however, in direct conflict with the fact that the proportion who say that education should be left to the school is not lower in the EHV than LSES group. It cannot even be maintained that different people are giving these apparently incompatible answers. At the time of writing we have not thought of any way of reconciling this apparent inconsistency.

We have seen that virtually all the Home Visited parents feel that parents should complain to the school about anything with which they are not satisfied. They are also more confident that the teacher would listen to their complaints (Table A48). However, they are no more likely to feel that they would be made welcome in the school if they asked to spend some time there so as to really understand what goes on (Table A49). (This was an activity which was almost universally advocated by the EHVs as a means of helping to ensure that their children would do well at school).

A more detailed analysis shows that there has been a significant increase in the proportion who feel they would be made welcome in one area, and a decline in another.

The Home Visitors appear to have had less impact on the role the parents think they should play in the child's education as he gets older (Table A50). However, such impact as they have had has, once again, had the effect of bringing the proportions who gave various types of answer closer to the HSES than LSES group. This effect runs across virtually all items, and its cumulative effect could be considerable. The same sort of pattern is also evident in their answers to the question about what they would do if they wanted their child to do better at school (Table A51). Nevertheless, rather pathetically, they don't actually feel any better equipped to help their children with their homework (Table A52).

A comment should, perhaps, be made about the fact that, when parents were asked a closed question about what they thought they would do *if* they wanted their child to do better at school, almost everyone said they would explain why it was important to do so and praise the child whenever he did something well, while, in response to other questions, the LSES group seems much less often to explain or praise or think it is important to explain or praise. Part of the explanation of the apparent discrepancy lies in the initial *if* in the question, for, as we have seen, LSES parents are less likely to think it is important for their children to do well at school. The rest of the explanation probably stems from the fact that, when parents were asked what they would do to motivate their children, they were unable to indicate how *often* they would do these things. Thus the LSES parents may well do them from time to time—but far less frequently than the HSES parents.

A smaller proportion of the Home Visited mothers than of the LSES mothers feel that they do not understand modern methods of primary education very well (Table A53). Nevertheless, although they feel they now understand modern methods of primary education better than they did, all but one of them wants to know still more about them.

The Home Visited mothers are also much less likely to feel that they need more advice on any aspect on child rearing or even on handling their own problems more effectively (Table A55). They are far more confident than even the HSES parents that they know how to help their children, how to intervene in the school system, and how to amuse their children and keep them out of mischief.

Table A56 shows that Home Visited parents are little more likely than other LSES parents to think that they are the right people to make decisions about what goes on in schools. Once again this reinforces the view that they think professionals know better than they do what should be done, are able to make better decisions, and should be left to get on with the work they are paid to do.

PART IIIC

SUMMARY, GENERAL DISCUSSION, AND POSSIBLE IMPLICATIONS OF THE STATISTICAL STUDY OF THE IMPACT OF THE LOTHIAN REGION EDUCATIONAL HOME VISITING SCHEME

CHAPTER 24

SUMMARY, DISCUSSION AND IMPLICATIONS
OF THE STATISTICAL RESULTS

We will now attempt to summarise what has been learnt from our statistical study about the effects of the Educational Home Visiting programme, tie the threads together, and explore their possible implications. Readers who are dipping into this book at this point should be cautioned that the implied changes which will be referred to below are *inferred* from differences between the responses of a sample of parents who had been Home Visited and a sample of other parents from the same areas of the city. The former are referred to as the EHV group, and the latter as the LSES group. For reasons which were explained in Chapter 14 it was neither possible to mount a before-and-after study, nor a study in which an experimental group was compared with a matched control group.

Attitudes, rather than Behaviour, Primarily Affected

The Educational Home Visitors (EHVs) seem to have had a dramatic effect on parents' attitudes and expectations, but much less effect on their reported behaviour.

A less "Fatalistic" View of Development

As far as attitudes and expectations are concerned the Home Visitors have apparently led the parents to be more likely to think that they are able to influence the course of their children's development—including the development of their characters and personalities and their intelligence.

More Importance Attached to Intellectual and Academic Activity

The Home Visited parents attach more importance than do other mothers from Low Socio-Economic Status (LSES) areas of the city to their children doing well at school. Indeed they think this is more important than do parents from contrasting High Socio-Economic Status (HSES) areas of the city. They also attach more importance than do LSES mothers to the development of intellectual qualities like thinking for oneself and to a large number of intellectually-oriented child-rearing activities like providing books in the home and reading to their children. They are also much more likely to think that intelligence is to be fostered by talking to, and reading to, children. They expect their children to take much more delight in intellectual activities like looking at books with their parents.

Role in Formal Education

Similar differences between Visited mothers and other LSES ones seem to have occurred in relation to the part they think a parent should play in promoting the educational development of primary school children.

The Home Visited parents attach more importance (even than HSES mothers) to their continuing the work of the school in the home and to the child reading and studying on his own when he is older.

There has apparently been a dramatic increase—in this case taking the Home Visited mothers still further away than other LSES mothers from our HSES mothers—in the proportion who think that they should teach their children things before they learn them at school, in the proportion who think that they should ensure that their child's teacher should stretch him to the full, and in the proportion who said they should talk about school as much as possible to their children.

A More "Schoolmasterly" Stance

The Home Visited parents also attach more importance to a number of other "schoolmasterly" activities (which are not particularly stressed by HSES parents) like punishing bad behaviour, and teaching their children to "respect" figures in authority and to respect property. They are also more likely to view asking questions about pictures in books as an opportunity to "test" their children and to see whether they are paying attention (and *not*, as the HSES mothers more often tend to do, as an opportunity to stimulate the development of the spontaneous tendency to think and seek to understand). They think it is slightly less important for children to learn to use books to find information which the children themselves want.

A More Child-Centred Approach

The Home Visitors do not appear to have led the parents they visited to be more likely to say that most of the child's activities are *joint* activities. But the Home Visited parents do seem to be more *responsive* to their children; they are more likely to say that they do things the child wants to do rather than things *they* want to do, they are more likely to say that they find themselves thinking about what the child is learning as he is playing, and they are more likely to say that it is *important* to study the things the child wants to know and then help him to find out.

A Narrower Developmental Stance?

In spite of their apparently greater child-centredness, it is at least arguable that the Home Visited mothers have come to think of "development" more narrowly than they did previously. We have already seen that, in at least some respects, the Home Visitors seem to have widened the gap between the HSES and LSES parents—but, so far, it is at least arguable that these apparent shifts will be conducive to adjustment to school. Unfortunately, there are other ways in which the Home Visited parents' attitudes seem to be *further* removed from those of the HSES group than were those of the LSES group. Not all of the differences seem likely to be conducive to the development of the independence, imagination, intrinsic motivation and general competence to cope with life which the project sought (in the long run) to foster in children. The lesser emphasis on *using* books to find the information one needs has already been mentioned. But the Home Visited parents also think it is even more important that their children *need* them—that is, they stress the importance of a relationship which involves dependence rather than independence. The Home Visited parents also place no greater emphasis on their children learning to be independent or confident and at ease in situations which they have not met before or on children learning to settle down and concentrate on the task in hand.

Although they are more likely than their LSES counterparts to think that intelligence is to be fostered by talking to and reading to children, the proportion who think that intelligence is to be fostered by giving the child plenty of attention and taking an interest in him is still less than half that found in the HSES group. The same applies to encouraging the child to use books as a means of fostering intelligence.

The Home Visited parents place only slightly less emphasis than do LSES parents on children having "respect" for their parents—and "respect" appears, from their answers to our questions about how it is to be fostered, still to be defined in strict disciplinarian terms which involve the parent insisting on respect and obedience, rather than earning it because their behaviour is commendable. They are also only slightly more likely to say that it is important to treat the child with respect or to *foster* respect by treating the child with respect, by being fair, or, in particular, by example. Their strategies of discipline tend to involve more rows and distraction from annoying activities, and less physical punishment, but they are no more likely to try to *explain* things to the child—perhaps because they find such intellectual activity difficult, perhaps because they do not value such activity, perhaps because they think it will make for difficulties later on, or perhaps because the child will not respond to such reasoning.

A Possible Interpretation

What this data may be telling us is that the mothers who have been visited have been led to attach greater importance to school education and intellectual activity defined as equivalent to success in the school system, but have not been led to attach any more weight to the *general* competence-promoting activities which also distinguish HSES from LSES parents. Not only do the Home Visited mothers not come to place more emphasis on the child learning on his own, they are no more likely to say that qualities like determination and respect are to be fostered through personal example. They are no more likely to think of *withholding* help so that the child learns to cope on his own. They are no more likely to give answers which are consistent with the theory that children learn by discovering that their actions are effective in helping them to reach their own goals—such as getting answers to their questions, finding the information they want, and learning to cope on their own. The suggestion that the general developmental activities engaged in by the HSES group have not been taken up is confirmed by the data we obtained by asking parents about which were the most important qualities that a child learned from his parents: the proportion who said things like initiative, friendliness, and being a good citizen is *not* greater in the EHV than in the LSES group. Nor is the frequency of mention of obedience and respect for authority as low as that found in the HSES group.

Instead of leading parents to think of themselves more often as *facilitators of* development, it would seem that the Home Visitors have led the parents to increase the *pressure for* development. They have led them to be more likely to insist that their children read, pay attention, and do as they are told. They are not more likely to create a climate conducive to development by encouraging the child's interests, treating him as an individual worthy of respect, encouraging independent learning, and participating in *joint,* child-initiated, activities. It can therefore be hypothesised that they are not much more likely to encourage the child to feel that he has a *right* to reason, communicate, or be listened to, to recognise the child's ability to reason and therefore feed the growth of that reasoning (thereby stimulating the development of high level (moral) reasoning), or to take the child's complaints seriously and attend to them themselves (thereby reinforcing for the child the value of reasoning) or intervene on the child's behalf if he has complaints about the school system.

It will be argued in Part IV that HSES parents seem to have a much more complex and indirect—though not necessarily better—view of child development than the LSES group. They focus more on fostering success indirectly—by fostering qualities like independence and confidence in dealing with new situations. These qualities may make for increased success at school and, quite independently, for increased success in life. The HSES group make more use of rewards—including the intrinsic reward that comes from successfully undertaking an activity and seeing that it produces the results that are desired. They make much more use of teaching by example—including the example portrayed by others who work hard, handle responsibility well, and themselves behave in highly commendable ways. They promote development by *responding* to the child and, possibly, thereby reinforce the child's tendency to take initiative, to reason, and to argue with authority. Not only is such behaviour likely to reinforce the child's tendency to engage in it, it is likely to lead the child to think of himself as someone who has a right to opinions and activities of his own, who can independently find information he needs, who is entitled to raise questions about the wisdom of his superiors, and to expect to guide his own behaviour by reference to the long term good of society rather than the dictates of an authority which both demands instant obedience and is not open to reason. The EHVs appear to have had little impact on these wider, more subtle, and more complex perceptions and expectations. Rather, they seem to have reinforced the parents' tendency to think that what might be regarded as evidence of HSES parents' success in their approach—success at school—is a *cause* of their children's success in life. And they seem to have reinforced their tendency to focus on qualities which are cognitively closely related to success in the school system rather than qualities which might make for success in life—and only incidentally for success in the school system.

Are They More Inclined to See Themselves as Their Child's Most Important Educator?

The Home Visited parents believe that it is important for them to do many more things to promote the cognitive development of their children: their perception of their role appears in this respect to have been enlarged. Nevertheless, they think that what their children learn from them, as parents, is *less* important than do the other LSES mothers, and the gap between them and the HSES parents, in this particular respect, is actually greater. *School,* and school-related activities, are important and they appear to think that they themselves may not be the best persons to foster the abilities required to succeed at such tasks. Although we did not ask what they thought the consequences of doing, or not doing, many of the things they believe to be important would be, it is perhaps significant that *only one* of the things which they feel *they* could do to promote the development of their children is likely to promote *school* success. Many of the things which they feel they could do are, presumably as a result of the Visiting, less often seen as having *any* connection with school success. Thus the Home Visited parents are *less* likely than other LSES mothers to think that asking the child questions about books and things he had seen will make for school success, they are *less* likely to think that looking at books with him will do so, they are *less* likely to think that his having educational toys is likely to do so, and they are no more likely to think that talking to the child a lot or treating him with respect as an individual entitled to interests and ideas of his own will do so. They are no more likely to spend time on joint activities such as playing with jigsaws and bricks, or looking at books together, and they spend less time teaching their children in a formal manner. They are only slightly more likely to say that they set out to teach their children things. The one exception to this pattern is that the Home Visited parents are more likely to associate encouraging the child to ask questions and seek reasons for things he is told with school success.

It is, perhaps, because of the Home Visited mothers' inability to see any more connections between things *they* could do and school success that the only *behaviour* which seems to have been markedly affected by the EHVs is the time they spend taking their children to nursery school or playgroup.

Language and Discipline Interaction

Although we have said that Home Visited parents are more likely to think it is important to talk to their children, the style of their language and discipline interactions seem to be very similar to those of other LSES mothers. Nevertheless, they are less likely to make use of physical punishment and more likely to give the children a row. This may be viewed as a transitional stage on the way to giving more explanations. As far as language activity is concerned, the main emphasis in the EHV group is still on issuing warnings and instructions. The Home Visited mothers appear to be even less likely to discuss the past or the future and less likely to discuss the activities which parent and child are undertaking together. Since the parents appear to be less likely to discuss the activities they are undertaking with the child it is possible that they are not talking about what they are thinking about, or giving the child an insight into the *way* they think—into the fact that they tend to think about obstacles they might encounter, where to get help, and the process of dredging about in one's mind for relevant past experience. As a result, the child may get even less insight than other LSES children into cognitive processes in action.

Formal Teaching

As far as what parents actually teach their children is concerned, the Home Visited group, despite not having spent as much time on formal education during the day immediately prior to the day of the interview as had the HSES or LSES group (who did not differ from each other), are much more inclined to say that they teach intellectual skills—counting, reading, and the names of things and colours. But the emphasis on teaching social skills and moral values is less. Even fewer Visited than other LSES parents say that they teach their children by example and the gap between them and HSES parents is greater than that between HSES parents and other LSES parents.

From these data it would seem that the Home Visited parents are *less* likely to see themselves as their children's most important educators; they have a narrower conception of what that phrase implies (specifically a more "teacherish" style with less emphasis on example, modelling, or facilitation of growth); that they feel less able to fill that new function and that they are more convinced that schools are the best learning environments for their children. The data raise serious questions about what it would be necessary for the EHVs to do if they wish to model mothering behaviour involving sensitive, transactional, reactive activity for the parents. To behave in this way it may be necessary for them to know the child—his interests, and the meanings and interpretations of minor cues in his behaviour—extremely well. And it may be necessary for them to have a great deal of time. It may therefore not be possible for anyone who is not the child's mother—or at least caretaker—to do these things, and this may mean that the conception of "encouraging the mother to play her unique and irreplaceable role in promoting the educational development of her children" in this way needs to be re-thought.

Failure to Communicate the Intent: the Medium is the Message

Just as the EHV's message that the *mother* is the child's most important educator appears, in many ways, to have been distorted in the process of transmission so as to support the parents' already dominant perceptions, so too have some of their other messages. LSES parents expect to have (and have) many more difficulties making contact with, influencing, and establishing satisfactory relationships with, their children than do the HSES group. The Home Visited mothers anticipate even more problems of this sort than do the LSES mothers. Many activities modelled by the EHVs (such as reading to children and talking to them) which the EHVs and the HSES parents see as promoting cognitive development (including the willingness to think, try to understand, imagine and concentrate) appear to be perceived by the Home Visited mothers primarily as ways of helping them to reach their goal of establishing better relationships with their children. Unfortunately, the Quality of Life data suggest they have not, in fact, become better able to reach that goal either.

Parents' Self-Images and Feelings of Competence and their Impact on their Children

The Home Visited parents' self-images seem to be dramatically better than those of other LSES mothers: they are much less likely to feel that they need advice on how to find out what schools are doing, how to help their children at school, how to influence schools, how to help their children to grow up to be the sort of people they would like them to be, how to develop the abilities needed to handle their problems, or how to amuse their children and keep them out of mischief. However, the fact that they are less likely to want advice on any of these things except handling their children and their problems than even the HSES group makes one wonder just how realistic they really are. It also makes one wonder if they might not have been at the receiving end of just too much, possibly impractical, "advice".

They are more willing to try to do something about the problems which plague them and they feel more confident that they would enjoy the intellectual and other activities involved in so doing. As a result they may portray for their children a more competent and confident style of behaviour. This may rub off on the children. They may "catch" the parents' attitudes. If they do, the Home Visitors may, through this indirect process, have had a substantial impact on the development of the children concerned.

Once again, unfortunately, it is necessary to caution against seizing on this result in isolation. Despite this apparently beneficial result of the Visiting, the quality of life of the Home Visited mothers has not significantly improved. Indeed, in many respects, they are more critical than other LSES mothers and are more dissatisfied with many aspects of their environment. While this dissatisfaction may be an essential precursor to activity designed to change those environments, it is significant that they are no more satisfied than the LSES parents with their ability to get on with their children—and a great deal less satisfied than their HSES counterparts. The same applies to their relationships with their close family, including their husbands, and their neighbours. In response to a question on the problems they expected as their children got older, it emerges that the Home Visited group actually expect *more* unruliness and rebelliousness from their children and expect them to have more problems at school. It would seem, therefore, that the Home Visitors may have sensitised the mothers to problems with their children, and in their environments, of which they were previously unaware. But, whatever may happen in the long run, it is clear that the Home Visitors have not been able so far to create environments which are physically, socially and psychologically more conducive to growth and development, and in which family relationships are more conducive to mothers spending time with their children in a way which is likely to promote the development of the psychological characteristics valued by the EHVs.

In the course of looking at this data we have uncovered what appears to be a serious dilemma for the EHVs. At the cost of over-simplifying the results, we can say that, in their role as *experts* the EHVs taught the mothers that it was important to do all sorts of new things with their children but that they have made the mothers feel less competent to do them. On the other hand, in their role as *friend,* the EHVs have, by trying to help the mother solve her own problems, led her to develop enhanced feelings of self-respect, confidence and motivation to tackle her own problems, although they did not lead her to feel more *able* to tackle them. From this it would seem that Educational Home Visiting programmes based on experts may convey knowledge, but, by making people feel incompetent in comparison with the expert, lead them to be *less* inclined to carry out the desired activities with their children and more inclined to hand their children over to professionals. Home Visiting programmes based on Home Visitors of similar status to the mothers themselves may, therefore, be more likely to enhance the mothers' feelings of confidence, and, if organised in an appropriate way, lead the mothers to discover the same *knowledge*.

Will the Parents be More Willing and Able to Support their Children whilst at School?

Having looked at the impact of the Home Visitors on the parents' ability to intervene effectively to promote the educational development of their young children, we may now move on to examine their impact on the parents' ability to support their children during their school careers.

As we have seen, the Home Visited parents are very much more likely than their LSES counterparts to think that a parent *should* teach her children things before they learn them at school. Unfortunately they are no more confident than other LSES parents— and a great deal less confident than HSES parents—that they will be *able* to help their children with their homework. Once again, therefore, the actual effects of the Home Visiting may have been to increase the parents' feelings of guilt and inadequancy, rather than to make them feel more adequate.

We have also seen that although the Home Visited parents are more likely than other LSES parents to think that they *should* help their children to do well by ensuring that the teacher stretches their children to the full, they are *less* likely to think that it is important to have a teacher who takes their views seriously (although they are more confident that their child's teacher would listen to them). And they have more confidence that their teachers know best. Again, then, it may be that the Home Visitors have created a dilemma for the parents.

The Home Visited mothers are also more likely to believe that a mother should help her children by finding out exactly what is happening at school—but they are again no more likely to feel that they would be made welcome if they visited the school to find out what was going on. Fewer Home Visited parents feel that they do not understand the modern methods of education very well—but feel they want to know more.

The Home Visited parents also place more value on their own school education. They feel it was of more relevance to them. They may, therefore, be less likely than other LSES parents to question the value of education in front of their children.

Finally, the proportion who think that there should be a change in the weight given to the various parties in the decision-taking process in education has not changed, though, of those who did think that there should be a change, more felt that the parents should have more say.

CONCLUDING DISCUSSION

The material we have presented may be summarised by saying that the EHVs appear to have had a dramatic effect on the mothers' beliefs, attitudes and expectations, but less effect on their behaviour. It is apparently a great deal easier to influence attitudes, perceptions and expectations than many people have suspected. Nevertheless, as is often the case, the effects of the attempt to influence attitudes and behaviours were greatest in those areas in which it was possible for the mothers to interpret the Home Visitors' "messages" in such a way as to reinforce their existing beliefs.

The effects of the programme were greatest in the areas which were originally, and largely remain, at the centre of the Home Visitors' attention. Nevertheless, even in this area, the effects on behaviour, as distinct from attitudes, appear to have been slight. The effect of the programme was still significant in relation to the goals which have become more central to the project as it has gone along—witness its impact on the mothers' feelings of confidence and competence to cope with their own problems. The project was least successful—and possibly even harmful—in relation to those potential goals of the project which have really only become clear for the first time in the course of discussing the background data we have collected.

One possible interpretation of the data is that we have a picture of adults in transition. The mothers' attitudes have been unfrozen. They now see things in different ways. But they have not yet developed the habit of *behaving* in new ways. We all know how difficult it is to do what we feel we should do and want to do. For us, as for the Home Visited mothers, there is a discrepancy between our beliefs about what it is important to do and what we actually do. Much of the data reported earlier is consistent with the hypothesis that the Home Visited parents have come to question old ways, but not yet learned new ways. They have questioned their old perceptions of schools and no longer feel so negatively about them—and they have come to place *more* trust in teachers than they did before. They have become dissatisfied with aspects of their environment which they previously accepted, and feel that they would *enjoy* the activities needed to do something about the problems they sense—but they still do not feel *able* to tackle them. They have come to recognise that it is undesirable to employ physical punishment with their children and have developed more positive *attitudes* toward explanation, but they have not yet learned *how* to explain and have, instead, fallen half way between and resorted to telling their children off rather than hitting them. They have become more conscious of their feelings about competitiveness and now say that they do not know how to foster it rather than that they are for it or against it.

If what we are seeing *is* a picture of adults in transition then it may be important to help the mothers concerned to translate their new beliefs into smooth habits. If, on the other hand, their failure to follow through beliefs into action is due to important impediments—such as an *inability* to think in a cognitively complex manner or an *inability* on the part of the child to grasp the logic of the reasons he is given, or to environmental constraints, or to acute value conflicts, then the EHVs would seem to be under a moral obligation to help the parents to adjust to the increased frustration they would be expected to experience as a result of their rising expectations.

But the data we have reviewed may not be best thought of as a picture of adults in transition. It may alternatively be construed as evidence that our current understanding of educational processes is grossly inadequate in relation to the wider educational objectives which almost everyone whose views have been canvassed hold most dear. Indeed it may be construed as evidence that the educational processes on which teachers tend to focus are actually destructive of the very competencies which most people think it is most important for teachers to foster. The educational system in general achieves the more limited goals which it sets out to achieve—goals like teaching reading or arithmetic—extremely well. It is less successful in the wider sense of leading children to develop the spontaneous tendency to transfer those skills to new problems. But it is arguable (from the scant evidence available) that it is actually destructive of the very qualities which most people think lie at the heart of the educational process—developing initiative, self-confidence, the ability to live and work with others, and the ability to make one's own observations and learn *without* instruction (Bronfenbrenner, 1974; Coleman, 1972; Raven, 1977).

It may seem absurd to measure a programme such as this against criteria which it did not set out to meet. But, as is becoming abundantly clear in ecological studies in general, if the unintended and unwanted side effects of a programme outweigh its benefits, then serious doubts are cast on the validity of the programme. At the very least questions are raised about ways in which the programme might be modified in order to avoid those unwanted side effects. We will explore what our bench-mark data may have to tell us about this question in the next section of the report. Here it is sufficient to underline the considerable responsibility which has fallen on the shoulders of the evaluators of social programmes. By not asking the right questions—questions which may well go beyond those asked by those who commission their work—and questions which are not capable of being "answered" in any unarguable sense given the current state of the social sciences—and by not reporting the results, however tentative, of asking those questions, they can so easily misrepresent the outcomes of a social and educational programme. It would be easy to dispute practically everything that has been said in this report. But to suppress it on the grounds that it is not above dispute would be irresponsible. It is much more important to put in hand a much larger programme of action research—conducted by practitioners and evaluators with a variety of very different orientations—and to publish the results of all these activities so that the time-honoured, self-correcting, procedures of science can do their work. It is no skin off the nose of a scientist to be proved wrong; indeed the only thing that a scientist can be certain of is that he *is* wrong! Nothing we have said in this report indicates that the action-research programme we have studied should be terminated. But neither does it indicate that it should be expanded as a service which purports to offer known benefits to parents. It *does* suggest that those responsible should consider a number of possible modifications, implement those modifications on a selective basis, and carefully monitor their impact. The evaluation of that impact, if properly conducted, would undoubtedly advance understanding of the processes and issues involved and suggest a further round of modifications. What this study also shows is that, just as it is not "too difficult" to influence parental attitudes, so, also, it is not "too difficult" to mount broadly-based evaluation exercises which contribute in important ways to our understanding of the objectives and process of social and educational policy. No one ever assumed that the Home Visiting programme would not be capable of improvement. Indeed quite the reverse. We only ask that the same charitable standards be adopted in relation to the, perhaps equally difficult, task of evaluating the project and that the mutually beneficial, if not necessarily harmonious, process should be much more widely adopted when attempts are made to improve policy.

There are several ways in which we ourselves are suspicious of these statistical results and conclusions. The most serious of these is that the results reported here differ from the impressions we formed in our own interviews with parents in one very important respect. We had the impression (see Part IIC) that Home Visiting led to a marked improvement in family relationships, and we thought that this would have major implications for the educational development of the children concerned. This impression was supported by the changes in family activities by the EHVs, by what the Home Visited mothers said to the interviewers who carried out the statistical study, and by what the Home Visited mothers said at public meetings. It is also supported by results reported by Palmer (1977) in the USA.

This issue is of particular importance because it is possible to argue that, if family relationships improve, parents will have time to discover how competent their children really are, and they will then both feed these competencies and take their children's complaints— whether at home or at school—seriously and do something about them. The result will be both to improve the environment in which their children live *and* to reinforce that tendency to reason and communicate.

Given the importance of the question, it is important to seek an explanation of the apparent discrepancy in the data. What might it be due to?

Firstly, it could be due to a measurement error. Each element of our statistical data is based on two or three questions buried in a longish section of the interview schedule which came at the end of the interview. It may, therefore, be that the questions are faulty—and this hypothesis could be tested through further work.

Our statistical data, however, also suggest another hypothesis. There is clear evidence that the parents now realise how enjoyable it is to spend time with their children—playing with them, talking to them, and reading to them. But the parents do not in fact spend any more time with their children. What their comments *about the Home Visiting* may, therefore, mean is that they do indeed treasure the moments they spend with their children more, but the fact that they are not able to extend the amount of time they spend with them may mean that, overall, they are no more satisfied with their relationship with them than they were before. Indeed it may lead them to be less satisfied with that relationship.

A third possible explanation has to do with the fact that our formal interviews did not, as we had intended, contain a section of the mothers' perception of the Home Visiting itself. Our own personal interviews, and the American interviews, did involve the mother in a discussion of this. What was most striking in these interviews was the warmth of the personal relationship which the Home Visitors forged with them. This warmth was extended to us and—in our conversations with them—seemed to flow over into their relationships with their children and husbands. What may have been happening was that this evident warmth was—either just in our own perception or in reality—spilling over *in the context of an interview about the Home Visiting*, but not into day to day living. Interviews conducted outwith that context, and sometime after Visiting had ceased, might, either because they failed to re-evoke the glow of Visiting, or because that glow had worn off, fail to record such an effect.

A final possible explanation is that in an interview explicitly conducted about the *effects of the Home Visiting* (as in our own personal interviews as distinct from a statistical study) parents feel obliged to say that the Visiting has had an effect on their relationship with their children precisely because that relationship is, as we have seen, so very, very important to them.

Because of the centrality of this impression that the scheme *did* have an effect on family relationships to our own and Van der Eyken's theorising about the probable long-term effects of the project, it is of the greatest importance to discover which of these is, in reality, the explanation of the discrepancy between our own, others', and the EHVs' impressions on the one hand and our statistical results on the other.

Practical Implications of the Results

Our data and discussion so far—and we will have more to say about this in Part IV—would suggest that, when considering ways in which the programme might be modified, those responsible should particularly consider the following points:

1. Whereas the project was based on the assumption that what prevented the mothers relating to their children in the way in which research studies had suggested it was desirable for them to do if the development of their children was to be optimally facilitated, was a *knowledge* deficit, perhaps aggravated by poor relationships between mother and child, it is now abundantly clear that values and environmental factors are at least equally important. The project staff may wish to devote time to thinking about how to come to terms with these facts.

2. As we have seen—and as will become increasingly clear in the next section of our report—even the *knowledge* deficit of the LSES parents *vis-à-vis* HSES parents seems to be more complex than had previously been assumed. If the complex

understanding of child development evinced by HSES parents is to be communicated to LSES parents, it raises serious questions about the strategy to be adopted.

3. Many of the EHVs' "messages" appear to have been "distorted" so as to reinforce the mothers' preconceptions. The research literature on communication may well have something to say about ways in which this effect might be reduced.

4. It is at least arguable that the mothers now have a narrower definition of their role in promoting the educational development of their children than they did previously. This is clearly contrary to the original objectives of the project, and ways in which this apparent effect could be reversed deserve discussion.

5. Likewise, it is arguable that—at least in relation to child rearing—the mothers are less confident in their ability to be their child's most important educator than they were previously. That this confidence may have been based on ignorance is not denied, but nevertheless the apparent effects of the Home Visiting in this area go squarely against the project's goals and ways of redressing the balance deserve discussion.

6. The parents' behaviour appears to have been affected much less than their beliefs, attitudes and expectations. This may be because of value conflicts, parental ability deficits, environmental constraints, or an absence of a lead or a response from the child. The validity of our observations and the weight to be assigned to each of these possible causes demands further research. But it is clear that both the first and the third *are* in some way involved. The mothers are still more likely than the HSES group to value dependence in their children. They are still less likely to have satisfactory relationships with husbands or others. They are still shorter of money. They are no better equipped to help their children with their homework. They still don't have gardens in which their children can run about in safety and play with sand and water. Their children are apparently still more difficult. Far from *helping* the parents to cope with the stresses which these problems generate, it is, therefore, at least arguable that the Home Visitors have increased the stress in their lives by leading the mothers to feel that they *should* be doing other things which they now believe

to be more important than they did before and think that their children will enjoy in the short term and benefit more from in the long term. Ways in which these problems could be ameliorated deserve serious consideration.

7. Given the environmental constraints on the mother's behaviour, and the fact that those mothers have not developed the HSES parents' complex understanding of ways in which competence is to be fostered, it is at least possible that the mothers have developed expectations which will not be fulfilled. It may therefore be desirable to pay some attention to thinking up ways in which they can be saved from the increased feelings of incompetence and failure which may follow in the wake of such a discovery.

8. Despite the absence of information on the long term consequences of the changes which have been documented, one is left in little doubt that the EHVs will prove to have had a substantial impact on the children's subsequent adjustment to school. Quite clearly, the children will be more likely to have been exposed to a school-marm-ish style of interaction and have learned to cope with it. Quite clearly their mothers are now much more favourably disposed toward intellectual and academic activity. But whether the changes which have been documented will serve to promote the growth of general competence in these children is a much more open question. If they have not, those responsible for the project lay themselves open to the accusation that they have entered horses in a race, and raised high expectations about those horses, while knowing that they are going to fall at the last ditch. Evidence of the effect of the programme on the growth of the children's general competence is, therefore, urgently needed.

9. There is, in fact, *no* evidence that the changes which have been brought about in parents' attitudes will have a substantial and general effect on their children. While there is clear evidence that parents' attitudes are, in general, markedly associated with their children's subsequent progress, the direction of causality has never been clear, and the evidence that changing parental attitudes and behaviour will lead to substantial changes in children's performance remains extremely shaky. To avoid misunderstanding, it is, perhaps, important to be quite clear about what we mean by such a statement. As we saw in Part I, although it is well established that teaching children to climb ladders, or to name colours, will lead to a

measurable increase in their ability to do these things, their advantage relative to other children rapidly disappears as the other children mature. From the fact that intelligence tests designed for young children contain items which assess their ability to name colours, stack blocks, and cut along lines, it follows that their scores at the time will increase as a direct result of a programme such as this. But it does not follow that such training has resulted in a general improvement in their ability to perceive relationships and educe correlates. Still less does it follow that enhanced ability to perform these simple tasks will help to ensure that the children maintain their head-start over others in achieving all the other tasks which need to be mastered if they are to get higher scores in aptitude and attainment tests when they are fourteen or fifteen years of age. Worse still, as is clear from the differing attitudes and behaviour of our HSES and LSES parents, there is every possibility that focussing attention on such direct teaching at the expense of other growth-promoting activities may actually *stunt* the development of the ability to perceive and think clearly. Support from this conjecture comes from the work of Stallings (1976), which shows that teachers who focussed on teaching arithmetic and reading got higher reading and arithmetic scores, but *depressed* scores on tests designed to assess the ability to perceive and think clearly. Conversely, teachers who created environments which facilitated exploration and the development of understanding, did indeed promote the development of the ability to perceive and think clearly (as measured by a test which did *not* contain items which parelled *any* of the activities which were undertaken), but depressed reading and arithmetic scores. Likewise, just as there is no doubt that the activities which parents undertake with their children will have a measurable effect on them, there is no doubt that their attitudes and expectations will also affect them. If these change—and remain changed—they will have effects on their children. But whether these effects will be of an order of magnitude which in any way compares with the well known correlation between parental attitudes and expectations and cognitive and intellectual performance is a very open question. As Raven (1977) has shown, there is every reason to believe that parents' attitudes and expectations reflect what they have observed in their children and are not directly a product of their own previous beliefs and expectations—and they do so in a way which makes it impossible to unscramble the effects of parents' beliefs and expectations in multi-variate cross-sectional studies. There is therefore a clear need to study this set of questions—and to study both the desired and desirable, and the undesired and the undesirable aspects of different types of intervention over a considerable period of time. (Note that, to do this, we need better measures of the styles of intervention adopted by the EHVs, and also—very interestingly—data on the extent to which the EHVs are able to vary their styles).

10. There is no evidence that parents are *able* to change their thinking and behaviours in ways which are most likely to be responsible for any environmentally-induced differences between the performance of HSES and LSES children. It might therefore be worth while devoting time to trying to invent ways in which these wider changes in attitudes, perceptions, and expectations and understandings might be brought about.

11. It is important to mount further research to find out whether a mother's failure to follow through on apparent changes in attitude are due to: (*a*) persistent value conflicts (they still value *dependence* in their children—but do they still expect school *success* to bring unhappiness?*); (*b*) environmental constraints; (*c*) ability deficits—such as *inability* to think in the cognitively complex manner in which HSES parents appear to think; or (*d*) *knowledge* deficits. On the answer to these questions rests the main decisions on the direction in which to proceed. Paradoxically, the answer to these questions can only be obtained by trying out strategies predicated on the various possible answers and assessing their impact.

---

*This is what we found in our pilot work for this enquiry, but were not able to pursue because of the need to limit the length of the interviews.

PART IV

POSSIBLE IMPLICATIONS OF THE BACKGROUND
DATA FOR HOME VISITING AND THE
DESIGN OF HOME VISITING PROGRAMMES

SO FAR, WE HAVE TREATED the data we obtained from our LSES and HSES samples mainly as bench-mark data against which to view the impact of the EHV programme. But this background data, and, in particular, the differences in attitudes and behaviour between these two bench-mark groups, may have something significant to tell us about the activities on which it might be important for Educational Home Visitors to focus. That, after all, was why we collected the data—with no intention of interviewing mothers who had been Home Visited as part of the statistical study. In saying that we hope to learn something of value to the EHVs from this comparison, we do not mean to imply that only the LSES group may be "disadvantaged". It may well be that *both* groups need Home Visitors, or that the Home Visitors have themselves something important to learn from what parents in both groups say and do. But it seemed to us that the contrast between the priorities, perceptions and expectations of these two groups might lead us to learn something significant about child-rearing and the processes which might be used to promote growth and development. In this section of our Report we will therefore re-examine the data we have already presented but focus mainly on the differences between HSES and LSES parents' responses and consider their possible significance and implications. Readers may like to recall that, as far as sample sizes are concerned, we are on much firmer ground in this section of our report than in assessing the impact of the Home Visiting, and the implications of the data for the design of Home Visiting programmes should therefore be considered very seriously.

CHAPTER 25

THE MALLEABILITY OF HUMAN NATURE

Figure 1 (p 111) shows that HSES mothers are much more strongly convinced of their ability to influence the sort of people their child will grow up to be than are LSES mothers. Although the majority of both groups say that it is *at least* "fairly possible" to influence the sort of person their child will grow up to be, only a minority of the LSES parents say that this is "very possible" whereas a majority of HSES parents do so. The difference is striking.

As can be seen from Figure 2 (p 111) *all* HSES parents say they believe it is possible to influence their child's values and beliefs, interests, friendliness and characters, and 75% of them believe it is possible to influence their child's intelligence. By contrast, in the LSES group, between 20% and 40% of parents believe that it is *not* possible to influence values, beliefs, friendliness, interests and character and 55% of them say that it is not possible to influence their child's intelligence. They are much more likely than the HSES group to think that intellectual ability is inherited, or otherwise "in them". "They have either got it or they've not", was a very common comment in the interview.

Discussion

It seems at first sight that the parents living in the HSES areas have a much more environmentalistic view of the factors which determine a child's development than the LSES group. But this may actually be an incorrect interpretation of the data. What the LSES group may be saying is *not* that the environment is any less important, but that *they* cannot influence the relevant aspects of that environment.

Nevertheless, both the fact that the difference between the two groups is most marked in relation to the development of character and intellect, and the parents' own comments, suggest that *both* processes are at work. The LSES parents are much less likely to believe either that it is possible to influence the course of their child's development or that they can counteract the effect of an adverse environment.

They may, of course, be much more likely than the HSES group to be exposed to evidence that both of these things are difficult. Their children are, quite obviously, much more often exposed to potentially damaging effects of the wider environment which they can do nothing about. They have much less choice of their neighbours or of the type and location of their house. As a result, they are much less able to choose a style of house which will make it possible for their children not to be under their feet all the time trying to engage in activities which are incompatible with their own. Nor are they able to choose a locality which will permit their children to explore their environment in safety.

LSES parents may also be more likely to be exposed to the most convincing evidence for a hereditarian position in relation to the development of intelligence. This evidence is that "bright" children regularly come from families which have not produced another bright child in living memory. If the home environment—and the parents' behaviour in particular—were responsible for the development of intelligence, how could such children possibly come out of such an unpromising environment? The child must have been born like it.

On the other hand, the very determination of the HSES parents to be *the* major influence on the development of their children may have a direct effect on their children. Their greater concern with the long term—the adults that their children will become—may also communicate itself to their children and lead them to more often think about the consequences of their actions and seek appropriate advice from books. On the other side of the coin, however, their determination to mould their children may lead either to cramping of individuality or rebellion. And their insistence on shielding the child from the adverse effects of the environment may deprive their children of the opportunity to learn to relate to others with different priorities and, in the long run, the willingness and the ability to live with others.

Possible Implications for the Design of Home Visiting Programmes

What do these results, and this discussion, suggest for the design of Home Visiting programmes? Firstly, they underline the importance of collecting good data to show whether HSES parents' confidence that child development can be significantly influenced by the action of individual parents is justified. The collection of data to study this question might well assume the role of a primary objective for an EHV programme. Secondly, since the available evidence on this point is, at best, tentative, and since it pays, at best, scant attention to the impact of the wider environment or counsels parents on how to counteract or exploit the impact of that wider environment, it suggests that Home Visiting programmes should incorporate some means of rescuing parents if they find that they have been inducted into an inappropriate life-style or that their new-found confidence in the view that individual parents can significantly alter the course of child development turns out to be ill-founded. Such a discovery may well be more destructive of their egos and their faith in intellectuals—and psychologists and teachers in particular—than any of their previous experiences. If it turns out that, through no fault of their own, they are unable to have a significant impact on the development of their children they may be even more inclined to regard themselves as failures. Thirdly, it underlines the need for Home Visitors to think carefully, not only about how it might be possible for parents to interact with their children in such a way as to promote the development of desired qualities, but also how parents are to counteract the adverse influence of the environment in which their children grow up. When they are doing this they should, perhaps, consider whether the activities they come to envisage in order to promote the development of one set of abilities are likely to be destructive so far as the development of other qualities is concerned.

CHAPTER 26

WHAT IS IMPORTANT IN CHILDREARING?

In this chapter we will review our material dealing with the importance parents attached to a number of goals and practices which might be important when bringing up children.

Reading to the child, talking to him a lot, having books at home, and asking him about pictures in books and things he has seen are the four most important items for the HSES parents (Table 1, page 113). Although lower down in priority, these are also seen as very important by many of the LSES group. Nevertheless there are striking differences between the proportions of HSES and LSES parents who think that these actions are *very* important; most of the *differences* amount to about 40%.

However, the three items seen as most important by the LSES parents do not appear on the HSES parents' list at all. Most important to these parents are: that their children need them, that they learn to respect property, and that they learn to stick up for themselves.

The overwhelming concern of the HSES parents with intellectual activity is striking. Whereas none of the "intellectual" activities are thought "very important" by significantly more than half the parents living in the LSES areas, there is virtual unanimity among the parents living in the HSES areas that their child should be *read to*, talked to, and have books in the home. (The fact that reading to children is more often thought to be "very important" than *talking* to them provides food for thought and discussion). All but two of the "top twelve" activities for parents living in the HSES areas have unmistakably to do with intellectual activity—and the others are at least supportive of intellectual activity. Moreover most of these activities are endorsed by two-thirds or more of the parents living in those areas.

By contrast, the main preoccupation of the parents living in the LSES areas in so far as it is revealed by this data, is, perhaps, not to feel redundant (which is what would happen if their children did not need them) and, perhaps, to retain control over their children by keeping them dependent on them.

The next two items (respecting property and sticking up for oneself) seem to reflect the alien nature of the LSES environments. Then comes the child being *read* to, followed by two items having to do with getting on with others and learning to respect authority.

Possible Implications for the EHVs

These striking differences prompt a number of thoughts.

At the very least, the apparent ecological appropriateness of some of the LSES parents' priorities should lead the EHVs to pause for thought before they seek to encourage more LSES parents to adopt the HSES parents' viewpoint. The data also raise the question, which we stumbled on earlier, of whether a change in the LSES parents' environment might not result in a substantial change in their values and priorities. If that were the case then it might be more appropriate for the EHVs to concentrate on changing the environment. Furthermore, if such intervention turned out to be unsuccessful, the EHVs would be forced to reconsider the justifiability of seeking to influence the LSES parents' values.

In order to underline the case for taking this question seriously, we may comment that not only may the LSES parents' priorities be appropriate to the environments in which they live, so, equally, the HSES parents' priorities may be appropriate *only* to *their* environments. How many books contain information which will in fact help LSES parents to lead their lives more effectively in the environments and jobs in which they find themselves—environments and jobs which are obviously not going to change all that much in the near future? How many find themselves in positions demanding independence? How many would not find themselves acutely frustrated if they thought of themselves as people who were entitled to interests and ideas of their own, or if they questioned the authorities with whom they have to deal? As Kohn (1969) has maintained, these attitudes, perceptions and expectations may have developed precisely because they are appropriate to the environment in which those concerned find themselves. While the development of alternative perceptions and expectations might help the parents concerned to move out of those jobs and environments, other people would probably have to move into them and adjust their views accordingly.

But equally, it may *not* be true that HSES parents' attitudes are appropriate *only* to their environment and that LSES parents have acquired attitudes which are appropriate only to theirs. The attitudes of HSES parents may be more appropriate to both environments, and LSES parents may not be capable of behaving in the way in which HSES parents behave. It may be that LSES parents, because of personal limitations, are unable to treat their children in the way in which HSES parents treat them. The *ability* to engage in intellectual activity—or the willingness to do so—may be dependent on other factors in the make-up of the individuals concerned or the environments in which they live. And, even if the parents were able to change their behaviour, their children might not necessarily become more able or more socially mobile.

That social status is, at least in part, a product of ability and temperament, rather than the reverse, is suggested by earlier research. Data published by Raven, Court and Raven (1977), shows that in respect of ability to perceive and think clearly children from different backgrounds show much smaller differences than do adults employed in different types of occupation. Some sort of selective process whereby people with different levels of ability find their way into different occupations seems to be at work. Similar data has been published in the area of values (Raven *et al*, 1975). This shows that socially mobile children tend to hold the values characteristic of the groups they are bound for as much as those of the group they left. These data support the view that social mobility, both upward and downward, is selective by ability and values. Other data are available to challenge the view that home background is responsible for the observed variance in abilities and values. Thus, Raven, Court and Raven (1977) found in one study that the lion's share of the variance in intellectual ability was between children who come from *similar* backgrounds, while Maxwell (1969) showed that the variance between children coming from the *same families* amounts to 65% of the total population variance in IQ.

We will return to this theme later. Here it is sufficient to note that the interpretation to be placed on these data *may not* be that LSES parents need to be taught to value engaging in intellectual activities with their children.

Parental Involvement and Schools as "Middle Class Institutions"

Several of those who have proposed intervention programmes of one sort or another have assumed that schools are "middle class" institutions and argued that one of their objectives must be to help working class children to accept, and adjust to, those middle class institutions in order to be able to take advantage of schooling.

On mulling over our own data on the values of the two socio-economic groups, it struck us that schools might not be such "middle class" institutions as is often assumed. It is true that HSES mothers are much more likely than LSES mothers to stress intellectual activities. However, even in this area, the sorts of activities stressed by HSES parents seem to differ markedly in character from most of the activities that go on in most schools known to us and in most of the secondary schools studies by Raven *et al* (1975), and by Raven and Litton (1976). The HSES parents' emphasis is on knowledge and skills chosen and selected by the child because that knowledge and those skills are relevant to his interests and problems, on unfettered, self-motivated, enquiry, and on the child's questioning his superiors and on their being able to help him answer *his* questions rather than on the child's answering the adult's questions. Books are a *tool* to be used to find information one needs, not things to be "mastered" because mastery of books is valued in and of itself.

This line of thought led us to sort out all the items which seemed to have a bearing on what parents might expect from schools and for which there is a marked discrepancy in the frequency of endorsement as "very important" by the HSES and LSES sample. These items are listed in Table 3.

TABLE 3

SOME DISCREPANCIES BETWEEN HSES AND LSES PARENTS

% Rating Item "Very Important"

	LSES	HSES
That your children need you	75	43
For your child to obey his parents without question	41	8
To teach your child to learn his place and know who's boss	43	13
To teach your child to respect figures in authority	49	23
For your child to be willing to use books to find information for himself	36	73
To teach your child to think for himself	41	68
To encourage your child to talk to you about what he is doing	38	68
For you to treat him with respect, as an individual in his own right entitled to pursue his own interests and ideas	37	63
To encourage him to be independent	40	60
For you to encourage your child to question and seek reasons for things he is told	28	58
To teach your child to be confident with people, situations and things he has not met before	23	55
To encourage your child to think clearly about what he is trying to do	25	40

Our subjective impression of schools is that they have a bias towards the views shown on this Table to be typical of LSES rather than HSES parents. At most schools, we suspect, children are expected to obey their teachers without question, to know their place and know who is boss, to respect (fear) figures in authority, to use books to cover ground prescribed by their teachers rather than to find information which is of value to them in solving their own problems, not to talk about what they are doing, to be circumspect about thinking for themselves and, in particular, questioning what they are told, and to be dependent on, rather than independent of their teachers. We also suspect that little effort is made to help children to be confident when dealing with people and situations they have not met before, and that teachers like to feel that their pupils need them rather than that they are independent of them. We do not deny that there are schools which make great efforts to foster the qualities more often valued by HSES parents—but we do suspect that the behaviour of most teachers in most schools approximates more closely to that which is more often valued by LSES parents. We would therefore argue that there is a strong case for research to check the assumption that the values which inform schools' activities are primarily those of the middle class.

Pending that research, we can only raise questions. What if we are right that schools tend to be "working class" not "middle class" institutions? Might the Home Visitors, by encouraging the parents they visit to adopt the HSES viewpoint, make life more difficult for the children they visit once they get to school? This is not an idle question: it is one which has haunted the Home Visitors throughout the time we have been working with them. (They have tended to resolve it by hoping that the parents will, as a result of their efforts, be able to bring pressure to bear on schools to get them to change).

Furthermore, if HSES children are successful *despite* the barriers which many schools place in the way of the types of growth their parents value, then the EHVs will be doing parents a disservice if they lead them to believe that developing such qualities will lead to school success, and, particularly, if they lead them to suppose that schools will help their children to develop those qualities.

Children from HSES backgrounds may do well in life because they have developed attitudes, values and competencies which have nothing to do with school— and they may do well at school for the same, or quite other reasons. Finally, if the EHVs *are* successful (and we have seen that they *are*) in influencing parents' values in the direction of those of the HSES group, and lead them to try to ensure that schools reinforce those new values, the EHVs may well find themselves—as some of them have found themselves—at loggerheads with other teachers whose behaviour is acceptable only because it conforms to the current expectations of LSES parents.

Whatever the data presented in Table 3 have to tell us about control of the overall climate in schools it also poses an interesting problem for those who argue for more parental involvement in schools—and this includes most of the Home Visitors. Although the differences between the HSES and LSES parents' responses are dramatic, the class-related variance documented here represents only a small proportion of the total variance in the importance parents attach to these abilities. The group differences conceal a great deal of variance *within* each of the groups. What is a school system to do with parents who value the development of such different qualities? Clearly, no school catering for a cross-section of children can create classroom environments which will make it possible to meet these apparently incompatible expectations. For example, one cannot at the same time encourage some children to question and seek reasons for things they are told and insist on instant obedience from others. Some form of individualised provision within classrooms might make it possible to cater for some of this variance—but, as our data on the features parents wanted in their physical and social environments shows, most parents are, in general, opposed to such individualisation of educational provision. So schools have a dilemma—a dilemma which will become acute if the EHVs lead parents to develop the strategies which are required to influence schools, without at the same time bringing them all to accept the HSES value system. Schools will be confronted with articulate parents making incompatible demands.

Home, Play, and Early Learning

Having briefly examined one or two possible implications of the broad sweep of our results, we may now focus on a series of topics in more detail.

Doubts about the value, if any, of play were revealed by the comments the parents made when they were asked how important it was not to interrupt their child while he was playing. Although most parents say they would not interrupt the child without good reason, others do not think it matters:

> "What? They're never doing anything important anyway, they just mess about and play all day. It doesn't matter if you interrupt them." (L)*

*Low Socio-Economic Status Parent

The lack of understanding of the growth which takes place through play could not be more evident and, in fact, as can be seen from Table A3, only 7% of LSES parents and 10% of HSES parents say it is very important not to interrupt a child whilst playing.

Although a small number (4%) of LSES parents think it is very important to let their children play on waste ground and building sites, 40% of both groups of parents say it is important *not* to do this (Table A4). This reveals conflicting interests between parents and children because a survey by Raven (*see* Hole, 1966) showed that this was the sort of place where children particularly liked to play. Safety is the main reason for disapproving of this. This concern with safety surfaced throughout the present enquiry and often conflicts with activities which are seen as positively beneficial to the child from a developmental point of view. The possibility of accident and injury was mentioned again and again in response to the question about the importance of giving young children tools, such as hammers and saws. As one mother in the Pilot Phase said when asked what she thought the consequences would be of giving her three-year-old such tools:

"You'd find his wee brother carved up in a corner somewhere." (L)

This fear explains why it is that only 2% of LSES parents and 13% of HSES parents say it is very important to give tools to a child, and why 29% of LSES parents and 2% of HSES parents say it is important NOT to do this. These figures, taken together with other data collected in the exploratory study, suggest that HSES parents trust their children's competence more than do LSES parents and are possibly more aware of the creative value of such opportunities to the child. The LSES children may, of course, actually be more ham-fisted, careless and destructive. The LSES families are, on the whole, larger, and the mothers in this group are more likely to expect fighting and aggressive behaviour from their children, and so, with shortage of space and adequate supervision difficult, many LSES mothers may be correct in thinking that damage and injury may occur as a result of giving their children tools. Nevertheless the stories mothers made up during the exploratory phase of the study about a picture of a child climbing a cliff revealed an extraordinary preoccupation with injury among LSES mothers in a situation which HSES mothers viewed as an opportunity to build self-confidence, independence and adventurousness. However it is also clear from the fact that many mothers said that such activities were "All right at the nursery" that their inability to supervise these activities is indeed one important consideration.

From these results it would seem that many parents—especially, but not only, LSES parents—have a none-too-positive view of the value of play. It is an idle way of filling idle time. In the context of the emphasis which both HSES and LSES parents place on formal instruction, it would seem that many parents will lap up any suggestion that play could be used to teach language, counting, or reading. The ground in which to sow any more subtle notion seems to be less fertile. Any notion that children, through play, might learn to concentrate, follow their interests single-mindedly, initiate action and monitor its effect, learn through that process to observe cause and effects, evolve ways of thinking about relevant variables, learn to effectively modify their goals as they see "what gives", develop confidence in their own abilities, or learn to gain the cooperation of others in order to pursue their own goals, seems to be foreign indeed. If the EHVs try to relay such messages—and such sometimes are the messages which "modern" educationalists seek to convey—there would seem to be good reasons for thinking that their message will not often be heard.

Education and School

When we turn to the school-related items in Figure 3 perhaps the most striking observation to be made is that most parents seem to have a relatively relaxed attitude toward school success. Only 27% of LSES parents and 30% of HSES parents say that school success is "very important".

Those who attach less importance to it often qualify their replies:

"Of course I'd *like* him to do well, but if he doesn't it's not the end of the world . . ." (H)*

"If he tries hard, does his best, that's what matters to me." (H)

"It would be nice, but if it's not in him there's no point in making a big thing of it." (L)

As is clear from these quotations, parents' answers to the question about the importance of school success are intimately bound up with their view on the origins of intellectual ability. Their answers suggest that the reasoning process which led at least some of them to answer in the way they did was "there is no point in getting worked up about something which you can do nothing about". If this is the case, the EHVs, by convincing parents that they *can* influence the development of intellectual ability, may lead parents to feel that something which was previously, at best, only a hope or a pipe dream could in fact

*High Socio-Economic Status Parent

become a realistic expectation. In that case the parents might be more prepared to say that it was important to them. And, indeed, the Home Visited group are much more likely to say that school success *is* important to them. Having raised such expectations, and led the parents they visit to believe that these are realistic expectations, are the Home Visitors going to be able to deliver the goods? And, if not, what are they going to do to help the parents to adjust to the frustration which they may have created? The case for Home Visiting programmes building in provision to follow through with parents seems to be strong indeed.

How is School Success to be Promoted?

How do parents think that intellectual development and school success are to be promoted? Neither group thinks school success is to be promoted by punishing children who do not do well there. 87% of HSES parents and 49% of LSES parents said that it was "important not to do this" (Table A4). Given that LSES parents are much less likely than HSES parents to think it is important not to punish their children for failure at school, it may be important for the EHVs to be particularly careful to avoid giving the impression that they in any way accept the view that children should be punished for failure. This may seem like an unnecessary comment, but one of the EHVs was observed smacking one of the children she visited for not sitting still and paying attention.

The fact that the HSES group is no more likely than the LSES group to think that it is important for their children to work and study on their own when they are older, or for them to continue the work of the school in the home, provides food for thought. Like the failure of the HSES group to attach more importance to school success than the LSES group, these findings suggest that the relative success of their children in the educational system may not be a result of pressure and hard work. Rather it may be a product of more basic abilities, attitudes and motivation which may be promoted by engaging the child in particular activities. Tomlinson and Tenhouten's (1976) data strongly support this conjecture, and draw attention to the importance of inter-personal behaviours which go far outside the cognitive realm. Such behaviours include making oneself and one's work known to authorities taking an interest in, and supporting, what the authority is doing, setting out to be different from others and therefore noticeable, and expressive behaviours of one sort or another.

The fact that the Home Visitors not only appear to have led the parents they visited to think that school success is more important than they did before, but also to think it is more important for the children to work and read on their own a lot when they are older (possibly in order to achieve that success) suggests that they may be selling a comforting Protestant ethic in which hard work is expected to be rewarded both in this world and in the next. More than that, as we have seen, they may be encouraging parents to see simple and direct links between parental behaviour and outcomes, rather than the much more indirect relationships which may be perceived by the HSES group and which may be behind the HSES group's relative success.

Evidence that the HSES group do see the process as less direct, more subtle, and more differentiated is also contained in Figure 3. Some of the most striking differences between the HSES and LSES groups are on the items dealing with books in the home, using books to find information for oneself, and promoting concentration and the ability to settle down. Only 14% of LSES parents said that this last was "very important" compared to 48% of HSES parents.

"That's one of the most important ways of preparing them for school. It doesn't matter if you teach them to read, write and do sums. They can learn all that when they get there anyway. But if you teach them to sit—and listen—and pay attention—you've given them all the abilities they need to learn." (H) (Teacher, mother of 3).

The value for sedentary intellectual activity isolated from action, knowledge as something to be absorbed rather than created, and knowledge as what goes on in schools rather than in life, could not be more apparent.

"Och, no! Not wee bairns like that. You can't tie them down at that age. They're always wanting to be up and about, never wanting to do the same thing for two minutes in a row. They just get bored if you make them concentrate on one thing." (L) (Father of 2, aged 4 and 6).

It is clear that HSES and LSES parents have very different expectations of their children at this age. The HSES parents expect their children to be able to concentrate, act responsibly, and reason. They regard them as possessing most of the abilities and motivations possessed by adults. LSES parents, in contrast, are less inclined to believe this: they are more inclined to think that their children lack these abilities and motivations and must be protected from injury and the effects of ignorance and coerced into whatever behaviours are essential to the smooth running of the family and society. The *indirect* process of promoting success—whether that success is to be defined in terms of school or anything else—by fostering concentration, the willingness to observe and think for oneself, the tendency to study casual sequences and find the information one needs in books and, perhaps above all, the ability to lead others to recognise the value of one's contribution, cannot, therefore, be used. It is a totally different way of thinking, and it is noticeable that the EHVs have not been particularly successful in influencing discipline expectations toward the assumption that the child is capable of reasoning and acting responsibly, leading the parents to focus on promoting the development of concentration, or bringing their children to see books as a potential source of help in coping with their problems.

Some of the parents who do not think about child development in this more complex way are not merely indifferent to it. They are actively opposed to it. For example, asked how important it was for their child to use books to find information for himself one LSES mother commenced:

"I wouldn't want that. You never know *what* he might come across, poking about in books. I'd rather he asked his father or his teacher." (L)

The fear of the consequences of original sin (curiosity) could not be more apparent. Attention may also be drawn to this mother's assumption about internalised controls. The child is not expected to have the ability to know what is bad for him. As another informant said, in the course of another study, when the author asked him about the importance of censorship of books and periodicals:

"Oh, yes—that's *very* important. I couldn't even trust *myself* with that stuff." (L)

Other comments made during the interviews also reveal that, in the absence of internalised controls, to which we will return later, independence *does* make for unruly behaviour.

From such comments it follows that, as the Home Visitors emphasise, and as other authors such as Hess and Shipman (1965), Brandis and Bernstein (1974) and, in a completely different context, Watts (1977) have emphasised, there is an extremely close connection between the promotion of active intellectual enquiry and discipline practices and expectations. As we have already observed, many secondary schools seem to have adopted the LSES parents' views on discipline, and Lynn's (1977) work might be taken to indicate that these are having the effects on intellectual development which the material reviewed here would lead one to expect.

If the Educational Home Visitors wish to lead the parents they visit (and therefore, perhaps, in the long run their fellow teachers) to adopt a more complex view of development and to see their children as more competent, capable of reasoning, and developing internalised, reasoned, moral codes, there are elements of their work, already stressed more by some EHVs than others, which could be strengthened. Demonstrating to parents that their children *can* concentrate, *can* reason, and *can* act responsibly are among them. Unfortunately the idea of demonstrating to parents that children can concentrate, reason and act responsibly poses a number of problems. In the first place, the EHVs often feel that they have to "cover ground" in their "lessons". They are frequently found leading children on to new things just as they become absorbed in one task. They are aware of the dilemma, but most have tended to resolve it either by arguing that they must introduce the parent to as many things as possible which *might* interest the child—or by arguing that it is necessary to introduce the child to a wide *range* of concepts and cognitive skills which are all of potential importance in cognitive development.

The concept of "concentration" is also inherently ambiguous. Children will often become absorbed in tasks—like playing with water—and persist at them for long periods of time despite the fact that they do not seem to be "learning" anything from them. Both the parents and some of the EHVs seem to feel that it is justifiable to interrupt a child involved in such activities in order to move him on to something else. What's more, schools also tend to favour the child who wants to concentrate on books and teachers, rather than the child who wants to concentrate on some idiosyncratic problem which is known only to him. What we may be saying is, therefore, that concentration is not a generalisable *ability*, but rather something which forms part of what we *mean* when we say that someone is *interested* in a particular problem or topic. The EHVs' task may, therefore, be to interest children in intellectual activity—and it may (or may not) be necessary for them to acknowledge that such interest will only come about at the expense of some other interest.

But, in conclusion to this section, we should emphasise that we ourselves are not convinced that the HSES group's perceptions and expectations are correct. It may well be that children *are* unable to reason, concentrate and act responsibly. Even if HSES children *are* able to do these things it does not necessarily follow that *all* children are able to do so. It may well be that LSES parents' children *need* to learn to concentrate on, think about, and practise *different things*— such as how to win a fight. It may well be that HSES parents are wrong to think that these more subtle processes of child rearing actually work. It may well be that what works, and is appropriate to, one group of children is not appropriate to another group. We have repeatedly pointed out that differences in parents' expectations may reflect real differences, not only in their children's behaviour, but also in their own experience. Morton-Williams *et al* (1968) and Raven *et al* (1975) found that early school leavers, and pupils who expected to enter low status occupations, regardless of their background, were much more anxious than others to have school activities in which they could move about and did not have to sit still all day. The conclusion to be drawn may therefore be that not all children should be expected to sit still and concentrate on books! It is therefore, once again, of the greatest importance to find out whether the EHV project has been able to *influence* such things as levels of concentration, interest in intellectual activity, and the ability to reason.

We may turn now to a discussion of the more directly school-related activities included in Figure 3. Despite our findings that HSES parents attach more importance to activities related to the promotion of cognitive development in their children, such as reading to the child, talking to him, and having books at home, no parents in the HSES group said it is very important to teach their child to read before he goes to school, compared to 12% of parents in the LSES areas. Indeed, 20% of HSES parents, compared to 6% of LSES parents, say it is important NOT to do this.

Altogether, responses to this question are very varied, both within and between groups. Many parents, especially in the HSES areas, attach "some importance" to teaching their children to read, qualifying their answer by saying "I would do it if she asked, or seemed interested, but not otherwise."

Other parents are worried that the child might get bored at school, or confused by being taught in a different way.

"She was always asking me— 'what's that word—what does this say?'—and so on, but I didn't like to take it any further in case her teacher didn't like it when she got to school." (L)

Many parents report having been told by teachers definitely *not* to attempt to teach reading.

On the other hand, it appears that a number of LSES parents attach great importance to teaching of reading, but, in some cases, lack the knowledge necessary to carry it out.

"I think it's very important, it gives them a start. But I got books, Ladybird ones, and tried to get him to read them. After the first day or two it would end in tantrums and screaming fits . . ." (L)

HSES parents, on the other hand, attach less importance to the actual teaching of reading and more importance to indirect "pre-reading" activities, such as matching, copying shapes, reading and telling stories, and increasing vocabulary.

Although the EHVs are clearly more inclined to share the HSES parents' priorities, the problem of what to do with those parents who wish to teach their children to read—presumably because of its direct relevance to school success—remains, for the EHVs have not been able to stop parents thinking it is important. In fact, discussion of this topic at the EHVs' meeting revealed that they were plagued by exactly the same dilemmas as the parents—and it is clear that this is a problem which cannot be tackled without involving the local schools. It is worthy of note that, since the Home Visitors—who are themselves teachers—have had so little success in gaining the schools' agreement and co-operation on this issue, one can hardly expect the parents to do so. Nevertheless, as it happens, it *was* the *parents* who persuaded the reception class teacher in one of the project schools to share her professional know-how in this area with the parents.

Discipline Expectations

Figure 3 also documents differences between HSES and LSES parents' expectations of their children and difference in their perceptions of their children's competence. The HSES parent is more likely to think that her child is open to reason, that he is capable of respecting his parents because of the quality of their behaviour rather than out of fear, more willing to accept the absence of instant compliance with commands—perhaps because she feels that the child will have good reasons for not complying with them, perhaps because she feels that the child needs to develop a view of himself as someone who has a *right* to question commands, or perhaps because she feels that what the child is already doing is important to him and that he has a right to continue with it, or that the development of important qualities will be stunted if he is forced to stop what he is doing, and less likely to think that punishment is essential in order to eliminate undesired behaviour and induce compliance. And there is further evidence that the LSES parents are less likely to think that their children are capable of learning by example: they are less likely to think that it is important for children to spend time in the company of people who handle responsiblity well and less likely to say that it is important for their children to see their parents working hard and being resourceful. While this may be because they feel themselves to be less capable than HSES parents of providing that example, we will shortly see that this explanation is not sufficient to cover all the items which have been studied.

The LSES parents' tendency to make use of a rather simplistic concept of motivation, and their tendency to make little use of personal example as an educational device, is going to become a recurrent theme in our report. It may well be important for the Home Visitors to help mothers develop a more complex understanding of development and the ways in which it is to be promoted. If this is to be done, it may be important, as Weikart (1978) has suggested, to provide the mother with new concepts to use to think about the qualities she wants her children to develop and the ways in which they are to be developed. As our pilot data showed, our LSES informants are a great deal less likely to read, and to read widely, than our HSES parents. They may therefore be particularly likely to lack the concepts and understandings they need. In the absence of an effort to supply such concepts and understandings it is unlikely that the Home Visitors will be able to lead the parents they work with to stimulate the development of high level competencies which in part may be responsible for the differential school success of children from HSES backgrounds and which may well also make a direct contribution to the subsequent life success of children from such backgrounds. In the absence of broadly based programmes of this sort it is possible that they may lead the parents they work with to think that purely cognitive activity will lead to the goals they so much desire—health and happiness for their children.

Nevertheless the magnitude of the task to be undertaken should not be underestimated. The LSES parents may have a relatively simplistic view of development because they are incapable of more complex reasoning. As Raven (1976) has shown, downwardly mobile children are more likely than others from their backgrounds to stress the need for firm rules and "discipline", and they are less likely to value independence, originality, and thinking for oneself. The necessary ideas may be altogether too complex for LSES parents. Even if they are not, it is certainly true that they have had much less practice at thinking in such complex terms. And even if both of these problems could be overcome (by, for example, making the necessary conceptual framework more explicit and comprehensible) it is also true that psychologists and educators have, apparently, not yet even caught up with the common sense thinking of the HSES parents in their understanding of these issues. And finally there is no evidence that if all these things *could* be changed that they would produce the desired effect. But none of this should be taken to imply that we do not think that an attempt should be made to work in this area. On the contrary, the glimmerings of understanding we are now coming to would not have been gained *without* the attempt to mount an intervention project in this area.

At a more down to earth level, the LSES parents' emphasis on control of their children makes one suspect (*a*) that if their children do *not* need them they may lose control over them, and (*b*) that they may in fact have considerable difficulty getting their children to behave in a reasonable manner. Both of these reflections suggest that the EHVs' message may fall on stony ground if they do not take account of the strength of the mothers' need to ensure that their children are dependent on, rather than independent of, them. The potential strength of this need can be underlined by reflecting further on the fact that, as can be seen from Figure 3, 75% of LSES mothers said that it was very important to them that their children needed them.

What else besides the need to retain control over their children could lie behind this? It is not simply a matter of family closeness, since *more* of the HSES than LSES parents said that it was very important for young children to spend a lot of time with their parents (48% compared with 23%).

Another possibility is that catering for children may be much more central to the LSES mothers' sense of worth. Whereas 90% of the HSES mothers had had some education beyond age 15, only 22% of the LSES mothers had. Many more alternative avenues to making contact with others and finding a high-status job will therefore be available to the HSES mothers. Conversely, the role of *mother* may be much more central to the LSES parents' self-concept—and if their children did *not* need them that central pivot would disappear.

Thus, encouraging *independence*, in the absence of strategies designed to develop internalised controls and, in particular, alternative sources of feelings of meaning and worth for the mothers, may be both difficult and potentially damaging to parent and child alike.

Discipline Expectations and Cognitive Growth

We have already remarked upon the fact that the Educational Home Visitors, previous researchers, and the present authors have become aware that there seemed to be some logical connection between discipline expectations and strategies and cognitive growth. The relationship is poorly understood. But it is at least plausible that involvement in discussion and decision-taking, involving reasoning and consideration of the long term consequences of one's actions, should result in the development of the spontaneous tendency and the ability to reason and consider alternatives.

Nevertheless, it is important to note that the "authoritarian" views documented in Figure 3 do not necessarily imply that the LSES parents do not think that their children should be consulted and expected to contribute to rational discussion and decision-taking. They only indicate that *when* an order *has* been given it should be obeyed. Both parents and children may actually be expected to engage in a great deal of intellectual activity *before* that decision is taken in order to ensure that it is a *good* decision.

This data does not, however, stand on its own. In the first place, although it cannot be seen from the table, LSES parents abhorred the notion that their children should learn to get people in authority to do what they wanted them to do. If the argument advanced in the last paragraph were correct they should be prepared for their children to do this *before* a command were given. Furthermore, as we have seen, LSES parents were also much less inclined than the HSES parents to say that the child should be encouraged to think for himself, question and seek reasons for things he is told and be treated as an individual with a right to opinions and interest of his own. It is therefore *unlikely* that LSES parents think that their children should be involved in discussions *prior* to decisions being taken and commands being given.

Once again, one starts to wonder what are the reasons for these priorities. It may be that the parents themselves are unable to engage in these complex reasoning processes or lack the complex interpersonal skills which are necessary to exert influence in a "democratic" structure. It may be that they do not value these patterns of interaction. It may be that they do not see the connection between one thing and another. It may be that their own experience is that their life style demands neither cognitive activity nor independence and internalised controls.

But, whatever the explanation, it is clear that any attempt to influence patterns of parent-child interaction with a view to promoting cognitive development will have to come to terms with these problems. More than that, if such activities are *successful* they may affect patterns of relationship, and expectation, which have very little obvious relationship to cognitive development.

More and more children, pupils, employees and citizens may come to question, and seek reasons for, things they are told. As Piaget (1932) and Kohlberg (1971) have observed, it may not be possible to divorce cognitive development from moral development. We may therefore ask whether the EHVs are doing sufficient to alert the parents they work with to the possibly far-reaching implications of what they are doing. Have they led the other teachers in the schools they work in to anticipate changed discipline expectations from parents and pupils?

Relationship to Authority and the Explanation of the Results of the Evaluation

There is one final comment which it may be worth making on Figure 3. The LSES parents' emphasis on their *children* learning to respect authority and know who's boss reflects their own feelings about authority. If the EHVs are—as they inevitable must be— regarded as authorities, then the mothers may feel under a very strong obligation to appear to have absorbed and accepted the EHVs' message. This effect would be expected to be greatest in relation to those areas for which the message was most explicit. And that process may go a long way toward accounting for results we have reported in Part III.

CHAPTER 27

"WHY, MUMMY?"

We now return to our data on *why* parents thought certain activities were important and what they thought the consequences would be if they, or their children, did, or did not do, certain things.

Why is it important to ask a child questions?

We have seen (Figure 3) that, although most parents feel it is important, HSES parents are much more likely than LSES parents to think it is *very* important to ask their child questions about pictures in books and things he had seen.

The reasons for thinking it is important to do this also differ markedly (Table A5). For the HSES group the most common reason is to encourage the child to understand, find out, and take an interest in things. This category includes replies like:

"It encourages him to form his own opinions." (H)

"They become more aware of what's happening, how things work ..." (H)

"He discovers things and relationships for himself." (H)

For the LSES group the reason most commonly given is to teach the child to recognise things, ie to teach him what they are, what their *names* are, so that he will recognise them when they recur. Replies included:

"It learns him what things are." (L)

"It helps him to remember the names of things." (L)

What the difference in emphasis between these two bench-mark groups seems to reflect is the difference between an emphasis on cognitive *processes*—understanding, observing, reasoning—and an emphasis on cognitive *knowledge*. The data might be taken to support Bereiter & Englemann's (1966) belief that LSES children need to be taught to *label*. Indeed it might be suggested that LSES parents already *know* that their children need such tuition (perhaps because they are slower than others) and Bereiter & Englemann's willingness to satisfy their felt need for it might account for the popularity of the materials they produced (DISTAR). This LSES emphasis on knowing the names of things may also account for the fact that our own EHVs devote a considerable amount of time to such activities. This would be in line with the author's earlier finding that teachers have a tendency to do what the parents of their pupils want, despite their own judgment (Raven, 1977).

But while the parents' emphasis on these activities *may* be correct so, also, it may *not* be. While their children's learning difficulties might be responsible for their emphasis on such activities, so the child's learning difficulties might be a product of his parents' not having adopted the wider viewpoint implied by the sorts of activities which were thought more important by the HSES group. Their perspective, like that of Spearman (1927) and Macnamara (1972), would suggest that one *first* encourages the development of qualities which many people would take to be synonymous with "intelligence" and that learning to recognise things, name them, and talk about them in appropriate ways, will then take care of itself.

An Educational Home Visiting programme based on one of these alternative viewpoints would obviously look very different from one based on the other, and the comparative evaluation of programmes based on them would provide useful data on their relative truth.

LSES parents are also more likely than HSES parents to think it is important to ask a child questions to see *if* he is learning, what he is learning and find out if he has been paying attention. Parents said things like:

"To see what he's taking in." (L)

"To see if he's understanding what you're on about." (L)

"To make sure she's remembering." (L)

This emphasis on "testing" the child may reflect a feeling that the child will not spontaneously take an interest in things and learn for himself. He has to be *forced* to do so and checked up on. Such a viewpoint is consistent with our finding that LSES parents generally have less confidence in their children's motivation and competence. By not *expecting* such interest and competence they may not find it and reinforce it. Alternatively, their failure to expect it may be a product of their children's lacking such competencies and interests. As a result, the parents' emphasis on teaching their children to recognise and name may reflect a greater anxiety that the child is not learning and developing as fast as he should. Once again, the EHVs might usefully enquire what perceptions, expectations and processes lie behind a set of attitudes which they appear to be reinforcing.

Why is it Important to look at Books with a Child?

We have seen (Figure 3) that more HSES than LSES parents think it is very important to read to their child and encourage him to use books. The reasons given by the two groups for thinking it is important to spend time looking at books with the child are very different, although both think it is educational (Table A6). Responses in this category include:

"It learns them." (L)
"Develops his mind." (L)

The biggest differences between the two groups are that the HSES group is more likely to say that it develops language, imagination, and creativity—the last three being much more highly prized by the HSES group and, as we have seen, potentially responsible for the differential school and life success of their children. HSES parents are also much more likely to say that it is of value because it is interesting and enjoyable.

It is clear that the EHVs have been extraordinarily successful in leading the parents they visit to think that such activities are valuable because they are interesting and enjoyable (Table A6). The fact that they have been less successful in reducing the other HSES/LSES differences suggest that they may, as Weikart (1978) has suggested, need to supply the parents with the constructs needed to think about these other qualities and, if possible, research data on the long term consequences of children developing them. Such data would help them to allay some of the parents' doubts about the consequences of leading their children to develop intellectual qualities. The EHVs may, of course, also like to consider whether the HSES parents are right in believing that looking at books with children does in fact lead them to the goals they mention, or whether this is mere wishful thinking. Research data would again be useful.

Why is it Important to Talk to the Child a Lot?

Figure 3 showed us that HSES parents are very much more likely than LSES parents to say that it is very important to talk to the child a lot.

There is also evidence that more HSES than LSES parents think that lack of conversation between parent and child will lead to poor language development, feelings of rejection, poor intellectual development, poor progress at school, boredom, and unhappiness (Table A8). HSES parents are also more likely to expect this to lead parent and child to fail to get to know each other so well, to problems in later years, and to lack of full enjoyment of their children's company. Indeed more than twice the proportion of HSES parents than LSES parents think that they and their children would not get to know each other so well if they did not talk to them a lot. Conversation, then, appears to be an important part of the parent/child relationship in all but a few of HSES homes. It must be remembered that there are a large number of parents in LSES areas who think this way also. However, there are also a large number who do not. Possibly some of these are the parents we have identified as lacking in self-confidence, those who cannot believe that anything they do, or do not do, can have as much influence on the child as his friends and teachers. As one LSES mother said:

"It wouldn't really matter. If I never spoke to him he'd pick it up outside anyway, or at school. They'll always learn somehow."

She could well be right. Perhaps the LSES parents have much more *evidence* that, if they do *not* talk to their children, the intelligence of the brighter ones still develops; they are not distant, unhappy, and bored. Nevertheless, it is hard to reconcile such an hypothesis with the fact that the LSES parents are much more worried about their children getting out of control and into trouble.

As far as the EHVs are concerned, the implications of the failure of the LSES parents to anticipate the all-pervading consequences which HSES parents expect if they do not talk to their children could be considerable. As High Status individuals themselves they cannot expect the parents they visit to share their own assumptions. Nevertheless, the accuracy of their assumptions, while mostly logical, is open to question. But, while more data are needed, the data available from this survey support the HSES mothers' contentions. Although the EHVs have led the LSES mothers to radically alter their view of the consequences of not talking to their children a lot, one cannot help wondering whether the LSES mothers anticipate that the consequences of, for example, their knowing their children better are the same as those anticipated by the HSES parents. Given what we have already seen, it is more than likely that LSES mothers may think that the implications of these "benefits" will be quite other than what the EHVs suppose.

Encouraging the Child to Question and Seek Reasons for Things he is Told

As can be seen from Figure 3, HSES mothers are twice as likely as their LSES counterparts to say that it is "very important" to encourage the child to question and seek reasons for things he is told (Item B24).

While most parents associate question-asking with the development of the tendency to work things out for oneself, developing one's own opinions, independence and responsibility, the HSES group is more likely to do all of these things (Table A9). They are also more likely to associate question-asking with the development of language.

As we have seen, the HSES group is also more likely to think that all of these qualities are "very important". Their tendency to encourage children to ask questions, and seek reasons, would therefore be expected to be very firmly linked to a supportive network of beliefs and attitudes, and therefore much stronger.

As far as the EHVs are concerned, however, the main import of these data is that it is not true that LSES parents do not see the *connection* between encouraging children to ask questions and seek reasons for things and cognitive and character development. They see the connection, but they don't particularly *value* the qualities which have been mentioned. What's more, less than half of either group feels that questioning, reasoning people will be more likely to get on at school or in life—which perhaps indicates that the HSES parents value these qualities for intrinsic rather than instrumental reasons. Indeed 20% of both groups feel that people (parents, teachers, etc.) would regard children who asked questions and sought reasons for things they were told as difficult.

Treatment as an Individual who is Entitled to Pursue his Own Interests and Ideas

We can see from Figure 3 that, while only one third of the LSES group think it is "very important" to treat a child as an individual who is entitled to pursue his own interests and ideas, just under two-thirds of the HSES group do so (Item A25).

Once again, most parents anticipate that this will lead the child to have opinions of his own, to work things out for himself, to be independent and responsible (Table A9). Despite the fact that the LSES parents do anticipate these things less than the HSES parents, therefore, the difference in the amount of importance attached to this activity is not to be attributed to a failure to perceive the consequences, but rather to differing evaluations of those consequences. If, as they do, the EHVs wish to encourage the parents they visit to treat their children with more respect, it is important for them to recognise the centrality of the values issue and to be sure that they can justify their value-judgments—to the parents they visit and to others. Alternatively, it may be important for them to try to help the parents bring about a situation in which schools and society value and cater for a wider variety of people with different value orientations.

Which Activities are Educational?

It is clear that the most *educational* activity of those we asked about is thought to be looking at books with the child. Jigsaws come next for the HSES group, but the LSES group put cutting out pictures and shapes next (Tables A6 and A11). The most *enjoyable* activity for the HSES group is playing with sand and water with the child, while for the LSES group it is rough and tumble (Table A10).

For the LSES group, looking at books and doing jigsaws are rarely seen as enjoyable (only 8% and 11%, respectively, say so) and even for the HSES group these things are much less enjoyable than playing with sand and water. Clearly, for both groups, activities which are *educational* are not enjoyable—and enjoyable activities are not particularly educational! The EHVs therefore seem to face a classic dilemma: Do they encourage *educational* activities, or do they encourage *enjoyable* activities?

CHAPTER 28

PARENTS AS TEACHERS

Teaching and Learning—General

The great majority of parents (92% of parents living in HSES areas, and 69% of those living in LSES areas) said that their children learned a lot from them (Table A25). Nevertheless about half the parents felt that it was best for the child to learn for himself rather than for them to teach him (Figure 7, p 139). These results, taken together with the finding that 60% of parents living in LSES areas said that what a child learned from his parents was very important to his future (Figure 3, Item B16), would seem to imply that there is little need for EHVs to convince parents that they are their children's most important educators. They do, however, highlight an extremely important research question—for only a third of the HSES parents said it was best for them to teach, while two thirds said it was best for the child to learn for himself rather than to be taught. Promoting growth may therefore have more to do with creating an environment in which optimal development can take place rather than with teaching (Figure 7).

The impression that parents expect to *follow* their children's interests is reinforced by the data presented in Table A34. This shows that 57% of HSES parents and 36% of LSES parents thought it was very important to study what the child wanted to know and then help him to find out, while only 17% thought it was very important to make sure that the child learnt the things that they wanted him to learn.

The question for research is whether parents or teachers are the best facilitators of growth. Or, more correctly, which strategies are best for achieving different sorts of goals. Teaching may be a good method of *conveying knowledge*, but, as we have seen, psychologists are none too clear about the connection between knowledge and cognitive development, let alone about the ways in which the growth of the sorts of competence we have been discussing in this report are to be promoted.

Parents' answers to our questions about what and how they taught their children should clearly be interpreted in the context of the

findings we have reported here, namely that *most* parents did *not* think
it was a particularly good idea to set out to teach their children (which
is, apparently, not the same thing as saying that they did not recognise
that their children learnt a great deal from them).

What do Parents teach their Children?

Parents' answers to our open-ended question about the sorts of
things they taught their pre-school children (coded in Table A27) are
mainly of value in showing that parents' answers to an open-ended
question lend support to the conclusion we have drawn from looking at
their answers to the closed questions we asked on the importance of
various possible goals in child rearing.

1. *Social Skills/Behaviour.* 65% of LSES parents, and 60% of
   HSES parents said they taught social skills and behaviour.
   Under this heading came table manners, politeness, how to share
   things, doing what one is told, not answering back and how to
   behave in different situations.

2. *Intellectual Skills.* After social skills, most responses of the LSES
   parents fell into this category (36%). Although this percentage is
   smaller than the 60% found in the HSES group, it still indicates
   that many LSES parents do pay attention to the development of
   intellectual skills in their children. Those mentioned were varied,
   but included reading, writing, counting, teaching 'new' words,
   teaching about animals, nature, 'the world', in fact anything that
   the child or parent was interested in.

3. *Moral Values.* 28% of LSES parents and 10% of HSES parents
   gave responses which fell into this category. The difference in
   emphasis supports the suggestion that HSES parents are less likely
   to expect undesirable influences in their child's immediate environment than LSES parents who have daily evidence that these exist:

   > "I try to teach them right from wrong. But sometimes it's like
   > battering your head against a brick wall. You say 'It's wrong to
   > swear' and he'll say 'But Jimmy's daddy says that.' I try to teach
   > them to bring their rubbish home, but when there's beer cans,
   > newspapers and fag packets lying all over the ground, and you
   > can't tell me it was bairns that done that—what can you do?" (L)

4. *Physical Skills and Independence.* This category included such
   things as tying shoelaces, going to the toilet alone, feeding oneself
   and managing cutlery, tidying bedrooms, washing dishes, helping
   with housework, dressing oneself, undressing oneself, using tools

and scissors, and things which included switching televisions on and off and using cameras. 26% of LSES parents, and 43% of HSES parents gave responses which fell into it. This supports our conclusion that LSES parents are less likely to value independence in their children than HSES parents. This may be because LSES mothers find that it threatens their role of mother and provider, or it may be that time pressures prevent them attending to the niceties of fostering "independence": it is quicker to do things for children. However, the following quotation, which was not isolated, supports the first of these interpretations:

> "They're not babies for long. I like to make the most of it. Before long they're off out the door with never a backward glance. That's when I always start thinking about having another one."
> (L, mother of 5).

How do Parents Teach?

After parents had told us what they taught their children, they were asked how they did this.

The results, shown in Table A28, suggest that *how* parents teach their children may be more important than *what* they teach them.

LSES parents are divided fairly evenly among four methods: Giving constant reminders (23%); Setting an example (22%); Punishing failures (22%) (which usually means smacking); and Giving reasons and explanations (20%).

The majority (67%) of HSES parents teach by setting an example, followed by 36% who teach by giving reasons and explanations and 28% by providing a stimulating environment.

Besides noting the HSES stress on teaching *by example* it is worth observing that the HSES parents have, by saying this, reinforced the message they conveyed in answer to our earlier question on whether it is best to set out to teach, or whether it is better to structure situations in which children can learn.

They are more likely to have confidence in their ability to influence their children with little persuasion or coercion, more likely to make use of positive reinforcement, and more likely than LSES parents to value reasoning. It has already been mentioned that many LSES parents appear to see reasoning and giving explanations as evidence of weakness and inability to exercise authority. Their more punitive attitude is expressed by the fact that 22% (compared with none of the HSES group) said they taught the child by punishing failures.

As we shall see later (Figure 10), 23% of LSES parents said they smacked their children often compared with no one in the HSES group.

LSES parents are also more likely to teach by giving constant reminders (often plain nagging) than HSES parents and are more likely to give threats and warnings.

The data in Table A28, as well as illustrating the differences in attitudes to teaching and learning held by many parents in the HSES and LSES areas, suggest possible reasons for differences in school performance between their children. If LSES children have been nagged and smacked, warned and threatened, in the course of their pre-school education, their attitude to learning is likely to be less positive at the age of five than their HSES counterparts who have been given reasons and explanations, provided with a stimulating environment, and have been praised and rewarded for good behaviour. The methods used by HSES parents are in some ways similar to those employed by infant teachers in reception classes (though not necessarily further up the school), and these children are therefore likely to make an easier transition from home to school. LSES children, however, many of whom may be already poorly motivated as far as formal learning is concerned, may take the absence of threats, nagging and smacking as an invitation to do as they please. As many teachers have been heard to complain, "Smacking is the only way to get through to some children".

The Educational Home Visitors could make use of these data as a basis for discussions with parents in order to suggest alternative methods of teaching and disciplining children which could well have a favourable effect on their future educational prospects. But perhaps the main thing that it suggests is that the EHVs should consider how adequately they are able to model *for the mothers* ways of teaching their children *by example.* In this context the fact that the EHVs have actually further depressed the frequency with which LSES parents mention teaching by example and increased their emphasis on formal instruction may be viewed as not entirely satisfactory—particularly if "formal instruction" involves "drumming things into them". On the other hand, who is to say that the LSES parents are not right? Some highly respected psychologists agree with them.

Asking Questions

37% of LSES parents and 60% of HSES parents thought it was very important to encourage their children to ask questions (Figure 3, Item A8). The HSES parents were more confident that they would be able to answer them (Table A31) and, although more than half of them sometimes find them a nuisance, they were less likely than the LSES parents to do so (Table A32).

Although in some cases it was the sheer number of questions which parents found a nuisance, in many cases comments showed that it was the *nature* of the questions, or their unfortunate timing which made them a nuisance.

> "What do you do when she asks you how Tracy's mummy's baby got in her tummy, right in the middle of the Post Office queue?" (L)

> "They ask things like: 'Why has that old man got a big spot on his face?', or 'Is that lady a witch?' in loud voices. You never know where to look." (L)

> "When she asks where babies come from I don't know what to say. My mother never told *me* that—I found it out myself in the end—so I don't know what I should tell her. I don't believe in that gooseberry bush stuff so I just say 'I'll tell you when you're older'. I suppose I'll have to tell her something soon—she keeps on about it." (L)

These sentiments were echoed many times by parents in the LSES areas but rarely by HSES parents who seemed to be less embarrassed by the questions, and also more at ease when answering in public situations.

> "They always choose the busiest shops, or the most crowded buses to ask the most personal questions or make embarrassing comments about people. I must admit it bothered me at first but now with three of them I've become immune. I just answer as if nobody else is there and ignore all the stares." (H)

Possibly this is because HSES parents have more confidence in their ability to answer questions correctly. Many said they had read books and articles on such subjects as telling their children where babies came from and would therefore feel more confident about telling the child about these things, knowing that other people shared the same opinions as they did. HSES parents also seemed more likely to have discussed this subject with friends and neighbours and on the whole to have a more relaxed attitude to subjects which were often "forbidden" topics of conversation for LSES parents.

Informants were also asked what they would be most likely to do if they didn't know the answer to a question the child asked.

26% of LSES parents (and none of the HSES parents) said they would make up an answer (Table A32). The most likely explanation of this difference is that LSES parents are less likely to know the answer, and the EHVs, by encouraging question-asking, may be adding to the parents' embarrassment on this score. Another explanation is that they felt that their authority would be undermined if they said that they did not know the answer—and we have seen how very important it is to many LSES parents to retain respect and authority in the eyes of their children.

However, the benefits of making up answers may be short-lived. The children may be even more disrespectful of their parents when they come to realise that they have simply tried to fool them. The message that is conveyed may be that it is acceptable to say (or do) anything which will get one out of a tight spot. It may frustrate the development of an enquiring mind in the youngster—and thereby lead to an inability to develop high levels of moral reasoning and internalised controls of behaviour. It may lead the child to rely on, and respect, his teachers more than his parents—and Fend (personal communication) has shown that one of the qualities which insulates HSES children from adverse comments at school is that they rely on their *parents'* evaluation of them when it conflicts with that of their teachers, whereas LSES children rely on their teachers' evaluations, despite the fact that these are more often negative.

8% of LSES parents and 2% of HSES parents would "put their child off". 27% of LSES parents and 57% of HSES parents would look up the answer in a book with the child, a result which could be interpreted to mean that the LSES parents had not come to use books as a source of information, but which may also reflect the absence of books or, as we have already seen, the desire to protect the child from the works of the devil which books contain.

39% of LSES parents and 40% of HSES parents would "tell him to ask someone else (eg his father)." Although this was sometimes used by busy mothers to let themselves "off the hook", often it was for better reasons.

> "If he asks anything about electricity, or how things work, I usually send him to his father. After all he's the expert." (H, Engineer's wife).

> "His father's the one to go to with questions about football. I know nothing and I tell him that." (L)

From these data it would seem that there may be a case for saying that it is important for EHVs to try to help parents to appreciate the possible consequences of making up answers to their children's questions. If the children are "bamboozled" in this way, if their attempts to think and reason are thwarted, if children recognise their parents' disinterest in accurate knowledge and come to recognise the contempt they have for their children's intelligence which is implicit in giving any old answers, they are unlikely to develop respect for their parents or respect for knowledge, let alone gain an appreciation of the efficacy of cognitive activiy.

Incidental Conversations

We have already seen that the way in which HSES and LSES parents and their children interact are very different. Table A37 shows what parents said they talked about to their children whilst engaged in some joint educational activity—such as doing jigsaws with their children or making things in the kitchen.

The most common type of dialogue between LSES mothers and their children takes the form of warnings and instructions from the mother to the child:

"Get lost!" (L)

"Telling him to hurry up—and what was coming on T.V. next." (L)

"What do you think you're doing? You're giving mum more work." (L)

"To put legs and eyes on the people he was drawing. To be careful—to watch things in the kitchen: the stove, the knife . . . . Showing him how to do things correctly." (L)

"Telling them to get out and stop trying to help. Asking them to tidy up their room." (L)

"Mainly giving her a row for doing things she's not allowed." (L)

"Not to get herself soaking. Not to break the dishes." (L)

"What to do next. What to do and what not to do." (L)

"To make less noise." (L)

While HSES mothers also issued warnings and instructions, these came in fourth place behind other sorts of conversation. By far the most common for them was discussion of the activities which were being undertaken.

"Talking about weighing out flour, putting in water, mixing and stirring. Dusting, cleaning, scrubbing, polishing." (H)

The second most common topic for HSES parents and children was the discussion of past and future events, followed by the mother praising and encouraging the child.

Both groups of mothers were equally likely to question the child about what he was doing but no HSES parent mentioned that the child questioned her, while 9% of LSES parents did so. This could possibly indicate that HSES mothers volunteer more information without having to be asked.

The mother teaching or explaining things to the child was not very common.

LSES mothers were more likely than HSES mothers to say they did not talk at all because mother was too busy or working elsewhere in the house:

"Nothing. It's the only time I get any peace. I let him do it himself." (L) (Child drawing)

The HSES were much more open and responsive, and demanded more independence, initiative and responsibility from the child:

"I asked her how she was going to begin; she told me, and then she got on and did it." (H)

Bernstein (1971), Tough (1973), Hess and Shipman (1965), and others have also drawn attention to such differences in the quality of the language in the homes of pupils who come from different backgrounds.

At the very least, these two patterns of interaction would be expected to lead the children to develop different expectations of, and attitudes towards, the use of language. The LSES pattern of interaction seems likely to lead the child to expect that, if someone speaks to him in the context of such activities, it will be to issue specific directions, commands and warnings—and he may well come to depend on such close supervision if he is to undertake such tasks. That the child should be dependent on his mother in this way is, of course, just what the mother intended. An alternative explanation of the difference is, however, that the LSES parents' behaviour is dependent on the fact that their children are, in general, less likely to be able to carry out such tasks satisfactorily without constant supervision and direction.

Before we obtained the data from the Home Visited sample, we noted that encouraging parents to talk to their children might result only in an increase in such specific, directive behaviour—and this is indeed just what we observed. There is therefore a clear case for encouraging the EHVs to consider more carefully the *type* of language interaction they encourage.

The case for doing this becomes stronger the more one reflects on the implications of the differences between the two groups. The biggest differences are in connection with the amount of discussion of activity with the child and conversations about what is happening, has happened, or will happen.

Conversations about what is happening, in addition to conveying knowledge, may give the child a great deal of insight into cognitive processes in action. The parent may share with the child her understanding of what is going on, her tendency to try to understand cause and effect, her tendency to think about what is likely to happen, her plans and her initiatives designed to take corrective action to achieve her goals, her tendency to monitor what happens and intervene appropriately if necessary, her rejection, or modification of, certain strategies if it becomes clear that they are going to encounter obstacles, and her feelings about the activity itself and the goals she hopes to achieve. In short, she may model for the child the components of competence and the springs of motivation in action. She imagines, she dredges in her mind for relevant past experiences and she anticipates the future. Her feelings, the past and the future, her plans and her knowledge are finely balanced determinants of present activity, and not separated from it. The whole process is most *un*like the formal separation of academic activity from action which is so clearly apparent in schools and in the thinking of many LSES parents. And all this is done in the context of encouraging the child to join in in his own way. How best should the EHVs model for parents this entire, integrated and finely balanced pattern of activity?

One should, however, be wary of generalising too far on the basis of our data. Our questions asked LSES parents what they talked about in the course of activities which they did not, in all honesty, believe to be of the greatest importance (although, they *are* the activities which the EHVs try to encourage them to undertake with their children). As we have seen, they were more likely to think it was important for them to ensure that their children were *dependent* on them and to learn to stick up for themselves. As we have commented, their behaviour seems ideally suited to the achievement of the first of these goals. And we have also seen that at least some LSES parents do go to some considerable lengths to *show* their children how to fight—and it may well be that, had we asked what they talked about whilst they were doing that, we would have found that they discussed cause and effect, the past and the future, the goals of life and the sort of person who was worthy of admiration. Likewise, had we asked them what they talked about whilst engaged in rough and tumble we might well have found that they talked about the pleasures of social contact, the importance of closeness and dependence, the importance of affiliation and how it could be promoted. We might have found them recalling past experiences and anticipating the future. In other words, as the author has argued more fully elsewhere (Raven 1977) it may be absurd to assess attitudes and behaviour except in relation to valued goals.

How much time did parent and child spend on selected activities on the previous day?

In order to assess the impact of the EHV programme on other aspects of parents' behaviour as well as on their thoughts and feelings, they were asked how much time they, or their children, spent on selected activities on the day prior to the interview. People do not always do what they think it is important to do, or what they would like to do. Parents may attach importance to activities which they rarely have the time, money or opportunity to carry out. And, for a variety of reasons, they may also do things which they do not consider to be very important. These reasons may include pressure from their children or from other people.

In accordance with normal survey practice, parents were asked about the previous day in order to minimise memory and other effects. The results are presented in Tables 4 and A39.

Table 4 shows the ten activities for each group, which were engaged in by most parents and/or children.

Most activities—playing with small toys, answering the child's questions, watching television, playing on his own, teaching names of colours, objects etc, looking at books, helping mother with housework, and teaching child to read or count (most parents said that it was counting, not reading, which they actually taught)—appear in all three lists, indicating that there are no *great* differences in the frequency of these activities between groups. Smaller differences do occur, however. More HSES parents answered their child's questions, looked at books with him, taught the names of colours, objects etc and taught him to count. (We can exclude reading for the present as the majority of parents said they did not teach this on the previous day). More HSES children played with small toys, played on their own, and helped mother with her work.

Almost all HSES parents spent time talking to their children about what they had done in the past and would do in the future (97%, compared to only 54% of LSES parents). 82% of HSES children spent time drawing and painting—in fact they spent as much time doing this as watching television and "helping" mother with the housework—whereas 62% of LSES children drew or painted on that particular day.

TABLE 4

ITEMS MOST OFTEN ENGAGED IN ON THE DAY PRIOR
TO THE INTERVIEW

Table shows % who spent some time at this activity

	E.H.V. Group	%	L.S.E.S. Group	%	H.S.E.S. Group	%
1	Answering his questions	100	Child playing with small toys	94	Answering his questions	100
2	Child playing on his own	95	Answering his questions	92	Child playing with small toys	98
3	Child playing with small toys	90	Child watching television	88	Looking at books with him	97
4	Child playing outside with his friends	76	Child playing on his own	83	Talking with child about things done in past, will do in future	97
5	Going to nursery or playgroup	76	Parent/child engaging in rough-and-tumble	79	Child playing on his own	95
6	Parent/child engaging in rough-and-tumble	76	Teaching him names of colours/objects	75	Teaching him names of colours/objects	87
7	Looking at books with him	72	Looking at books with him	70	Child watching television	82
8	Child helping with housework	67	Talking about what he has seen on television	69	Child drawing or painting	82
9	Child watching television	66	Child helping with housework	66	Child helping with housework	82
10	Talking with child about things done in past, will do in future	62	Teaching him to read or count	64	Teaching him to read or count	80

Discussion

Talking about things that have been done in the past or will be done in the future is engaged in more often by HSES parents than LSES parents, and HSES children are likely to spend more time drawing and painting, and do it more often than LSES children *in the home.* Other differences, though not so large, occur between groups in items of the type said by educationalists to promote cognitive development in children. HSES children are more likely to spend time playing with bricks and Lego with a parent, being encouraged to notice how things work, being taught the meanings of words, such as "on", "under", "over", and "behind", playing with jigsaws, sand and water, and cutting out pictures and shapes. They are also more likely to look at books with their parents, and for longer, than LSES children.

This consistent and cumulative press toward intellectual activity and on parent and child working together in the HSES group is striking—and very much in line with the "importance" ratings we looked at earlier. Also noticeable is the infrequency with which our HSES parents engaged in a number of activities which some educationalists believe to be of central importance from the point of view of fostering cognitive development, and this, too, is in line with our observation that they tend to adopt a relatively *indirect* means of promoting development. However, the fact that they did not take place *yesterday* does not mean either that they *never* took place, or even that they took place too infrequently to stimulate the desired growth. What it does mean is that adult educators should beware of going overboard in their desire to increase the frequency of such activities. The data also suggest that it is important for more people to discuss the role which such activities may play in promoting the growth and development of children.

LSES children are more likely than HSES children to engage in rough-and-tumble with their parents, and watch television. They are also more likely to play outside with their friends, be taken shopping (although *less time* is actually spent on this, possibly due to proximity of shops in LSES areas), and be taken to visit friends or relatives. This supports our conclusion that family and friends tend to be very important to the LSES parents as does the development of the ability to stick up for oneself, which, as we have seen, LSES parents see as a consequence of playing outside and a benefit of rough-and-tumble play.

The main conclusion to be drawn from these data is, therefore, that apart from the EHV group, there are no serious discrepancies between parents' behaviour tendencies and their values and perceptions. This suggests that our reflections on the possible consequences of differences in emphasis in child rearing deserve to be taken seriously. And, in the context of these data, it would seem more urgent to ask why there is a discrepancy between professed ideals and behaviour in the case of the EHV group, what the implications of that explanation may be for Home Visiting, and what can be done either to reduce the discrepancy or to handle the problems to which it may give rise.

CHAPTER 29

PARENTS' ATTITUDES TOWARD
FORMAL EDUCATION

The objective of the Lothian Educational Home Visiting Scheme was to "encourage parents to play a more active role in promoting the educational development of their children". One interpretation of that phrase, frequently repeated by the project's co-ordinator (Leslie Thomson) was that parents should be more involved in their children's schooling. This was explicitly interpreted to mean that the EHVs should encourage parents to bring pressure to bear on schools to gain more control over what went on. How do parents perceive their role vis-à-vis the school system? How important do they think it is for their children to do well at school? What do they think the consequences would be if they did not do well at school? How do those parents who think it is important for their children to do well at school expect to help them to do so?

Importance of Child doing well at School

Figure 3, Item B10, showed that only about one quarter of parents thought it was very important for their children to do well at school—compared with much higher proportions who thought other things were very important. In this context, the fact that about three-quarters of the parents do not think it is *very* important for their children to do well at school is significant. It suggests that some children may not get a great deal of encouragement at home, and it may indicate that those who control our school system should consider how best to cater for a sizeable minority of pupils who cannot be expected to share the dominant ethos. Such pupils may not only find themselves in conflict with the schools' values, they may force teachers to establish classroom procedures which disrupt the growth of other children.

Table A44 shows that, although only about a third of parents think it is very important for their child to do "well" at school (perhaps because of the competitive overtones in the word "well"), 70% of HSES mothers and just over 53% of LSES mothers think it is very important for primary school children to learn the things they are taught, even if they don't pass the examinations. The content of primary education is, therefore, generally thought to be more important than the content of secondary education (Raven *et al,* 1975a, 1975b), but even then, half the LSES parents do not think it is very important.

We may turn now to the reasons which people give for thinking it is important for their child to do *well* at school. This question was finally approached by asking parents what they thought would happen if their child did *not* do well at school. The results are presented in Table A45.

The most frequently anticipated consequence of failure to do well at school is failure to get a good job. About a third of the parents think that failure at school will lead to problem behaviour. That there is a connection between school failure and problem behaviour is, of course, well supported in the literature, although it is not clear which is cause and which is effect. It would seem to follow from our data that many—but still a minority—of parents are motivated to do what they can to ensure that their child does well at school in order to avoid this fate. Although a number of parents in both groups anticipate that "his intelligence would fail to develop fully", and that "he'd get bored", a slight majority of HSES parents expect these things to happen. They are also more likely to expect the child to feel rejected. Less than a quarter of the parents feel that the child will not learn to fend for himself or that his language will fail to develop (cf Bullock, 1975).

It would seem from these data as a whole that, for both groups of parents, success at school is thought to be a pre-requisite to getting a good job. It has less to do with the growth of competence: for a small majority of the HSES group, and a minority of the LSES group, it has something to do with promoting the development of intelligence, but neither group usually sees it as promoting the development of language or the ability to fend for oneself. As far as these data go—which is not very far—schooling is about getting jobs, and only very secondarily about growth. The data support the view—though they obviously do not prove it—that what many people are buying when they vote for schooling is a ticket to a job, not a programme of personal development. If true, the implications are serious for, at the every least, they indicate that many parents can be expected to place little value on schooling if it becomes clear to them that *their* children are not going to be able to use the school system in order to get jobs. The same applies to the pupils themselves. Similarly, if schooling is about getting jobs, many pupils and their parents can be expected to resist growth activities if these either detract from their chances of getting the certificates needed to get jobs *or* seem to offer some children a greater advantage than others in the scramble for jobs. Getting jobs is the name of the game, and anything else is, at best, icing on the cake, and, at worst, a positive handicap in the race.

As Bernstein (1975) has pointed out, the interaction between attitudes to the instrumental functions of schooling and beliefs about the growth-enhancing functions of educational institutions produce a number of very different patterns of attitudes, perceptions and expectations. These are of great significance from the point of view of understanding the operation of the Lothian Region Educational Home Visiting Scheme.

Parents (or pupils) may accept or reject the instrumental (or occupational placement) goals of education and, independently, the goals of education which lie in the area of fostering motivational dispositions, attitudes, perceptions and expectations. The present author refers to the latter as *competencies;* Bernstein refers to them as "expressive goals of schools"—a term which, like the label "affective goals", both belittles them and detaches them from the development of cognitive capacities and the growth of competence (which involves both cognitive and affective activities).

Be that as it may, parents may accept or reject either or both the instrumental and competence-promoting goals of schools. And schools and teachers vary from one to another in the emphasis they place on achieving these two sets of goals.

But not only is there variation between parents, pupils and teachers in their emphasis on these goals, there is also variation in their understanding of the means to be used to achieve them (although, as we have seen, this variation in understanding appears to be less than might have been suspected).

Then there is a third set of variables—the parents', pupils' and teachers' acceptance of the *particular* means which a specific school or practitioner proposes to use to reach the goals. Thus, one may think it is important for children to develop initiative, understand that it is proposed to foster it by Outward Bound programmes, but still not believe that this is the best way to foster it.

Bernstein uses this framework to distinguish five types of pupil involvement—or uninvolvement—in school activities. Our concern is with parents.

Those parents who do not think that the instrumental functions of schooling are particularly important, but who value the growth of competencies—like intelligence, initiative and self-confidence—cell

B in the accompanying diagram, (which represents a sub-set of Bernstein's categories)—would be expected to respond very positively to Home Visiting programmes, and school curricula, which stress the growth of general competence rather than the abilities required to gain instrumental benefits of schooling (examination certificates) with the

ATTITUDES TO THE INSTRUMENTAL
FUNCTIONS OF SCHOOLS

minimum effort. Those parents who value schooling primarily because of the role it plays in developing the qualities required to get a good job, but who also value the growth of competence (a sub-group of parents falling into cell A, and which we may label cell A1), can be expected to be highly ambivalent and even to appear two-faced. They would be expected to welcome the Home Visiting Programmes but to oscillate in their focus. Those parents who value the instrumental benefits of schooling, believe that educational institutions do indeed promote the growth of competence, and value the growth of competence (a second sub-group of parents falling into cell A, which we may this time label cell A2), would be expected to be most receptive to those Home Visitors who adopt a "facilitative" rather than a "teacherish" style. And those parents who neither value the instrumental benefits of schooling nor the growth of competence (cell D) would be least likely to respond to any type of Home Visiting programme. The majority of parents involved in the present Home Visiting Scheme would appear to fall into cells A1 and D.

The minority of parents for whom schooling is *both* about growth *and* about getting jobs (Table A45) (cell A2) are likely to press for rather different forms of curriculum to those found in most schools. They (and their children) are likely to be outraged by those who seek to "beat the system" for their own advantage by satisfying assessment criteria without developing the competencies to which those assessments are deemed to testify. In pressing schools to broaden their curricula to perform *educational,* as distinct from social and instrumental, activities, such parents are likely to find themselves at odds with many other parents. This disagreement may be so great that if they are to be encouraged to experiment with new *educational* practices, they may need to be provided with opportunities to do so unimpeded by those who have a more narrowly utilitarian or instrumental view of the educational system.

Parents' Evaluation of their own Education

Whether parents encourage their children to work hard at school is obviously liable to be influenced by their feelings about their own education.

Whereas 58% of HSES parents say that their own education was of value to them in helping them to get a good job, only 18% of LSES parents do so, and a similarly small number say that it helped them to do that job well. Very few parents from either group feel that their education was of value to them in living their day to day lives more effectively—whether that meant running a home, enjoying their leisure, personal development, or contributing to society (Table A47).

In the eyes of most of our respondents, therefore, education is mainly about getting a good job. For the LSES group, their own education is thought neither to have been very good at getting them good jobs nor beneficial from the point of view of helping them to do their jobs well. Small wonder that such parents don't always seem to encourage their children to slave over their school work.

If the Educational Home Visitors are to find ways of encouraging parents to continue to encourage their children in circumstances in which it seems that more education is *not* going to lead to a good job, it would seem that their *first* task may well be to enlist the support of parents to ensure that the educational programmes offered by schools do in fact help children to develop the general competencies which most parents think it is so important for their children to develop—and which *would* be of value to them in the home, in their leisure activities, and in the wider community.

The Parents' Role in Formal Education

Parents were asked what part they thought a parent should play in a primary school child's education. Since, when answering this question, parents often suggested making contact with the school, they were also asked whether they thought the teachers they would deal with would be responsive and welcoming. In addition they were asked an open and a closed question about how they would help their children to do better at school.

Our data show that almost all parents think that a parent of a primary school child ought to see that he does his homework (Table A47). 95% of HSES parents, and 71% of LSES parents say that a parent should complain about anything with which they are not satisfied. Similar proportions say that a parent should find out exactly what happens in the school and insist that the child does his best. A majority of both groups (about three-quarters of the HSES and just over half of the LSES) also think it is important to talk about school as much as possible and to make sure that the teacher stretches the child to the full. Rather fewer think that a parent should visit the school regularly. Just under half of the LSES group say it is important to leave education to the school *and* that a parent should teach a child things *before* he learns them at school. It is not clear how these two statements are to be reconciled, but it may be that what they are saying is that parents should give children a head-start *in the early stages* by teaching children things *before* they learn them at school but, *once the child is at school,* leave education to the school. This ambiguity may be important to the EHVs for the notion that LSES parents think—as Morton-Williams (1966) also found—that education should be left to the school, may strike them as dysfunctional while their own activities are sometimes capable of being construed by parents as supporting the view that the way to help children is "to give them a head-start by teaching them things *before* they learn them at school", and then all will be well without much further attention from them.

As will be clear, many of the activities which parents think that a parent of a primary school child *should* do involve making contact with the school. How effective and welcome do they think that such actions would be?

We have already seen (Table 2, p 150) that only 8% of LSES parents and 13% of HSES parents are very satisfied with the extent to which teachers take their views seriously. Table A48 shows that about a third of the parents are confident that *if,* when their child started school, they went to see his teacher about something with which they were not satisfied, she would respond. Since it is well established that LSES parents are less likely to go to see their teachers (Morton-Williams, 1966) it is clear that the anticipated response is not what deters parents from going to see teachers, but rather their feeling of inadequacy and the contempt in which they believe their views are held.

Again, about half the parents feel they would be made welcome *if* they asked to spend time in the school (Table A49). However, only between 5% and 10% of parents are very confident that, if they tried to persuade their child's teacher to change her general approach, she would respond (Table A48). A further third are "fairly confident". The LSES parents are actually more confident than the HSES, and the EHV group are the most confident of all. Most parents feel that it is "not their place" to interfere with the teacher in this way and say they would only do so if they thought it was really necessary. The results of this question are based on hypothetical situations; the majority of mothers said they had never even considered doing such a thing: "She'd think I'd a right cheek if I just walked in and told her how to run her class." (L)

When they were asked an open-ended question about how, if at all, they expected to help their own child to do well at school when he was older, only 8% of our parents said that they did not expect to help in any way (Table A50). 60% of those in HSES areas, and 51% in LSES areas, said that they intended to help with homework and any other school-work in which the child was involved within the home. Next in popularity with both groups was showing interest and providing general encouragement. Parents said they would listen to the child, answer his questions, talk about school, and try to become involved in what he was doing.

A small number in both groups said they would keep in touch with the school and the child's teacher, although the number was higher in the HSES group. The latter were more inclined to mean that they had established or intended to establish a relationship with their child's teacher which involved regular informal meetings and discussion of the child's progress, whereas the LSES parents attended, or expected to attend, the annual parents' meetings faithfully. Few of the LSES parents with older children had successfully established a comfortable relationship with their children's teachers. Many said that they came away.disappointed from meetings as they had not really found out what they wanted to know and had difficulty communicating with the teacher. Although this was by no means always the case, this was mentioned sufficiently often to merit attention. Clearly there is room for the EHVs to explore ways of involving parents in education, particularly in LSES areas (although the problem was by no means confined to them). One other comment may also be made. It is clear from the interviews that few parents want to "take over and run the place" in the way that many teachers anticipate (Raven et al, 1975).

Helping with Homework

We have seen that the most commonly suggested way of helping the child to do better at school was to help him with his homework. Table A52 shows that the HSES group were more likely than the LSES group to feel that they were well equipped to help their children with their homework. Previous research (Raven, 1975) shows that LSES children were much more likely than HSES children to say that they would like facilities for, and help with, their homework at school. Perhaps the EHVs might consider trying to bring such support into being.

Discussion

While there are again indications that the HSES group is more facilitative of development and less pressurising (they are more likely to speak about providing reference books for their children and a quiet place in which to study and less likely to support crude pressurising techniques like telling their children that others will leave them behind), it is clear that the main method which was more likely to be used by the HSES group is that of making contact with the school and teachers. If the EHVs are able to lead the parents they visit to feel less guilty about, and more comfortable with, this type of contact they may well have a significant impact on the subsequent development of the parents' children. And, as Table A47 shows, that is exactly the effect they do have (although, as anticipated, they also lead the parents to be still more likely to endorse the "Headstart" philosophy).

But one wonders if they might not also adopt other strategies. Although they do not mention it, it is probable that the HSES parents make use of the fee-paying school system to move their children into classrooms in which high standards of academic performance are the rule. As Coleman (1961) has shown*, such climates markedly

* See also Rutter (1979)

influence the way in which able children will exert themselves, and Nash (1973) has demonstrated a frame of reference effect by which children move themselves up or down to put themselves back where they belong relative to other pupils. The interesting thing is that they put themselves in the same *position* in "able" and "less able" classes.

Other possible means of influencing academic achievement motivation have been outlined in Raven (1977). They include the possibility of exposing children to real or imaginary role models who value academic achievement and in which such activity brings rewards the children desire. They also include the possibility of encouraging children to enjoy the delights which can come from such activity. Once more the EHVs may care to review such possibilities more systematically and consider whether to share such insights with parents.

PARENTS' FELT NEED TO UNDERSTAND EDUCATIONAL METHODS AND HOW TO PROMOTE THE EDUCATIONAL DEVELOPMENT OF THEIR CHILDREN

If parents are to help their children as they would like it is clear that they need to understand the *methods* which are used by teachers. Tables A53 and A54 show that there is a widespread feeling among parents that they do *not* understand them and *would* like to know more. The EHVs have clearly a major role in this area.

Parents' Felt Need for Advice

Table A55 indicates the felt need for advice on various aspects of child rearing and day to day living. It is striking that nearly everyone wants advice on how to find out more about schools and how to help their children, and that more than half the LSES parents want advice on *all* topics. It is also striking that so many parents, particularly HSES parents, want advice on how to *influence* schools.

1. *How to find out more about what schools are doing*

83% of LSES parents and 75% of HSES parents say they would welcome advice on this. Competence-focussed activities designed to help parents develop the abilities required to *find out* about what schools are doing might be more useful than those which actually *told* them what they were doing, as this would lead them on to find out about other things that they wanted to know. Although the EHVs have had a marked impact on this, the fact that more than half still feel in need of advice on this point means that still more needs to be done.

2. *How to help your child to do well at school*

As Table A55 shows, there is a strong felt need for this sort of advice. This is also supported by pilot data, and also by answers to the question: In what ways, if at all, do you expect to help your child to do well at school when he's older? Many parents, especially in LSES areas, were only aware of a limited number of ways of helping their children, while others were under the impression that: "There's nothing much I can do. I don't understand the ways of teaching nowadays" (L). While the EHVs have again had a dramatic effect in leading parents to feel more confident about this, there is still no room for complacency.

3. *How to help your child to grow up to be the sort of person you'd like him to be*

The need for this sort of advice is felt far more strongly by LSES parents than by HSES parents who, as we have seen, have more confidence in their ability to influence their own destinies and those of their children.

4. *How to develop the abilities you need to handle your problems more effectively.*

The fact that 52% of LSES parents and only 33% of HSES parents felt a need for advice on this once more suggests that LSES parents have more problems and difficulties, or lack the ability to tackle them, or both. It is obvious from both this item and the last that LSES parents have less confidence in their ability to cope with their difficulties and gain control of their lives and their destinies. It is very interesting to note that, whereas the data we presented earlier suggested that the major problems which the LSES group have to confront have to do with their relationships with authorities, these data demonstrate that they have major problems with their own families. While it has already been suggested that these problems may be attributable to the environment in which they live, it may also be that they *are* a product of personal incompetence. Given that their problems are clearly both personal and environmental one possible avenue which the EHVs might pursue would be to help the parents they visit to grow in *general* confidence and competence (not areas of knowledge) and that this might be done *either* through pre-school work *or* through community work. Whatever was done in one area would be expected to have implications for the other.

5. *How to influence what schools do*

This is the only area in which HSES parents feel more need of advice than LSES parents. The result is supported by similar findings in the pilot study.

From talking to LSES parents in all stages of the study it is obvious that many of them think it inconceivable that they should have any influence in their child's school. This is not so true of HSES parents, many of whom did have some influence and wanted more, and many of whom had little influence but wanted some. Some typical comments from LSES parents were:

> "I'd just make a fool of myself, standing up in these meetings." (L)

> "If them that are trained for it can't do it properly, what chance have we got?" (L)

The EHVs could provide opportunities for parents to develop public-speaking skills, and the skills required to get authorities to do what one wants. They could try to increase the self-confidence of the parents involved and bring them to feel that they had something useful to say and a right to be listened to. They could help them to see that a three-year teacher training course does not really set teachers apart from ordinary mortals.

6. *How to amuse your child and keep him out of mischief*

Although the least urgent of the six items, 40% of LSES parents and 45% of HSES parents say they would welcome advice on how to do this. All mothers know that ideas soon become stale and that children become bored easily. As we have seen, the EHV programme has been welcomed by many mothers for no other reason than because it introduced them to new ways in which to amuse their children and keep them out of mischief.

THE PARENTS' ROLE IN EDUCATIONAL DECISION MAKING

Table A56 shows that, on the whole, LSES parents are more satisfied that the right people decide what goes on in schools than are HSES parents. It will be recalled that HSES parents were more likely to want to learn how to influence schools. This supports our tentative conclusion that schools' actions are more closely in line with LSES than HSES values.

Who Should Have More Say?

The majority of the parents we interviewed in HSES areas would like parents to have more say in education (Table A57). However, there are those who disagree with parents having any say, possibly fearing that those more articulate and outspoken than themselves will take over:

> "Parents would make it worse. They'd be fighting between themselves. One would say one thing and the next would say something quite different." (L)

> "Parents aren't qualified." (L)

A number of parents think that class teachers should have more say in deciding what goes on in schools.

Giving parents more power in education would therefore mean displeasing a minority of parents albeit a very small one. However, as we have seen, while the majority of parents approve of this in principle, the data we presented earlier on the variance in parents' priorities make one suspect that those parents who felt that it would be impossible to get consensus may well be right.

Discussion

These data in general support the other evidence which suggests that parents, particularly in HSES areas, *want* more say in their children's education than they have at present. The EHVs may care to consider whether they agree with the parents' views and, if so, how they might help them to translate their feelings into practice. When considering this question it may be particularly important for them to reflect on how the fears of those who said that giving parents more say would give an advantage to the more articulate and the more powerful are to be handled. Indeed, it would seem that their *primary* task is to find a way of reconciling this felt need for more influence over what is going on in schools with the fact, documented in Chapter 16, that different parents want their children to develop very different, indeed incompatible, qualities and the widely shared belief that teachers should not treat different children in different ways (Chapter 22). One of their central tasks may, therefore, be to influence parents' civic attitudes and expectations, parents' knowledge of the variance in the qualities other parents want their children to develop, parents' respect for the legitimacy of such alternative viewpoints, parents' understanding of the varieties of competence possessed by children and needed by society, parents' understanding of the ways in which these competencies are to be fostered, and parents' understanding of educational practices and procedures which would make it possible to foster different qualities in different children in accord with the variety of parents' wishes and the abilities, aspirations and interests of their children.

CHAPTER 30

A TAILPIECE TO PART IV

In this chapter we will briefly discuss one further topic on which the data reported in Part IV has led us to reflect.

Inventiveness, Inquisitiveness, Adventurousness, and Need Achievement

While, as we have seen, the HSES mothers were much more likely than LSES mothers to teach even such things as respect and responsibility by example and by providing children with an opportunity to evolve and practice the desired behaviour, we were struck by the apparent failure of even the HSES group to seek to teach what may be some of the most important qualities for the future of our civilisation—inventiveness, inquisitiveness, and adventurousness—in these ways.

(1) *Inventiveness*

No parent—even from the HSES group—said that children could be encouraged by example to be inventive—whether that example took the shape of a parent, a friend, or a character in a story. This is surprising since McClelland (1961) and MacKinnon (1962) have shown that one of the most important factors in the backgrounds of inventive and creative people is exposure to just such role models. Nor did any parent mention the possibility that children might be exposed to people—or read stories—in which inventive, creative, activity paid off and brought satisfaction, enabled people to reach their objectives or to contribute to society, or gain extrinsic rewards such as the esteem of others or financial benefits. The fact that none of even the HSES parents mentioned such possibilities—although they *did* mention them in relation to other qualities—may well be in part responsible for the plight in which Britain currently finds itself.

Nor did any parent mention the possibility of fostering the *components* of inventiveness—imagination, persistence, sensitivity, preparation and incubation—or the need to link inventiveness to follow-through activity to ensure that its benefits were reaped.

Also possibly significant is the infrequency with which even HSES parents mentioned supporting children's normal play. In play, many children are extremely inventive at finding ways of doing things and using things for new purposes. Creating opportunities for such play— and, in particular, creating situations in which children can practise being inventive in the course of reaching goals which they particularly care about—may be another way in which inventiveness could be elicited and reinforced. Play may be the ideal situation in which children can be optimally motivated to engage in such activities in relation to goals they care about. As a large number of researchers (summarised in Rogers, 1962) have shown, a high level of extrinsic pressure stifles inventiveness. Many teachers at secondary school level would give the world to be able to create such an optimally motivated, individualised, competency-oriented educational programme to foster this very quality. It would be a pity if parents were not encouraged to capitalise upon it.

(2) *Inquisitiveness*

Inquisitiveness seems to be thought of as purely questioning and getting into things; it does not seem to be thought of as a basis on which to build the development of a scientific understanding. It is not seen as a basis on which to build a systematic enquiring mind. Nor is it linked to the growth of intelligence.

It is clear that the LSES parents will be fairly receptive to the idea of fostering *verbal* inquisitiveness, but the message that inquisitiveness involves more than verbal activity and that it is to be fostered by structuring an environment which is conducive to, or at least non-stunting of, growth would seem to be less welcome. Most parents do not seem to be sufficiently concerned about the development of this aspect of their children's competence to re-arrange their houses and life-style in such a way as to allow children to exercise this type of ability. If we are satisfied that non-book oriented inquisitiveness is indeed an important quality for children to develop, and if we are satisfied that it is to be promoted, as White (1973, 1976) and some of the parents we have interviewed would suggest, by creating an environment in which it can be practiced, the data suggest that there is an important information gap.

(3) *Adventurousness*

Adventurousness, it seems, is yet another quality which is not highly prized in our soceity (only 15% of HSES parents and 7% of LSES parents thought that this was very important). Even if it is valued, it is to be fostered by the not-very-sophisticated procedure of throwing the child in at the deep end and *allowing* the child to adventure (79% of HSES parents who thought this quality was important and 25% of the LSES parents who thought this gave this answer). Its development is to be *facilitated* rather than stimulated. There is little evidence of parents possessing a cognitively complex understanding of the qualities which are required to adventure successfully. These might include the recognition that "planning" as conventionally conceived is altogether too constricted a concept. By definition an adventure involves not knowing where one is going or how one is going to get there. The successful adventurer relies on his ability to sense what is going to lead somewhere, his ability to continuously adapt his behaviour depending on whether his route seems to be moving him forward in a productive manner, and his ability to retreat and try another route at an appropriate time. He has to be able to recognise, and *re-define* "success" as appropriate and to take steps to *ensure* that his actions *are* successful in one respect or another. He has to acquire the ability to be an astute student of his environment and confidence in what his feelings tell him.

One of the problems which our society faces may be that altogether too few people have an adequate intuitive grasp of what is involved in adventuring, with the result that we surround the potential scientific or business adventurer with a set of constraints which are altogether too restricting. As a society, we may be behaving like LSES mothers. Because we have not created opportunities for our fellow citizens to show how competent they are, we may not trust them. Because we have failed to give them an opportunity to develop internalised controls over their behaviour, they may not be very good at knowing when things are going wrong and knowing when to set corrective action in motion. As a result we, like LSES mothers, may keep checking up on them and telling them that we know better than they do what they should be doing, and what is going to yield significant benefits—so that they never develop the sensitivity needed to decide for themselves what they should be doing.

The Other Components of Competence

The *ability* to adventure into the unknown is, of course, only part of a wider set of components of competence. If it is true, as the author has argued elsewhere (Raven, 1977), that these components of competence—like the sensitivity to minor cues which form the basis of new insights and the ability to adventure—can only be fostered in relation to the goals people care about, then it becomes important for educators—whether parents or teachers—to be able to recognise and encourage the special interests of children.

If children are not encouraged to pursue their special interests it is unlikely that they will be able to practise doing such things as concentrating, persisting, inventing, finding or inventing the specific information they need, gaining the co-operation of others to achieve their goals, observing and thinking for themselves, studying cause and effect, examining relationships and educing correlates, or learning without instruction. If they do not practise these competencies in relation to goals they care about they are unlikely to develop them. Yet only 5% of HSES mothers and 1% of LSES mothers said it was very important for their children to develop interests and tastes which were different from those of other people, and only 15% and 3% respectively said that it was very important to them to have a school system which could meet their own personal wishes if these differed from those of other people. It may be that another question on the importance of discovering and finding children's particular interests would have produced more enthusiasm, but the data we do have do not lead us to suspect that the support for doing so would be very strong.

If, then, the EHVs are to be effective they may need to help parents to accept that it might be desirable to help children to develop special interests and to study, think about, and reinforce their children's interests, and to help them to think about, and reinforce, these competencies in relation to those interests. In doing this they would, of course, be encouraging parents to think of educational programmes as competency-oriented and individualised, and, in this respect, be seeking to induct parents into a way of thinking which, as we have seen, is actually opposed by many of them and is not, in fact, understood by many of their children's teachers.

General Conclusion on Competence

If what we have said is correct, the EHVs may have a most important role to play in leading parents to adopt child rearing practices which would foster qualities conducive to economic and social development—and not just in LSES children!

PART V

RECOMMENDATIONS FOR ACTION
AND FURTHER RESEARCH

CHAPTER 31

SOME REMAINING QUESTIONS:
FURTHER ACTION AND RESEARCH

There is little need for a general summary of our findings other than, perhaps, once again to draw attention to the extent to which our statistical data support the conclusions we drew from our "illuminative" study—except in the crucial area of improving family relationships. Given the central role which we assigned to such improvement when we discussed the probable effects of the project, the failure of our statistical study to confirm these effects calls into question many of the benefits which we expected to follow from the programme. The reasons for the discrepancy can only be discovered through further careful research.

Despite our research, a large number of questions remain. The first of these is the obvious question of how far the results we have reported would be replicated if larger numbers of parents who had had Home Visits had been interviewed. But, despite the importance of this question, our own first priority would not be to increase the number of Home Visited mothers who were interviewed—for, because the results hang together and support each other so well, we would be fairly confident that they *would* replicate. Rather, our priority would be to modify the questionnaires so that we could explore some of the questions listed below *as well* as replicating—and extending—the study we have already undertaken.

These additional questions include: what effect *does* the programme have on family relationships? To what extent does it set in train cyclical processes of interaction between parent and child which confer long term benefits on the children? How do mothers perceive the Home Visitors and the visiting itself? To what extent are schools influenced? To what extent will the programme influence the communities in which the schools are sited? What are the differential effects of the different styles of visiting—on parents, on children, on schools and on communities? What follow-through activities would help to ensure that parents take up the activities which they now believe to be important and lead the effects of the programme to become more permanent? What are the *long term* effects of the visiting which has already been completed on the children's social and educational development, on the parents' patterns of family relationship, on the EHVs, on the schools, and on the communities?

If we are to begin to answer these questions it would seem to be essential for further evaluation activity in relation to this project to:

1. Assess the impact of the existing programme on the children. Does a programme which has such a clear impact on the parents have the expected effects on the children? As in the present study, it would seem to be the essence of wisdom to assess these effects in a comprehensive manner—to look at the programme's effects on the development of such qualities as initiative and the ability to work with others as well as its effects on IQ, school attendance, and school performance. It seems to us that this could be done by working with teachers from the schools the children will be attending in order to develop ways of assessing these wider qualities.

2. Assess parents' reactions to the visiting and to the Home Visitors themselves. We were not able to do this in our own statistical study because we did not have time to modify our interview schedules in an appropriate way after we had completed our interviews with the background sample. Study of the patterns of relationship which the parents build up with the EHVs, the effects that the programme has on the network of support available to the mothers, and the effects of the programme on the mothers' feelings of depression, isolation and loneliness should be accompanied by a more detailed study of the effects of the programme on family relationships.

3. Encourage the Home Visitors to diverge more sharply in their approach and then compare the relative effects of the different styles of visiting. The styles of visiting which it would be desirable to compare are:

   (i) A style based on the hypothesis that what young children primarily need is cognitive knowledge, cognitive skills and language. (This knowledge, and these skills, are to be taught in a formal manner).

   (ii) A style based on the hypothesis that cognitive development is to be facilitated by creating a situation in which a child is encouraged to be optimally motivated to pursue his own interests, in pursuit of which he will spontaneously engage in cognitive processes. (These cognitive processes can then be fed and the relevant knowledge provided. If mothers are to be encouraged to facilitate cognitive growth in this way it may be necessary to do more than show them how to do it. It may be necessary to give them the necessary concepts to think about the nature of growth, and the way in which it is to be fostered. To do this, it may be necessary to involve them in ongoing activities in mothers' groups or in nursery schools).

(iii)   A style based on the hypothesis that there is a great deal more to growth than cognitive development. (Other important qualities include initiative, the ability to adventure into the unknown, self-confidence, leadership, sensitivity to the unverbalised feelings of others, and the ability to persuade authorities to do what one wants. The development of all these qualities is to be "facilitated" rather than "taught". If mothers are to facilitate growth in these many directions, it may be necessary for them to be able to get together to make explicit the ways in which their children grow psychologically, and the ways in which those types of growth are to be facilitated. Again, therefore, it may be necessary to supplement the Home Visits by parents' groups, possibly involving participation in nursery school activities where the parents could observe other parents at work, and practise new styles for themselves in a situation which they would find less threatening, and more supportive, than activities with their own children in the isolation of their homes).

(iv)   A style based on the Plowden Social Surveys (1968) and the work of J.W.B. Douglas (1968). (Both of these studies laid particular stress on the parents' supporting the work of the school throughout the child's educational career. Some of the Home Visitors have already paid considerable attention to trying to find ways of leading their schools to encourage parental support of this sort, and this aspect of the work might well be strengthened. Alternatively the Home Visiting itself might incorporate a follow-through component designed to encourage parents to find ways of supporting the later educational development of their children).

(v)   A version based on the hypothesis that bringing the mother to understand and tackle her problems more effectively—preferably in the child's presence—should lead her to create either a better environment for the child, or to her being able to portray cognitive and other psychological processes in action for the child to copy, or both.

(There are two sub-versions of this theme:

(a)   A version based on the hypothesis that the mothers' problems lie primarily within the family and arise from such things as depression, poor family relationships, and ability deficits. This version would assume that the primary problem was to help the parent to cope with these problems—either at home or in a group—and that, once these problems have been dealt with, she would automatically tend to engage in the complex mothering activities vis-à-vis her children that the Home Visitors so much wish to promote.

(b)   A version based on the hypothesis that, by helping the mother to gain control over her own life, she would come to recognise the importance of cognitive activity, and grow in confidence and competence. She would then portray cognitive and other processes in action for her children. Group activities might be envisaged to help her to think about relevant behaviours on her own part and understand how her own growth and development is to be promoted. Once she understands the nature of her own psychological competence and its growth and development better, she might find herself in a very strong position to facilitate the growth of her children in relevant ways. One way in which Educational Home Visitors might set about promoting this sort of growth and development on the part of mothers might be to create groups of parents in which two or more of them could work together to solve these problems *without* the aid of an expert, who might well have a tendency to make them feel more *incompetent*.)

4. Assess the stability of the changes in attitudes and expectations over time, and with different types of follow-through activity. Such

follow-through activity might include continued Home Visiting—albeit on a less frequent basis—as the child progresses through school, the institution of parents' groups and other activities (possibly including Mother-Home-Visiting exercises or Community Development activities), or changes within the schools which would focus either on alternative approaches to the children or alternative approaches toward promoting parental involvement or both.

5. Assess the way in which both the activities of the EHVs and the effects of the Home Visiting would change if a group of HSES parents were included in the Home Visiting scheme.

All that has been said so far is directly related to further evaluation activity in relation to the Lothian Region Educational Home Visiting scheme. But, in Part IV of our report, we raised a large number of questions which could, and should, be explored in their own right, whether as part of an evaluation of an Educational Home Visiting scheme or not. Such questions include the absolutely fundamental question (which gets to the heart of the theoretical basis of the EHV programme—but to which we do not appear to have anything more than a glimmering of an answer) of "what *are* the effects of alternative styles of caretaker/child interaction?" What *are* the effects of the different styles of interaction which are so obviously more common among mothers from certain socio-economic status groups than others? What leads the mothers to behave differently? What *are* the effects of what we have called a "teacherish" style of interaction, and how do these differ from more facilitative "mothering" styles of interaction? Any such study should, of course, cover the types of possible activity which we have dealt with here—and more besides. Lest that be thought to be an impossible task, we may conclude by remarking that *all* the evaluation work reported here and in McCail's companion reports (including all the interviewing, analysis and typing) was undertaken in a project which involved, at the outside, seven man-years of work—dedicated work, involving a great deal of "overtime" admittedly, but, given the significance of the problem from the point of view of the future of our society and health and happiness of its population, the investment that is needed is a small enough investment by any standards.

REFERENCES

Atkinson, R.C. and Shiffrin, R.M. (1968), "Human Memory : A Proposed System of its Control Processes" in *The Psychology of Learning and Motivation*, Vol 2 (eds. K.W. Spence and J.T. Spence), New York : Academic Press.

Bereiter, C. and Englemann, S. (1966), *Teaching Disadvantaged Children in the Pre-School*, New Jersey : Prentice-Hall.

Berg, I. (1973), *Education and Jobs : The Great Training Robbery*, London : Penguin Books.

Berlyne, D. (1970), "Children's Reasoning and Thinking" in *Carmichael's Manual of Child Psychology* (ed. P. Mussen), New York : John Wiley.

Bernstein, B. (1971), *Class, Codes and Control*, Vol 1, London : Routledge and Kegan Paul.

Bernstein, B. (1975), "Class and Pedagogies : Visible and Invisible" in *Class, Codes and Control*, Vol 3, London : Routledge and Kegan Paul.

Bloom, B.S. (1964), *Stability and Change in Human Characteristics*, New York : Wiley.

Bloom, B.S. (1971), "Mastery learning" in *Mastery Learning* (ed. J.H. Block), New York : Holt Rinehart and Winston.

Bonsfield, W.A. (1953), "The Occurrence of Clustering in Recall of Randomly Arranged Associates" in *Journal of General Psychology*, Vol 49.

Bower, G.H. and Bolton, L.S. (1969), "Why are Rhymes so Easy to Learn?" in *Journal of Experimental Psychology*, Vol 82, No 3.

Bower, G.H. (1972), "Mental Imagery and Associative Learning" in *Cognition in Learning and Memory* (ed. L.W. Gregg), New York : John Wiley.

Brandis, W. and Bernstein, B. (1974), *Selection and Control*, London : Routledge and Kegan Paul.

Bronfenbrenner, U. (1974), "The Roots of Alienation" in *Scientific American 231*, pp. 53-61.

Bronfenbrenner, U. (1974), *Two Worlds of Childhood*, London : Penguin Books.

Bronfenbrenner, U. (1975), "Reality and Research in the Ecology of Human Development" in *Proc. Amer. Philos. Soc. 119*, pp. 439-469.

Bronfenbrenner, U. (1978), *Proposal for an International Intervention Project*, Washington : National Institute of Education.

Brown, B. (1977), *Long term gains from early intervention : an overview of current research*, United States Office of Child Development.

Brown, R. (1973), *A First Language: The Early Stages,* Cambridge (Mass): Harvard University Press.

Bruner, J.S. *et al* (1966), *Studies in Cognitive Growth,* New York: John Wiley.

Bruner, J.S. (1976), "Nature and Uses of Immaturity" in *Play* (eds. J.S. Bruner *et al*), London: Penguin Books.

Bullock Report (1975), *A Language for Life:* Report of the Committee of Inquiry appointed by the Secretary of Education and Science, London: HMSO.

Cazden, C.B. (1974), "Concentrated versus Contrived Encounters: Suggestions for Language Assessment in Early Childhood Education" in *Language and Learning in Early Childhood* (ed. A. Davies), London: Heinemann, 1977.

Cazden, C.B. *and* Brown, R. (1975), "The Early Development of the Mother Tongue" in *Foundations of Language Development,* Vol 1 (eds. E.H. and E. Lenneberg), New York: Academic Press.

Chomsky, N. (1975), *Reflections on Language,* New York: Random House.

Cole, M. *et al* (1971), *The Cultural Context of Learning and Thinking,* New York: Basic Books.

Coleman, J.S. (1961), *The Adolescent Society,* New York: Free Press.

Coleman, J.S. *et al* (1966), *Equality of Educational Opportunity,* Washington, D.C.: Government Printing Office.

Coleman, J.S. (1972), "How do the Young Become Adults" in *Review of Educational Research,* Vol 42, No. 4.

Coleman, J.S. (1972a), "The Children have outgrown the Schools" in *Psychology Today,* February 1972.

Coleman, J. (Chairman) (1974), *Youth: Transition to Adulthood.* Panel on Youth of the President's Science Advisory Committee, Washington: Government Printing Office.

Davé, R.H. (1963), *The Identification and Measurement of Environmental Process Variables that are Related to Educational Achievement.* PhD dissertation, University of Chicago.

Davie, R., Butler, N. *and* Goldstein, H. (1972), *From Birth to Seven,* London: Longman.

Donaldson, M. (1978), *Children's minds,* London: Fontana/Collins.

Donnison, D. (1972), "Research for Policy" in *Minerva* 10, pp. 519-537.

Douglas, J.W.B. (1968), *The Home and the School,* London: MacGibbon and Kee.

Emery, F. (1974), *Futures We're In,* Canberra: Centre for Continuing Education, Australian National University.

Emmerich, W. (1966), "Continuity and Stability in Early Social Development, Part II, Teacher Ratings" in *Child Development,* Vol 37, pp. 17-27.

Feshback, S. (1960), "Aggression" in *Carmichael's Manual of Child Psychology,* (ed. P. Mussen), New York : John Wiley.

Flavell, J.H. *et al* (1966), "Spontaneous Verbal Rehearsal in a Memory Task as a Function of Age" in *Child Development,* Vol 37, pp. 283-299.

Flavell, J.H. (1970), "Developmental Studies of Mediated Memory" in *Advances in Child Development and Behaviour,* Vol 5 (eds. H.W. Reese and L.P. Lipsett), New York : Academic Press.

Flavell, J.H (1970a), "Concept Development" *in Carmichael's Manual of Child Psychology* (ed. P. Mussen), New York : John Wiley.

Fraser, E. (1959), *Home Environment and the School,* rev. ed. 1974, London : University of London Press.

Hagen, J.W. (1972), "Strategies for Remembering" in *Information Processing in Young Children* (ed. S. Farnham-Diggory), New York : Academic Press.

Haney, W. (1976), *An analysis of Interim Follow-Through Reports,* Cambridge (Mass) : Huron Institute.

Havighurst, R.J. *et al* (1962), *Growing up in River City,* New York : John Wiley.

Hawkridge, D.G. *et al* (1968), *A Study of Selected Exemplary Programs for the Education of Disadvantaged Children,* Washingtom, D.C. : Department of Health, Education and Welfare.

Hess, R.D. *and* Shipman, V.C. (1965), "Early Experience and the Socialization of Cognitive Modes in Children", *Child Development* 36, pp. 869-886.

Hole, V. (1966), *Children's play on housing estates,* National Building Studies Research Paper 39, London : HMSO.

Hope, K. (1976), *Merit, Advantage and Deprivation in Scotland* Unpublished Manuscript, Scottish Council for Research in Education.

Jayne, E. (1976), *Research Report : ILEA Educational Home Visiting Project, Deptford,* London : ILEA Research Unit.

Jensen, A.R. (1974), "How biased are culture-loaded tests?" *Genetic Psychol. Monogr.* 90, pp. 185-244.

Keddie, Nell (1971), "Classroom knowledge" in *Knowledge and Control* (ed. M.F.D. Young), London : Cassell and Collier MacMillan.

Kellaghan, T. *and* Archer, P. (1973), *A Home Intervention Project for Two and Three Year Old Disadvantaged Children,* Dublin : Educational Research Centre, St Patrick's College.

Kellaghan, T. *and* Archer, P. (1975), *A Study of Home Intervention for the Preschool Disadvantaged,* Dublin : Educational Research Centre, St Patrick's College.

Kellaghan, T. (1977), *The Evaluation of an Intervention Programme for Disadvantaged Children,* Slough (Bucks) : National Foundation for Educational Research.

Kelly, G.A. (1955), *The Psychology of Personal Constructs, Vol 1: A Theory of Personality,* New York: Norton.

Kendler, H.H. *and* Kendler, T.S. (1961), "Effects of Verbalisation on Discrimination Reversal Shifts in Children" in *Science,* Vol 134, pp. 1619-1620.

Kendler, T.S. (1963), "Development of Mediating Responses in Children" in *Basic Cognitive Processes in Children,* Monographs of the Society for Research in Child Development, Vol 28, No 2, pp. 33-51.

Kinsey, A.C. (1948), *Sexual Behaviour in the Human Male,* Eastbourne: W.B. Saunders.

Kohlberg, L. *et al* (1971), "Moral Development and Moral Education" in *Psychology and Educational Practice* (ed. G. Lesser), Glenview (Ill): Scott, Foresman and Co.

Kohn, M.L. (1969), *Class and Conformity: A Study in Values,* Illinois: Dorsey Press.

Kreutzer, M.A. *et al* (1975), "An Interview Study of Children's Knowledge about Memory" in *Monographs of the Society for Research in Child Development,* Vol 40, No 1, Serial 159.

Kuenne, M.R. (1946), "Experimental Investigation of the Relation of Language to Transposition Behaviour in Young Children" in *Journal of Experimental Psychology,* Vol 36, pp. 471-490.

Labov, W. (1970), "The Logic of Non-Standard English" in *Language and Poverty* (ed. F. Williams), Chicago: Markham Publishing Co.

Lazar, I. (ed.) (1979), *Lasting Effects after the School,* Washington: U.S. Government Printing Office.

Lenneberg, E. (1967), *Biological Foundation of Language,* New York: John Wiley.

Levenstein, P. (1970), "Cognitive Growth in Preschoolers through Verbal Interaction with Mothers" in *American Journal of Orthopsychiatry,* Vol 40, No. 3.

Levenstein, P. (1972), "But does it Work in Homes away from Home?" *Theory into Practice,* Vol 11, No. 3, New York: Verbal Interaction Project.

Levenstein, P. (1975), *The Mother-Child Home program,* New York: Verbal Interaction project.

Levenstein, P. *and* Madden, J. (1976), *Research Proposal 1976-1979 and Progress Report 1973-1976,* New York: Verbal Interaction Project.

Levenstein, P. (1978), *Developmental Continuity Consortium, Follow-up Study,* New York: Verbal Interaction Project.

Love, J. *et al* (1976), *National Home Start Evaluation: Final Report: Findings and Implications,* Cambridge (Mass): ABT Associates Ltd.

Lynn, R. (1977), "Selective Emigration and the Decline of Intelligence in Scotland" in *Social Biology* 24, pp. 173-182.

Macbeth, A.M. (1978), *Why have a PTA?* Scottish Parent-Teacher Council, Edinburgh, Booklet 2.

McCail, G. (1980), *School Start: an account of an Educational Home Visiting Scheme for Pre-School Children,* SCRE (forthcoming).

McCail, G. (1980), *The Processes of Educational Home Visiting,* Edinburgh: SCRE (forthcoming 1980/81) (mimeo).

McClelland, D.C. (1961), *The Achieving Society,* New York: Van Nostrand.

Mackinnon, D.W. (1962), "The Nature and Nurture of Creative Talent" in *American Psychologist* 17, pp. 491f.

Macnamara, J. (1972), "Cognitive basis of Language Learning in Infants" in *Psychological Review* 79, pp. 1-13.

McLaughlin, D.H. (1977), *Title 1, 1965-1975 : A Synthesis of the Findings of Federal Studies,* Palo Alto (California) : American Institutes for Research.

Mann, A.J. *et al* (1977), *A Review of Head Start Research since 1969 : and an annotated bibliography,* Washington (DC) : Department of Health, Education and Welfare, Publications No (OHDS) 77/31102.

Marris, P.D. *and* Rein, M. (1972), *Dilemmas of Social Reform : Poverty and Community Action in the United States,* London : Routledge and Kegan Paul.

Maslow, A.H. (1954), *Motivation and Personality,* New York: Harper.

Maxwell, J.N. (1969), *Sixteen Years On,* Edinburgh: SCRE.

Moore, S.G. (1975), "Some Reflections on the Old and the New in the Education of Young Children"; Manuscript for *A Tape of the Month in Early Childhood* Series, Arlington (Va): Childhood Resources Inc.

Morton-Williams, R. (1966), "A Survey among Parents of Primary School Children", Appendix 3 in *Plowden Report 'Children and their Primary Schools' Vol 2 : Research and Surveys,* London : HMSO.

Morton-Williams, R. *et al* (1968), *Young School Leavers* (Schools Council Enquiry 1) London : HMSO.

Moynihan, D.P. (1966) in Coleman, J.S. *et al, Equality of Educational Opportunity,* Washington, D.C. : Government Printing Office.

Nash, R. (1973), *Classrooms Observed,* London : Routledge and Kegan Paul.

Newson, J. *and* E. (1968), *Four Years Old in an Urban Community,* London : Penguin.

Newson, J. *and* E. (1978), *Perspectives on School at Seven Years Old,* London : Allen and Unwin.

Palmer, F.H. (1977), *The Effects of Early Childhood Educational Intervention on School performance :* paper prepared for the President's Commission on Mental Health.

Peaker, G.F. (1967), "The Regression Analyses of the National Survey", Appendix 4 in *The Plowden Report, 'Children and their Primary Schools',* Vol 2, Research and Surveys, pp. 179-221, London : HMSO.

Peaker, G.F. (1971), *The Plowden Children Four Years Later*, Slough (Bucks) : National Foundation for Educational Research.

Piaget, J. (1932), *The Language and Thought of the Child*, London : Kegan Paul.

Piaget, J. (1932), *The Moral Judgement of the Child*, New York : Harcourt, Brace and World.

Piaget, J. (1950), *The Psychology of Intelligence*, London : Routledge and Kegan Paul.

Piaget, J. *and* Inhelder, B. (1969), *The Psychology of the Child*, New York : Basic Books.

Pines, M. (1969), *Revolution in Learning*, London : Allen Lane, the Penguin Press.

Plowden Report (1966), Central Advisory Council on Education : *Children and their Primary Schools*, Vols 1 and 2, London : HMSO.

Poulton, G.A. *and* James, T. (1975), *A Commentary on Educational Home Visiting* (mimeo). Department of Sociology, University of Southampton.

Poulton, G.A. *and* James, T. (1975), *Pre-School Learning in the Community*, London : Routledge and Kegan Paul.

Raven, J. (1959), *Adaptability, A Study in Social Assessment and Behaviour*, B.Sc. thesis, University of Aberdeen.

Raven, J. *and* Haynes, K.J. (1966), "Social Contact, Loneliness, and Club Going among Old People" in *Town Planning Institute Journal* 52, p. 94f.

Raven, J. *and* Molloy, E. (1969), *Report on exploratory work carried out prior to initiating a programme of research into values, attitudes and social structures associated with the development of different types of society.* Dublin : Economic and Social Research Institute, Memorandum Series, Paper 73.

Raven, J. Ritchie, J. *and* Baxter, D. (1971), "Factor Analysis and Cluster Analysis : their Value and Stability in Social Survey Research" in *Economic and Social Review*, Vol 2, pp. 367-391.

Raven, J. (1973), "The Attainment of Non-academic Educational Objectives" in *International Review of Education*, Vol 19, pp. 305-344.

Raven, J. (1973), "Some Results from Pilot Surveys of Attitudes, Values and Perceptions of Socio-Institutional Structures in Ireland" in *Economic and Social Review* 4, pp. 553-558.

Raven, J. (1975), "The Role of Social Research in Modern Society" *in Administration* 23, pp. 225-250.

Raven, J. (1975), "The Institutional Structures and Management Styles Required for Policy-Relevant Social Research" in *Administration* 23, pp. 251-268.

Raven, J. *et al* (1975), *Pupils' Perceptions of Educational Objectives and their Reactions to School and School Subjects,* Dublin : The Irish Association for Curriculum Development, ("A Survey of Attitudes of Post Primary Teachers and Pupils", Vol 2.)

Raven, J. *et al* (1975), *Teachers' Perceptions of Educational Objectives and Examinations,* Dublin : Irish Association for Curriculum Development, ("A Survey of Attitudes of Post Primary Teachers and Pupils", Vol 1).

Raven, J. (1976), *Pupil Motivation and Values,* Dublin : Irish Association for Curriculum Development.

Raven, J. *and* Litton, F. (1976), "Irish Pupils' Civic Attitudes in an International Context" in *Oideas,* Spring 1976, pp. 16-30.

Raven, J., Whelan, C.T., Pfretzschner, P.A. *and* Borock, D.M. (1976), *Political Culture in Ireland. The Views of Two Generations,* Dublin : Institute of Public Administration.

Raven, J. (1977), "Government Policy and Social Psychologists" in *Bull. Br. Psychol. Soc* (1977) 30, pp. 33-39.

Raven, J. (1977), *Education, Values and Society,* London : H.K. Lewis ; New York : The Psychological Corporation.

Raven, J. (1977), "On the Components of Competence and their Development in Education" in *Teachers' College Record,* Vol 78, pp. 457-475.

Raven, J. *and* Dolphin, T. (1978), *The Consequences of Behaving,* Competency motivation Project, Edinburgh.

Raven, J.C., Court, J.H., *and* Raven, J. (1977), *Manual for Raven's Progressive Matrices and Vocabulary Scales,* London : H.K. Lewis and Co. Ltd.

Rogers, E.M. (1962), *Diffusion of Innovations,* New York : Free Press of Glencoe.

Rutter, M. (1979), *15,000 Hours: secondary schools and their effects on children,* London: Open Books.

Smith, G. (ed.) (1975), *Educational Priority, Vol 4: The West Riding Project,* London : HMSO.

Spearman, C. (1927), *The Abilities of Man,* London : Macmillan.

Stallings, J.A. *and* Kaskowitz, D.H. (1974), *Follow Through Classroom Evaluation 1972-1973,* Menlo Park (California) : Stanford Research Institute.

Stallings, J.A. *et al* (1976), *Phase II : Instruments for the National Day Care Cost-Effects Study : Instrument Selection and Field Testing,* Menlo Park (California) : Stanford Research Institute.

Stevens, F. (1960), *The Living Tradition,* London : Hutchinson.

Taylor, P.H., Exon, G. *and* Holley, B. (1972), *A Study in Nursery Education,* Schools Council Working Paper No 41, London : Evans/ Methuen Educational.